Demography in Early America

Demography in Early America
Beginnings of the Statistical Mind, 1600-1800

James H. Cassedy

Harvard University Press
Cambridge, Massachusetts
1969

To My Mother

Mrs. William A. T. Cassedy

Preface

This book deals with a phase of the social, intellectual, and scientific history of seventeenth- and eighteenth-century America. It is an inquiry into the introduction and growth of statistical methods and ideas in early America, mainly insofar as they were applied to human vital events and population movements. My focus is primarily on the use of these statistics in public health and medical settings. Still, for this period before 1800, it is impossible and undesirable to consider such uses separately from their application in economic, religious, or other governmental and intellectual contexts.

In the twentieth century, the carrying on of many aspects of business, government, disease control, scientific research, and other activities of contemporary civilization is virtually inconceivable without the use of huge amounts of data carefully collected, compared, and analyzed. At the personal level, most persons in modern America find themselves involved somehow in the public opinion polls, racing odds, stock market averages, or other statistics relating to their everyday lives. Many use such statistics happily, even hungrily. Some, however, like Jacques Barzun, consider this "statistical living" to be among the most baneful manifestations of our civilization. He regards the obsession with statistics as a moral and spiritual retrogression of the human race:

> At every turn statistics tell us the chances of death or disease, success or failure, accident, suicide, or crime to which we are exposed, not to say expected to conform. . . . Men, as we say, are expendable; the next one is not anyone in particular, not even an enemy; he is "one of a thousand lifeless numbers," a unit to be turned into a cipher. . . . This bland indifference is linked with the industrial sense of the replaceability of parts and the ready supply of raw materials. How absurd in this frame of mind seems the old notion of each human life as a responsible pilgrimage.[1]

An understanding, by either partisan or critic, of the nature, extent, and depth of the statistical approach to our life and thought must take into consideration something of its roots. Up to the present, little basis for such an understanding has existed. The historical origins of American statistical institutions and, to an even greater extent, of our habits of thinking about people and things in the aggregate remain inadequately studied.

This volume attempts to identify those earliest Americans who looked at demographic and related matters from a statistical or quantitative viewpoint and to determine the extent of this phenomenon. Even though the word "statistics" did not come into the English language until nearly the end of the eighteenth century, there was from earliest times a widespread interest in America in the characteristics and movements of quantities of people and in the sig-

1. Jacques Barzun, *Science: The Glorious Entertainment* (New York: Harper and Row, 1964), pp. 44, 188.

nificance of their vital events. Throughout the seventeenth and eighteenth centuries there was a continuous transmission to and implantation in the New World of European vital statistics institutions, practices, and concepts. Demographic problems rose from the beginning; Americans thought about and dealt with these problems in various ways. I view these statistical ideas and activities both as phases of America's early intellectual development and as elements of the ordering processes of early American society in its confrontation with the New World wilderness environment.

The period before 1800 in America was a time of planting basic statistical institutions and habits, not of their flowering. It was a time of proposing uses for vital statistics but not of applying them very far. It was a period of small demographic numbers, unsophisticated techniques, and simple theories. It was the day of the generalist and the dedicated amateur. In short, the statistical mind was in its embryonic stages. Its growth up to maturity after 1800 was another, later stage, which belongs to a second volume, now in preparation.

Since this history covers a span of some two hundred years, I have presented the subject in a broadly chronological framework. At the same time, the nature of the material seemed to require topical chapters, a treatment which violates the time sequence to some extent. I have devoted four chapters to discussing the various imperatives —social, political, and economic—behind the early legislative enactments and institutional developments in American demography. A fifth chapter examines the demographic implications of the American Revolution. The other six deal in detail with some of the important subelements of colonial demography: census-taking, parish registers, population theory, life probabilities, bills of mortality, and medical statistics.

All these topics are presented as integral parts of the history of seventeenth- and eighteenth-century American life and thought. The total work is not a volume of historical demography per se; it does not attempt to analyze the statistics of American history but rather the statisticians of our past. Nor is it a history of genealogy; genealogists are concerned with records of people as individuals, while demographers and vital statisticians deal with the data of groups of people. Again, it is not really a study of life and death in America, though no attempt is made to play down the poignant implications which the data of such human events carry.

Preparation of the present volume has suggested a variety of subjects for further historical study. A general survey of the colonial development of commercial and other non-demographic statistics would be a useful supplement to this volume. At the same time, there is much need for detailed local studies of vital statistics legislation, population enumerations, and demographic ideas in the various colonies. There is also need for further study, in vital and demographic data, of the transfer of European habits, ideas, and institutions to America. Finally, such matters as the efforts to obtain vital statistics legislation or to carry out census enumerations may profitably be examined for their potential illumination of early lawmaking and enforcement, of shifting local-state-federal relationships, and of the roots of the welfare state or of other aspects of centralism in American life.

My interest in early American intellectual and social history was given impetus and direction many years ago by

Professors Reginald L. Cook, Edmund S. Morgan, and Donald Fleming. Since then many scholars have contributed, albeit unknowingly, to the substance of this work, as I gladly acknowledge in the bibliography. Others have contributed more directly by their generous responses to my questions about specific matters. Their observations have often helped materially in defining or presenting the project as well as in identifying materials. Particular help and encouragement has come from Drs. Whitfield J. Bell, Jr., William G. McLoughlin, and Richard H. Shryock. Librarians at many institutions both in the United States and Great Britain have also given me unstinting aid and advice. Mrs. Barbara S. Cassedy has helped materially in the preparation of the manuscript. Dr. Conrad Taeuber was kind enough to read and comment upon it in its entirety.

J. H. C.

Contents

Demography in Early America

Chapter I

The Demographic Factor

in an Age of Colonization

The Englishmen who founded Virginia were, not surprisingly, intimately familiar with the facts of life and death in their time. Many also were well informed about the statistics of these events and were concerned with the numbers of populations. The counting of populations and accounting for their movements were matters of ever-increasing importance to the sixteenth- and seventeenth-century European state. These activities took on importance not only in the state's competition with its neighbors but in its colonization ventures in newly discovered lands. At the same time, the church and the state alike had long since found it desirable in a well-ordered community, for legal purposes, at least, to record the facts of birth, marriage, and death of their constituent members. The process of American colonization, which involved a transfer and displacement of populations, was accompanied from the beginning by efforts to collect and record population data. It also included steps to establish in the New World the registration and other demographic practices which had become standard at home.

Renaissance energies had stirred up in Europe a new interest in numbers and their uses. Scientists were stimulated, partly by a new reading of ancient writers, to seek knowledge of the universe inductively through experimentation and accumulation of observed facts, rather than through deductive reasoning. Other scholars found from classical literature how people and their vital events had been recorded in ancient Greece and Rome. Some noted the registers of birth which had been kept in the temples of Juno Lacina and the death registers which had been kept in the temples of Libitina.[1] Statesmen found particular meaning in the long series of censuses which had been conducted by imperial Rome, and noted their utility both for the well-being of the modern state and for governing far-off domains. Consolidation of small principalities into large kingdoms, as well as increasing commerce, called for improvements in administration, finance, and information-gathering. Accumulations of general and vital data also became increasingly necessary as exploration led to colonization.[2]

1. See August Meitzen, *History, Theory, and Technique of Statistics*, trans. Roland P. Falkner (Philadelphia: American Academy of Political and Social Sciences, 1891), p. 17; James Bonar, *Theories of Population from Raleigh to Arthur Young* (London: Allen & Unwin, 1931), p. 169; and Cornelius Walford, "Early Bills of Mortality," *Transactions of the Royal Historical Society*, 7 (1878), 213.

2. The history of statistical developments in Europe, particularly governmental or official statistics, has been discussed in some detail in a number of volumes, such as Meitzen, *History of Statistics*; John Koren, *The History of Statistics* (New York: Macmillan, 1918); and Harald Westergaard, *Contributions to the History of Statistics* (London: P. S. King & Son, 1932).

Every patron, explorer, and colonial governor, whatever his nationality, quickly learned that he must gather quantitative as well as qualitative data about his discoveries or domains if he was to hope for continued support or additional settlers for the new colonies. The people at home were avid for detailed information, not only about gold, silver, and precious stones, but about the climate, land, animal life, and, perhaps most of all, about the people who had been discovered. Sea captains, missionaries, soldiers, and settlers contributed to the flow of information about Spanish America both before and after Philip II's ambitious survey of that area in 1579. English explorers, officials, and settlers ultimately followed the same practice.

No English, French, or Dutch report of the period ever rivaled in statistical interest the astounding bit of information sent back to Spain soon after the conquest of Peru. The scholars and priests who followed close upon the conquistadores reported that the Incas had a highly developed system by which they recorded quantities of facts. This system used intertwined colored strings and knots known as "quipus." Besides their applications in agriculture, business, and finance, the quipus were used in carrying out census enumerations and in collecting routine demographic data. The historian William H. Prescott described it as a method "which has scarcely a counterpart in the annals of a semicivilized people. A register was kept of all the births and deaths throughout the country, and exact returns of the actual population were made to government every year by means of the *quipus*." [3] The quipus,

3. Quoted in *Handbook of Vital Statistics Methods* (New York: Statistical Office of the United Nations, 1955), p. 4. See also L. Leland Locke, *The Ancient Quipus, or The Peruvian Knot Record* (New York: American Museum of Natural History, 1923). Sixteenth-century accounts of the quipus included those by Pedro Cieza de León and Garcilaso de la Vega.

however, along with the rest of Inca civilization, were quickly supplanted by Spanish institutions, in this case by vital registers and censuses.[4]

In New Spain, as in most other places, the first months and years of colonization were strenuous periods of work, fighting, and sickness during which survival hung precariously in the balance. The occasional gentlemen or other idlers who tried, as in Virginia, to shun the work and fighting could not escape the sickness. Leaders of colonies during these periods became painfully aware of the human quantification of their enterprises: the size of the sick lists, the rapidly increasing number of graves, the slow arrival of relief ships. The earliest documentation of these events had to rest upon informal rather than formal statistical data, upon information hastily noted in diaries, letters, or other accounts written by the participants. More often than not, the information emerged in the form of rough guesses rather than as precise totals or exact registration. Roanoke provides an early example.

The exploratory expedition which Sir Walter Raleigh sent to Virginia in 1584 took back two Indians for the edification of Elizabethan England. More important, the captains of the enterprise reported briefly upon the decimated state of the Indian population on Roanoke, a condition which apparently had been caused by tribal wars. Later observers, however, noted that there were still considerable numbers of Indians in the vicinity. Ralph Lane, writing to Richard Hakluyt in 1585, though filled with wonder at the novelty of the adventure, still had an eye

4. As early as 1554 the Spanish historian Sarmiento wrote of the provincial returns of births, marriages, and deaths which were made annually to the Peruvian capitol at Cuzco. *Handbook of Vital Statistics Methods,* p. 213.

for human numbers: "It is the goodliest and most pleasing Territorie of the world: for the continent is of an huge and unknowen greatness, and very well peopled and towned, though savagely, and the climate so wholesome, that wee had not one sicke since we touched the land here." Later, Lane provided some details about nearby Indian tribes and their towns. The largest of these, Chawanook, he noted, by itself could furnish some seven hundred fighting men.[5]

Lane's figures marked the beginning of many years of counting and guessing — but chiefly guessing — by the English of the numbers of North American Indians. The data were needed in 1585, as in succeeding generations, to provide a basis for self-protection in the bloody confrontations between the two groups. The Indians themselves were at a disadvantage here. They sometimes were known to use strings of colored wampum to register events or to take counts of people, animals, furs, and other objects for various empirical purposes. But, unlike the Incas, they made no regular or systematic enumerations. Nor did they keep cumulative data. As Thomas Hariot noted in 1586, the Indians on Roanoke had "no letters nor other suche meanes as we to keepe Records."[6]

In 1587 reinforcements were sent out from England to give the Roanoke colony new vigor. John White, the Governor, shortly sent back his famous note, which might be regarded as the earliest birth certificate issued in British America: "The 18 [of August, 1587] Elenor, daughter to the Governor, and wife to Ananias Dare one of the Assist-

---

5. See *Hakluyt's Collection of the Early Voyages, Travels, and Discoveries of the English Nation*, 5 vols. (London: Evans, Mackinlay, & Priestley, 1810), III, 310, 311, and 312.

6. *Ibid.*, p. 336. See also Locke, *The Ancient Quipus*, p. 54.

ants, was delivered of a daughter in Roanoak, and the same was Christened there the Sonday following, and because this child was the first Christian borne in Virginia, she was named Virginia." [7] White also included a list of the ninety-odd men and seventeen women who remained as settlers after he returned to England. When, a few years later, relief expeditions failed to find any trace of the Roanoke settlers, White's 1587 list turned out to be the earliest bill of mortality for English America.

Raleigh, the patron of Roanoke, like other late fifteenth-century Englishmen, was concerned with demographic matters in general as well as with colonization.[8] The two interests merged as these men sought answers to the social malaise of Elizabethan England. It is now evident that events like the sale of the monasteries, the enclosure movement, and the rise in the wool trade caused serious population disruptions. Although the country may not have been actually overpopulated during these years, many people got the impression that it was. Large numbers of rootless persons — tramps, beggars, idle soldiers — stirred up widespread terror. Although they had little quantitative data about such groups, some observers were persuaded that colonization could provide relief. Thousands of English poor were consequently sent to Ireland under settlement schemes, and as the New World opened up, it appeared that English colonies there also could relieve overpopulation at home.[9]

7. *Hakluyt's Voyages,* III, 345.
8. See Bonar, *Theories of Population,* chap. 1.
9. Englishmen were not all of one mind about this. By fairly early in the seventeenth century, in fact, the view prevailed that England could not afford to lose its manpower to the colonies. As late as the 1630's, however, many people still believed England to be over-populated. John Winthrop, for instance, gloomily wrote in 1629 that

Demographic factors also helped lay the groundwork in England for the scientific study of vital data. Bills (published summaries) of mortality began to appear in London early in the sixteenth century.[10] Although the precise date of this beginning remains obscure, clearly it was stimulated by the almost constant presence of the plague. While the plague terrorized most of the British Isles and the Continent, it had a special impact in London, where tramps had greatly swollen the population. To obtain a better idea of the effect of the disease on the city, the Lord Mayor of London began to require weekly reports (bills of mortality) of the number of plague deaths in each parish of the city. The guild of parish clerks (church functionaries who had advanced from singers and actors to administrators) was given the duty of obtaining the returns, preparing the

---

"this lande growes wearye of her Inhabitantes, so as man which is the most pretious of all the Creatures, is here more vile and base, then the earthe they tread upon." Quoted in Carl Bridenbaugh, *Vexed and Troubled Englishmen* (New York: Oxford, 1968), p. 397. For further discussion, see Marcus L. Hansen, *The Atlantic Migration, 1617–1860* (Cambridge: Harvard University Press, 1940), pp. 25–30; and Howard M. Jones, *O Strange New World* (New York: Viking Press, 1964), passim.

10. Many authors have attempted to trace the beginnings of the London Bills. Graunt in 1662 set the commencement sometime in the 1590's, while Maitland in 1739 put it at 1562. Ogle, Christie, and Creighton, all writing in the 1890's, variously found bills going back to 1528, 1532, and 1535. By 1956, Charles Mullett had found the existence of a bill of 1519. See John Graunt, *Natural and Political Observations Made upon the Bills of Mortality* (London: Tho. Roycroft, 1662); William Maitland, *The History of London* (London: S. Richardson, 1739); William Ogle, "An Inquiry into the Trustworthiness of the Old Bills of Mortality," *Journal of the Royal Statistical Society,* 55 (1892), 437–460; Charles Creighton, *A History of Epidemics in Britain,* 2 vols. (Cambridge University Press [Eng.], 1891–1894); and Charles F. Mullett, *The Bubonic Plague and England* (Lexington: University of Kentucky Press, 1956).

reports, and publishing and posting them. Over the years the bills of mortality were expanded slightly, particularly to include data on christenings. Up to the end of the sixteenth century, however, only the deaths from plague were singled out on the bills; in fact, bills were issued only intermittently, during visitations of the plague. Around 1600, the weekly bills not only began to appear regularly but began to include data, such as it was, for other diseases or causes of death.[11] Some sixty years later, John Graunt first sought by systematic analysis to extract scientific, social, and political meaning from the accumulated bills.[12]

The terror of the plague not only existed side by side with the excitement produced by the sixteenth-century voyages of exploration, but it doubtless helped feed the excitement. For Englishmen who lived through the horrors

11. The shortcomings of the bills, both in their simple early form and after they began to include diseases besides plague, have been discussed by many writers. The chief inadequacies after 1600 seemed to center around the "ancient women" hired by the parish clerks to view dead bodies and report upon the causes of death. Even if these untrained persons could have given a fair idea of different diseases, which they could not, "a cup of ale or double fee" apparently often affected the nature and accuracy of their reports. See the accounts in Graunt, *Natural and Political Observations*; Ogle, "An Inquiry . . . ," *Journal,* Royal Statistical Society, 55 (1892), 437–445; and Mullett, *The Bubonic Plague,* p. 107, n. 2.

12. Graunt, *Natural and Political Observations.* Citations throughout are to the edition prepared by Walter F. Willcox and published in 1939 in Baltimore by The Johns Hopkins Press. The long controversy over the respective roles of Graunt and Petty in the writing of the *Observations* has been summarized recently and authoritatively by D. V. Glass, "John Graunt and His Natural and Political Observations," *Proceedings of the Royal Society of Biology,* 139 (1963), 1–37. Even more forcibly than such statisticians as Charles Hull (1899), Walter Willcox (1939), or Major Greenwood (1948), each of whom considered the matter, Glass concludes that there is "little reason to doubt that the volume . . . was in all essential respects Graunt's work" (p. 22).

of plague visitations and who read the awesome death figures in the weekly bills of mortality, the risks of a long
sea voyage to the New World may well have seemed the
lesser of two evils. Some persons must have hoped to find
in the Americas not only gold but an absence of plague.

Taken together, the ferment of plague fears and exploration excitement — in the setting of Renaissance curiosity
and Reformation adjustment — helped produce a lively
concern for the quantitative data of human life and death.
In England, Francis Bacon was only one, but possibly the
most persuasive, of the thinkers of the day who advocated
the quantitative approach for every area of experiment and
observation. Although Bacon showed no special awareness
of the scientific possibilities of the bills of mortality, his
general proposals for the exploration of natural phenomena
placed large emphasis upon counting, weighing, and enumeration.[13]

The late sixteenth- and early seventeenth-century beginnings of industrialism in England were likewise accompanied by new demands for enumeration and precision:
for careful records, exact quantities, and exact distances.
Turn-of-the-century Lords Treasurer were already trying
to ferret out quantitative data on the coal trade from
London customs officials. And the latter, to satisfy the
demand, not only began to use books instead of rolls to
record ship cargoes, but before 1600 began preparing
statistical summaries and tables of such records. These and

13. See, for example, Bacon's *Advancement of Learning* (1603–4),
Novum Organum (1620), and *New Atlantis* (1624). Bacon's proposals
for research included quantitative and experimental studies of long-
lived persons in order to bring about the prolongation of life. See
his *The Historie of Life and Death* (London, 1638), pp. 8–14. Des-
cartes played a role in France roughly comparable to that of Bacon
in England as an advocate of the quantitative approach.

other activities during that period, Professor Nef points out, marked "the beginnings of that interest in the exact quantitative expansion of trade that has since become characteristic of practical economics." [14]

But the age of Bacon, Raleigh, and the new merchant class was also the age of Shakespeare and Donne. The high regard which people of that age had for drama and poetry perhaps helped make more bearable the lot of the ordinary man who could not hope to escape plague or poverty by going to the New World. By the time English colonization was getting well started in the seventeenth century, even the bills of mortality had passed sufficiently into common currency to serve as topics in the poetry of the day. For every birth, marriage, or death in the Royal Family around the turn of the century, the wits at Oxford and Cambridge "got out *epithalamia, gaudia,* or *threnodia* celebrating the happy or lamentable event in hexameter or elegiacs." [15] More characteristic poetic responses to the plague, however, were the grim verses in Henry Climsell's "London's Vacation, and the Countries Terme":

> This day the weekly bills come out
> To put the people out of doubt

14. John U. Nef, *Cultural Foundations of Industrial Civilization* (Cambridge University Press [Eng.], 1958), p. 16 and passim. In another work, Nef writes: "The direct forces behind industrial civilization are to be found, I suggest, not only in the spirit of capitalism but in a novel emphasis on quantity as the principal purpose of production and on precise measurement and mathematical statement as the major methods in scientific inquiry." — John U. Nef, *The Conquest of the Material World* (Chicago, Ill.: University of Chicago Press, 1964), pp. 216 and 121–239 passim.

15. Samuel Eliot Morison, *The Intellectual Life of Colonial New England,* 2nd ed. (New York: New York University Press, 1956), p. 23.

How many of the plague do die;
We sum them up most carefully.[16]

When permanent English colonies were established in North America, the general concern for the quantification of human vital events carried over naturally and easily to them from the mother country. To be sure, harassed settlers had little energy for writing poetry about bills of mortality, or even for preparing such bills. They had even less opportunity to make scientific observations about vital data. Theoretical contributions were far in the future, but there were immediate demands for quantitative information, however rough. The first settlers met these demands in various ways.

Whatever his personal qualifications, Captain John Smith was among the best placed of the early Jamestown leaders to inform the British public about the new colony and its New World setting. In 1612, five years after the settlement was launched, he set about to do just that. In that year he published his account, *A Map of Virginia, with a Description of the Countrey, the Commodities, People, Government and Religion.*[17] The volume is noteworthy, at least in the context of this discussion, because

16. Extract quoted in Mullett, *The Bubonic Plague,* p. 191. Similarly, John Taylor's "The Fearful Summer of London's Calamity" was all too specific:

> Thus passeth all the week, *till Thursday's bill*
> Shows us what thousands death that week did kill.
> That fatal bill, doth like a razor cut
> The dead, the living in a maze doth put. — *Ibid.,* p. 169.

17. Published in *Travels and Works of Captain John Smith,* ed. Arber and Bradley, 2 vols. (Edinburgh: John Grant, 1910). Over the following dozen or more years Smith added to his original account with supplemental observations.

of its character as a compendium. In it, Smith gave a survey of the plants, animals, trees, minerals, rivers, and other natural phenomena of Virginia, as well as a description of the colony itself and its short history. By no means a unique kind of publication in Europe, Smith's compendium was nevertheless the forerunner in America of the almanac, the directory, and the statistical register. It is one of the earliest of a long series of histories, geographies, and other descriptive works by colonial and later writers which depicted British North America more or less statistically.

The work also had a certain statistical distinction in its survey of the Indians of Virginia. Smith early tried to ascertain the number of actual or potential enemy forces in each of the villages and tribes. On the basis of observation, counts of houses, and reports from friendly Indians, he drew up rough estimates. He then concluded: "The land is not populous, for the men be fewe; their far greater number is of women and children. Within 60 miles of *James* Towne there are about some 5000 people, but of able men fit for their warres, scarse 1500. To nourish so many together they have yet no means, because they make so smal a benefit of their land, be it never so fertill." [18] Here, despite the crude data, is the hint of a pragmatic theory about the population of America, a seed which did not really sprout until Franklin nourished it one hundred and forty years later.

Bruce has noted the discrepancies between Smith's estimates of the Indian population and those of William Strachey, who also left a fairly extensive account. Strachey, who wrote a few years after Smith, reported a larger num-

18. *Ibid.*, I, 65. Smith later also made substantial surveys of the Indian tribes of New England. His population estimates formed prominent parts of his accounts of that region.

ber of Indians, since he included certain areas and tribes which Smith had not visited. Both, however, were concerned principally with the numbers of fighting men rather than with the total Indian population.[19]

Apart from their concern with the strength of the Indian populations around them, the leaders of Jamestown found that their responsibilities required them to quantify the human events of the colony itself in various ways. During the first critical years, such reckonings could hardly have been much more than the daily roll call to ascertain how many had died, how many were sick, and how many were left to work or to guard the settlement. Insofar as they were able, however, responsible persons sent back, in their letters to England, a growing variety of numerical information about these events. This included numbers and names of new settlers or ships arriving, "lists of the dead in the several plantations," and details of an occasional "exact muster of the people and cattle." [20]

The human data which found their way back to the London Company in the early letters and reports were consistently rough in quality. Some kinds were almost invariably grim. Mortality, in fact, was so consistently and shockingly high that the Company dared not make the figures public.[21] The writings of Smith and others disclosed something of the truth. Smith reported fairly accurately that three fifths of the original complement of the colony (sixty out of some one hundred persons) had died within

19. Philip A. Bruce, *Economic History of Virginia in the Seventeenth Century*, 2 vols. (New York: Macmillan, 1895), I, 140–145.

20. See *Calendar of State Papers, Colonial Series, America and West Indies, 1574–1660* (London: Her Majesty's Stationery Office, 1860), pp. 22, 57, 72, 89, 117, 175, and 201.

21. Stella H. Sutherland, *Population Distribution in Colonial America* (New York: Columbia University Press, 1936), p. 184.

less than a year, fifty of them between May and September of 1607. He also related with some gusto the macabre case of the man who killed, "powdered" (salted), and ate part of his wife, and was in turn executed. Smith further reported that while the population in 1625 had climbed to 1232, nearly 8000 had perished along the way. Peter de Vries observed that a somewhat comparable mortality still prevailed in 1633; out of thirty-six English vessels loading tobacco at the mouth of the James River that year, the captains of fifteen had died.[22]

None of the leaders or reporters had an exact idea of the causes of the early mortality. At the same time, Smith and George Percy agreed that most of the early deaths were from famine. Percy was certain that some also succumbed to fever.[23] After the first few years, disease became the principal factor; the mortality from disease and general "seasoning" continued to be harsh through much of the century. The cruel fact, a recent historian has commented, was that "many had to emigrate in order that a portion might survive." [24] Ironically, as Governor Wyatt wrote in 1623, those who survived the rigorous natural selection of the seasoning process enjoyed an average length of life "as great as in the most wholesome parts of England." [25] The situation was much improved by 1671, when

22. Smith, *Travels and Works*, I, 90–100, and II, 498; and Sutherland, *Population Distribution*, p. 185.

23. Bruce, *Economic History*, I, 133. George Percy was one who wrote from firsthand experience about the first settlement of Jamestown, including the diseases. See "Percy's Discourse of Virginia," ed. Albert B. Hart, *The Founding of Jamestown* (New York: Simmons, 1907), pp. 3–16.

24. Abbot E. Smith, *Colonists in Bondage* (Chapel Hill: University of North Carolina Press, 1947), p. 8.

25. Quoted in Bruce, *Economic History*, I, 138. Wyatt's conclusion obviously resulted from empirical observation rather than from firm statistical data.

an estimated 80 percent of the newcomers survived. Yet, as late as 1700 there were still only an estimated 60,000 to 75,000 people, although over 100,000 had immigrated and natural increase had contributed many additional thousands.[26]

Although observers like Smith and Wyatt ventured their estimates of the grisly mortality taking place around them, these were informal, personal observations. The colony had no organization like the London parish clerks to prepare bills of mortality, with such regular and systematic data as these could provide about deaths from particular diseases.[27] The colony did, however, at an early date initiate means for recording the bare legal facts of its deaths, along with those of the other vital events, that is, its births and marriages.

The disastrous mortality of the first few years after 1607 was related in part to the general administrative weaknesses of the colony. In order to salvage Jamestown from near anarchy, the London Company in 1611 drew up a detailed prescription for government, discipline, morals, and civil institutions. This became known as Dale's Code, after Sir Thomas Dale, who introduced and tried to enforce it. As part of this formula for bringing order to the colony, the Code provided for the registration of vital data. Specifically, it required each minister to

. . . keepe a faithful and true Record, or Church Booke, of all Christenings, Marriages, and Deaths of such our people as shall happen within their Fort, or Fortresse, Townes or Towne, at any time, upon the

26. See Thomas J. Wertenbaker, *The Planters of Colonial Virginia* (Princeton, N. J.: Princeton University Press, 1922), pp. 36–41.
27. This lack continued throughout the seventeenth and eighteenth centuries as well as much later. See discussion in Chapter VI.

burthen of a neglectfull conscience, and upon paine of losing their Entertainment.[28]

Such a provision was an entirely logical clause to appear in an early seventeenth-century English code of law. The keeping of parish registers, which was already a substantial, well-established practice in Spain before Columbus discovered America, became compulsory throughout the Catholic Church after the Council of Trent.[29] Grandfathers and fathers of the first Jamestown settlers, moreover, had been alive in 1538 when the English Crown required the practice in the churches of that country. If monks had been the principal recorders of vital human events during the Middle Ages, under Henry VIII parish priests of the state church took over the task. By the time Jamestown was established, English law had set penalties for the non-reporting of such events and had specified that registers be kept on durable parchment to ensure against deterioration. It also specified that registers be kept from Sunday to Sunday in coffers under three sets of locks and keys—one kept by the clergyman, the others by not always literate church wardens. Queen Elizabeth and her counselors (like many succeeding generations of English rulers) made several vain attempts between 1562 and 1590 to establish a central registration office for these and other data. Despite their failure, by 1611 the concept of parish registers as the official legal records of vital personal events had been

28. Quoted in George E. Howard, A *History of Matrimonial Institutions,* 3 vols. (Chicago, Ill.: University of Chicago Press, 1904), I, 236.

29. Everywhere in Spanish America, not just in Peru, the practice spread quickly on the heels of the conquest. Catholic registers in Saint Augustine, Florida, were probably the earliest kept within the present area of the United States.

thoroughly established. Although these were usually records of religious ceremonies — baptisms, church weddings, and burials — rather than of natural events (births, marriage unions, and deaths), they were considered adequate for legal purposes.[30]

It was natural for functionaries back in London to prescribe the keeping of colonial vital statistics registers. It was another thing to expect that a tiny band harassed by hunger, sickness, low morale, fatigue, and a multitude of fears would be able to comply with this part of the Code. Admittedly, we know little or nothing about when and how this provision was put into effect, and nothing about the earliest actual registers. It would, in fact, be surprising if either continuous or accurate registers were actually kept during the first decade or more of the colony's existence.

The keeping of registers in early Virginia, not in itself a difficult matter, nevertheless presented serious obstacles. Frequently, it was as basic a problem as the illiteracy of church wardens or the shortage of ministers. Those preachers who did come to Virginia sometimes had little energy for record-keeping after the physical demands of scratching out a living had been met. Then, as the popula-

30. No thorough history of vital statistics registration exists. There are, however, a number of partial studies which together provide much information. Works already referred to include: *Handbook of Vital Statistics Methods*; Howard, *Matrimonial Institution*; Meitzen, *History of Statistics*; Koren, *History of Statistics*; and Creighton, *Epidemics in Britain*. Other important secondary sources include: John Southerden Burn, *The History of Parish Registers in England* (London: Edward Suter, 1829); Leslie G. Pine, *American Origins* (Garden City: Doubleday, 1960), 28ff and 292ff; J. Charles Cox, *The Parish Registers of England* (London: Methuen, 1910); and P. Granville Edge, "Vital Registration in Europe," *Journal of the Royal Statistical Society* (London), n.s., 91 (1928), 346–376.

tion spread out along the rivers, the minister often lost close contact with the vital occurrences in his large parish. Sometimes the problem was as simple as the failure to obtain record books or other supplies from England.[31]

Public burial grounds near every settlement were required in Virginia beginning in 1623. Names of persons interred in these places, which were usually located near the parish churches, could be expected ordinarily to appear upon the parish burial registers. The case was frequently different with many of the plantations and distant homesteads. Because of their remoteness from parish churches, these places often maintained their own burial areas. It is apparent that the burials in such places, whether of family members, servants, or slaves, had a good chance of escaping entry in any kind of list or register, unless perhaps in the family Bible.

However serious the obstacles, leaders in the colony as well as those back in London were early persuaded that vital statistics registration was essential in an orderly society. They accepted the prevailing view that the government had a responsibility to require and oversee such registration. And, as good members of the state church, they continued the tradition of carrying out the registration within the framework of ecclesiastical rites and functions.

As early as 1619 the colonial Assembly passed its own registration bill. This Act required the clergy not only to record all christenings, marriages, and burials (the latter instead of deaths), but called for annual quantitative reports of these events. An Act of 1631–32 made church wardens jointly responsible with the ministers for submitting the annual returns each June 1 to the quarter

31. Registration difficulties in remote areas of the world today are little different from those encountered in seventeenth-century America.

court. Readers as well as ministers were given registration duties in 1661–62. The 1657–58 law required the vestry of each parish to provide adequate registry books. Later statutes continued these provisions in substantially similar form, while over the years, still other statutes provided for the keeping of auxiliary vital records of such events as the publication of banns, obtaining of marriage licenses and certificates, and payment of fees for marriage or burial services.[32]

Like the keeping of the parish registers, the mechanics of keeping track of people were relatively simple in the early years of the colony, when most of the settlers remained close to each other. The total of 4914 persons listed on the "official" census of 1635 (the only one identified as such in colonial Virginia) is probably accurate. Likewise, there is no reason to feel that other population enumerations were not substantially correct up through the 1640's.[33]

32. The Act of 1619 is noted in the Minutes of the Assembly, 1619, p. 26, in *Colonial Records of Virginia*, State Senate Document, Extra, 1874. For discussion of this and other acts, see Philip A. Bruce, *Institutional History of Virginia in the Seventeenth Century*, 2 vols. (New York: Putnam's, 1910), I, 186; and Howard, *Matrimonial Institutions*, I, 231–232, and II, 225–235.

33. Historians have identified a variety of population enumerations, estimates, lists of settlers, and "censuses" in colonial Virginia besides the official census of 1635. In addition to details in Bruce, *Economic History*, Sutherland, *Population Distribution*, and Wertenbaker, *Planters of Colonial Virginia*, extensive accounts may be found in Franklin B. Dexter, "Estimates of Population in the American Colonies," *Proceedings of the American Antiquarian Society*, 5 (1888), n.s., pt. 1, 22–50; W. S. Rossiter, *A Century of Population Growth* (Washington, D. C.: Government Printing Office, 1909); and Evarts B. Greene and Virginia D. Harrington, *American Population before the Federal Census of 1790* (New York: Columbia University Press, 1932). Greene and Harrington provide an exhaustive index to almost every colonial population count or estimate ever made. Their lists of sources are invaluable both for actual figures and for the varieties of demographic activities.

After that time the population became so dispersed that enumerations were highly subject to error. In any case, they relied heavily upon estimates.

Simple and irregular as they all were, some of the enumerations nevertheless produced, even in the early years, a certain variety of population data. The census of 1624–25, for instance, out of a population figured at 1202, distinguished servants and gave their ages. Other counts reported variously upon males and females, numbers of children, white males of fighting age, and, later on, Negroes. In many of the estimates made from at least the middle of the century, calculation of the total population was made from the annual county lists of titheables. The customary formula used in these calculations was three inhabitants for each known titheable.[34]

Throughout the seventeenth century, the painfully slow increase in population remained a central concern in Virginia. Deliberate efforts were made to augment the population, mainly for economic and security reasons. These efforts contributed to a number of demographic movements, notably of white servants and Negro slaves. Of these, the servant traffic was of particular statistical concern to the colony in the early decades.

The head-right system, which sought to stimulate immigration by granting individuals fifty acres (later decreased) for each person they brought to the colony, had a certain success. Operation of the system also resulted in administrative controls which were at least partially quantitative in nature. As early as 1619 the Virginia Assembly attempted to institute some means of recording the contracts made

34. Philip A. Bruce, *Social Life of Virginia in the Seventeenth Century*, 2nd ed. (New York: Frederick Ungar, 1964), pp. 14–15.

with servants before their departure from England. The Virginia Company provided such a registration at London in 1622. In 1645, customs houses in England were ordered to keep registers of all outgoing passengers, while Parliament the next year instructed colonial governors to return certificates of the actual arrivals of such persons. The city of Bristol, beginning in 1654, maintained a compulsory registry of departing servants, an example followed in the next century by London and a few other ports. The national Registry Office established by Parliament in 1664 existed throughout the eighteenth century, but due to its optional character accomplished little in regularizing the servant trade.[35]

The colony of Virginia at an early date also attempted to regularize its procedures for obtaining and centralizing various other kinds of quantitative data. Among these steps, the office of Register of the colony was established by 1637. The first occupant was Mathew Kemp. He and his successors inspected tobacco and other exports, kept records, and sent detailed yearly statements of exports to the Lord Treasurer in England. For a time the Register received a fee of two pence per cask of tobacco loaded. Somewhat later he became responsible for the registry of land patents as well.[36] By 1640 the Secretary of State had also acquired a variety of record-keeping obligations. An Act of that year specified that he receive and maintain for the entire colony not only records of such transactions as court orders, land patents, and wills, but also of "all Births,

35. See discussion of this matter in Abbot Smith, *Colonists in Bondage*, pp. 16, 70–80.
36. See *Calendar of State Papers 1574–1660*, pp. 245–246 and 287. Several other colonies also established the office of Register. For Edmund Randolph's activities in such a post, see Chapter IV, below.

Burials, Marriages, and Persons that go out of the country." [37]

The fact that such offices were established to record vital statistics and a variety of other data was no more an indication of the amount or completeness of the data actually received than was the fact that parish registers were prescribed. A vast gap existed throughout the colonial period, and even longer, between prescription and performance, between good statistical intentions and enforcement under the law. This was true not only in Virginia and neighboring Maryland, where conditions were similar, but also in New England with its particular background and special motivation. [38]

37. Robert Beverley, *The History and Present State of Virginia,* ed. Louis B. Wright (Chapel Hill: University of North Carolina Press, 1947), p. 245. See also Bruce, *Institutional History,* II, pp. 396–398.

38. The General Assembly of Maryland passed a vital statistics registration act before 1650. See Eugene F. Cordell, *The Medical Annals of Maryland, 1799–1899* (Baltimore: Williams & Wilkins, 1903), p. 642

Chapter II

Vital Events of a Puritan Community

The leaders of other English colonies in North America found as much use for statistics as the Virginians did, and they were equally concerned with demographic matters. They carried out population enumerations and provided for various kinds of statistical registers according to the needs and capacities of their colonies. There were similarities in vital record-gathering and-keeping activities from one colony to another. Yet differences existed, particularly in the political setting of and motivation for such activities. This was notably true of the New England colonies. While Virginians collected vital data largely to fulfill their obligations to Company, Church, and Crown in England, New Englanders did so chiefly to satisfy their own internal needs and aspirations as a self-conscious community. The rather full development of these activities in

Massachusetts Bay, which set the pattern for the whole region, illustrates these differences.[1]

As in the case of Virginia, a number of explorers and settlers gathered information about the geography, resources, Indian tribes, and other characteristics of New England.[2] Demographic details about the settlers themselves came out in a number of now-famous histories or journals written by leading participants in the planting of the New England settlements. William Bradford's history of Plymouth, like John Smith's account of Virginia, constitutes a kind of demographic record. Bradford's well-known description of the terrible mortality of the Pilgrims' first winter admittedly is not expressed in numbers. It conveys nonetheless a vivid cumulative impression of vital human events: "But it pleased God to visit us then with death daily, and with so general a disease that the living were scarce able to bury the dead and the well not in any measure sufficient to tend the sick."[3] The appendices of his memoir, prepared in 1650, are more exact. There Bradford furnished a kind of bill of mortality of the original 101 persons who had come to Plymouth on the *Mayflower*. It was a summary of those who had married and of how many children they had had; of those who had died, giving their ages and usually the causes of death; and, finally, of the thirty who remained.

John Winthrop's account of New England was every bit

1. Although no systematic state-by-state survey of legislation is intended, early registration in the Carolinas, New York, New Jersey, and Pennsylvania will be discussed briefly in Chapter III.

2. Among the early general accounts were those of Captain John Smith and Ferdinando Gorges. See also G. P. Winship, ed. *Sailors' Narratives of Voyages Along the New England Coast 1524–1624* (Boston: Houghton, Mifflin, 1905).

3. William Bradford, *Of Plymouth Plantation, 1620–1647*, Samuel Eliot Morison, ed. (New York: Knopf, 1952), p. 95.

as much a record of vital human events as Bradford's history.[4] Kept as a journal, the work includes notations of marriages, deaths of prominent persons, reports of the numbers of smallpox deaths among the Indians, and a wide variety of fatal accidents at sea and on the land. But neither Bradford's nor Winthrop's recording of such matters was at all unique in New England. Many literate persons took it upon themselves to note in diverse places the intimate human events of the community. While leaders remarked such occurrences in their journals or in sermons, ordinary citizens recorded them in family Bibles or in letters back to England. Some even resorted to verse, as did Samuel Sewall in his diary entry of November 8, 1706:

> This morning Tom Child, the Painter, died.
>
> Tom Child has often painted Death,
> But never to the Life before:
> Doing it now, he's out of Breath;
> He paints it once, and paints no more.[5]

With these informal kinds of notice being taken in the community, the chances were good that vital events in New England did not pass without a record being made by someone, quite apart from any official provisions. The reasons for this widespread individual interest lay at least partly in the settlers' identities as Puritans as well as in their heritage as Englishmen.

Puritans, whether Separatists or non-Separatists, had

4. John Winthrop, *Winthrop's Journal, "History of New England," 1630–1649*, James K. Hosmer, ed., 2 vols. (New York: Scribner's, 1908).

5. *Diary of Samuel Sewall, 1674–1729*, in *Collections of the Massachusetts Historical Society*, 5th ser., vols. V, VI, VII (1878, 1879, 1882), VI, 170.

had their interest in the numbering of vital events sharpened by years of controversy, first with Catholics and then with Anglicans.[6] The tradition of a learned clergy and an informed laity which both Puritan branches cherished enabled them to hold their own in these controversies. It also gave their members a heightened awareness of the value of recording vital occurrences. Close study of the Testaments made Puritans familiar with the experiences of Biblical peoples in enumerating tribes and nations. The Old Testament in particular provided frequent reminders of the religious and genealogical importance of vital data. For a people who came to regard themselves as a chosen group it was imperative to preserve records of their vital data in order to maintain the continuities they had perceived between earlier chosen people and themselves.

The systematic maintenance of vital records had, moreover, at least a methodological kinship with an important element of Puritan theology. Amesian logic, a systematic classification of religious doctrines by heads and subheads, was the orderly method used by the Puritans to reveal the proper meaning of God's past words as recorded in the Bible.[7] It followed that the Puritans welcomed any

6. Pine believes, but without providing much evidence for his belief, that the development of parish registers in Protestant countries in general was stimulated by the need for written records and other data to help in proving Roman Catholicism wrong. Pine, *American Origins*, pp. 28ff.

7. For a discussion of the influence of William Ames and Petrus Ramus in shaping this concept in New England, see Perry Miller, *The New England Mind: The Seventeenth Century* (Cambridge, Mass.: Harvard University Press, 1954), pp. 111–153 and 188–190. See also Joseph Dorfman, *The Economic Mind in American Civilization, 1606–1865*, 2 vols. (New York: Viking Press, 1946), I, 36–37; and Keith L. Springer, "Technometria: A Prologue to Puritan Theology," *Journal of the History of Ideas*, 29 (January–March 1968), 115–122.

method which might help reveal God's present meaning or intentions with any comparable degree of precision. In the study of the churches' vital records, some Puritans found a tool which came close to meeting these specifications.[8]

As Englishmen, the Pilgrims and Puritans who migrated to New England were entirely familiar with the mandatory registers kept in the home parishes. Indeed, more than one of their pastors must themselves have kept registers in English parishes. It was thus an entirely natural matter for congregations on their own initiative to keep registers in the New World when part or all of their members were transplanted. Someone connected with First Church, Boston, began keeping a record of the baptisms and other events of the church's members in 1630, soon after their arrival. In 1634 Thomas Leverett, one of the ruling elders, "was keeping both church and town records."[9] The Reverend John Eliot, at the First Church in Roxbury, helped set the early pattern of records for the New England churches. Beginning in 1630, he personally kept records not only of persons received into communion and of matters of church discipline, but also of baptisms, serious accidents, and deaths.[10] Samuel Danforth continued the series after Eliot's death. John Lothrop, first pastor of the Scituate and Barnstable churches, kept a detailed

8. See further discussion in Chapter V, below.

9. Noted by Darrett B. Rutman, *Winthrop's Boston* (Chapel Hill: University of North Carolina Press, 1965), p. 65. See also [City of Boston], *A Report of the Record Commissioners, Containing Boston Births, Baptisms, Marriages, and Deaths, 1630–1699* (Boston: Rockwell and Churchill, 1883).

10. [City of Boston], *A Report of the Record Commissioners, Containing the Roxbury Land and Church Records* (Boston: Rockwell and Churchill, 1881).

manuscript of similar events from 1634 through 1653.[11] Similarly, in other churches, someone, usually but not necessarily the pastor, maintained records of this kind and often included accounts of special providences as well.[12] Keeping records of religious events such as baptisms was one thing; keeping legal records of vital events was another, so far as Puritans were concerned. The radical solution of this matter in Massachusetts was part of the colony's working-out of a special church-state relationship.

Reformation leaders from Luther and Zwingli to William Perkins and John Milton took progressively extreme positions in denying that rites connected with vital human events were properly church functions. At first they rejected only the notion that marriage was a sacrament of the church. By 1608, however, when the Scrooby Separatists went to Holland, they found that the Dutch Calvinists were extending the notion to burials.[13] Pastor Robinson and the Pilgrims found these concepts entirely congenial. They accordingly agreed among themselves "that the ceremonies of marriage and burial, being common to all men, whether Christian or heathen, were no part of the services of the church, and should be performed . . . by a civil magistrate."[14] In America, both the Pilgrims and

11. [Amos Otis], "Scituate and Barnstable Church Records," *The New England Historical and Genealogical Register*, 9 (1855), 279–287, and 10 (1856), 37–43.

12. See further discussion of church registers in Chapter V.

13. For a brief general discussion of the views of Reformation leaders, see Nelson M. Blake, *The Road to Reno: A History of Divorce in the United States* (New York: Macmillan, 1962), pp. 1–35. William Bradford noted that marriage in Holland had by 1590 been formally and legally turned into a civil ceremony (*Of Plymouth Plantation*, p. 86).

14. Quoted in Arthur W. Calhoun, *A Social History of the American Family*, 2nd ed., 3 vols. (New York: Barnes and Noble, 1960), I, 48.

the Puritans continued the practice of civil marriage from the beginning. By extension, it was a matter of simple logic for them to regard the registration of marriages as an essentially civil matter. And by further extension they came to feel that the registration of births and deaths for legal purposes was a state rather than an ecclesiastical responsibility, though they did not deny the interest of the church in recording events of such true religious significance as baptisms.[15]

The admitted variance from English law of their own marriage practices made the leaders of Massachusetts Bay colony understandably reluctant, in the first years, to adopt legislation on marriage which might invite interference from the English authorities.[16] Nevertheless, by the late 1630's, when the colony decided to regularize all its record-keeping mechanisms, marriage records were included. This legislation came in Massachusetts before the adoption of a broad internal code of laws (the Body of Liberties), but at a time when internal crises in England were already diverting the attention of its officials.

On September 9, 1639, the General Court of Massachusetts Bay provided "That there bee records kept of all wills, administrations, & inventories, as also of the dayes of every marriage, birth & death of every pson [sic] within this jurisdiction." At the same session, the General Court made provision for keeping land and housing records, for re-

15. In practice, New England Congregationalists sometimes considered burials to be religious as well as civil acts. Accordingly, some church records of the seventeenth century include burials as well as baptisms. On the other hand, few included marriages in their records until after 1686, when marriage received status as a religious ceremony as well as a civil action.

16. See the well-known passage of John Winthrop, *Winthrop's Journal,* I, 324. See also the discussion in Edmund S. Morgan, *The Puritan Dilemma* (Boston: Little, Brown, 1958), passim.

cording all court proceedings, and for publishing banns — the latter to be read at a public lecture or town meeting or placed upon a public post erected for the purpose, but specifically not at churches.[17] The law charged the recorders of the various towns with performing the registration; Stephen Winthrop, a son of John Winthrop, "was chosen to record things at Boston."[18] Subsequently, a law of 1642 gave the responsibility of recording births and deaths to the Clerk of the Writs in each town (after 1693, the Town Clerks) and to make annual returns to the court recorders in their areas. Magistrates were required to report the marriages they performed directly to the recorders. The law provided for fees to be paid for each entry, set the responsibility with the clerks for obtaining and forwarding complete returns to the General Court, and provided penalties for failures. Modifications by 1644 made the ordinary citizen responsible for reporting vital events and for some reason eliminated the central collection of such records.[19]

Though the work of a tiny outpost of civilization, the Massachusetts registration system represented several note-

17. See *Records of the Governor and Company of the Massachusetts Bay in New England,* Nathaniel B. Shurtleff, M. D., ed. (Boston: William White, 1853), I, 275–276.

18. Quoted in *Guide to the Public Vital Records in Massachusetts* (Boston: Historical Records Survey, 1942), p. 283.

19. For a thorough study of the development of Massachusetts vital statistics registration, see Robert Gutman, *Birth and Death Registration in Massachusetts, 1639–1900* (New York: Milbank Memorial Fund, 1959). An older but a reliable and concise account is that of Robert Rene Kuczynski, "The Registration Laws in the Colonies of Massachusetts Bay and New Plymouth," *Journal of the American Statistical Association,* VII, n.s., no. 51 (September 1900), 65–73. Nothing comparable to either of these reviews of the relevant legislation exists for any of the other colonies or states, although some efforts have been made to unravel the record of Rhode Island.

worthy statistical innovations. Most important scientifically, no doubt, was the change in the nature of the data to be gathered, from the recording of such religious ceremonies as baptisms, weddings, and burials to the demographically more meaningful events of births, marriages, and deaths. Most significant socially and politically was its abandonment of reliance upon ecclesiastical mechanisms for registration and the transfer of these processes to government clerks. Making the individual citizen, instead of ministers or clerks, responsible for reporting the vital events was also a significant departure from prevailing practice.[20]

Such innovations had considerable influence outside Massachusetts. The General Court of Connecticut adopted similar provisions for civil vital statistics in 1644 and in 1650. Town clerks were ordered to keep local registers and to make annual returns to a central register in Hartford.[21] Plymouth followed with comparable legislation in 1646. In that colony the clerks or other record-keepers were ordered to "exhibit a true and pfect Copy fairely written annually at March Courte unto the sd Courte of all the birthes, marriages and burialls of the yeare past."[22] By 1647, even Rhode Island, regarded by many as the backwater of New England, had adopted registration legislation.[23]

20. These innovations were pointed out in *ibid.*, p. 73.

21. See Ira V. Hiscock, "The Background of Public Health in Connecticut," in *The Heritage of Connecticut Medicine,* ed. Herbert Thoms (New Haven: Whaples-Bullis, 1942), p. 137.

22. Quoted in David Pulsifer, ed., *Records of the Colony of New Plymouth in New England,* vol. II, *Laws, 1623–1682* (Boston: William White, 1861), 52–53.

23. The precise beginning of marriage registration in Rhode Island is known to have been in 1647. Although pertinent records are missing, it is probable that birth and death registration was

Even the mother country followed the Massachusetts example. Under Cromwell's Commonwealth, various acts, culminating in the 1653 Civil Marriage Act, brought about a system of civil vital statistics registration in England. Despite ridicule from Royalist pamphleteers, the county clerks and other laymen selected as registers in England generally brought such reforming zeal to their work that "more orderly records were secured during the Commonwealth than existed before it or after." [24] The regime even began to substitute English for Latin in the registers and other vital documents. The Restoration, to be sure, brought a quick return to ecclesiastical registration in England. The New England colonies, however, were able to retain their civil arrangements.[25]

The original vital statistics legislation of Massachusetts Bay was revised or renewed seven times between 1639 and 1692. This continuing concern attests to the high standing that vital registration had among the Puritans. The orderly methods implicit in the systematic collection and recording of vital data fitted in well with the concepts of thrift, hard work, sobriety, and piety which characterized the Protestant Ethic. At its best, the system worked wherever there was a fairly high degree of civic responsibility along with a considerable amount of clerkly initiative in reminding citizens of that responsibility. Samuel Sewall has told us in his famous Diary how the system functioned in the Boston of his day:

legislated for within a few years of that date. See *Guide to the Public Vital Statistics Records: Births, Marriages, Deaths in the State of Rhode Island and Providence Plantations* (Providence: Historical Records Survey, 1941).

24. Howard, *Matrimonial Institutions*, I, 426.

25. See discussion in *ibid.*, pp. 61ff.; Nelson Blake, *Road to Reno*, pp. 35ff.; and Calhoun, *A Social History*, pp. 61ff.

January 8 [1717/18]: At Mr. Prout's, upon his mentioning it, I enter'd the Death of my dear Wife, gave him a Shilling.

February 25, 1720/21: Went to Mr. Joseph Prout, Town Clerk, and gave him the Certificat of Marriage of the Rev'd. Mr. William Cooper and Mrs. Judith Sewall.[26]

On the other hand, the fact that registration legislation repeatedly had to be revised suggests that such neighborly arrangements were not always an unqualified success. Not all citizens, by any means, were as conscientious, cooperative, or informed as Sewall. And while there were other clerks as thorough as Joseph Prout, many were not. A few colonial writers claimed that there was "general neglect" of certain registration acts. While this may have been exaggerated, it remains that there were wide differences in the way the legislation was carried out. The reasons for this state of affairs are not entirely clear, but they involve more than personal differences.[27]

26. *Diary of Samuel Sewall*, VII, 158 and 282. Besides Prout, four individuals served as Clerk for Boston and Suffolk County between the 1650's and 1709. These were Jonathan Negus, Joseph Webb, Captain Ephraim Savage, and William Griggs. Concord had seven clerks between 1649 and 1719. Of the eight clerks in Braintree between 1643 and 1776, Benjamin Thompson, who was both a physician and a schoolmaster, brought far more than ordinary talents to the job.

27. Mid-twentieth-century scholars who are beginning to study in detail the demographic history of given New England towns are revealing something about specific registration deficiencies. Kenneth Lockridge found that in Dedham, Massachusetts, births and marriages were relatively well recorded between 1636 and 1736, while deaths were "radically underrecorded." He noted that "spinsters simply do not appear in the vital or in the town records, nor —

One difficulty may well have been the close relationship of township and parish. Since township and parish boundaries were frequently identical, the vital records which the town kept were often, at least at first, the same as those for the parish — that is, the church congregation as a social and legal entity. They were, accordingly, often kept by the same person, a convenient arrangement.[28] In practice, however, the recollection that the clergy used to keep the official parish records in England, and the assumption that energetic ministers still concerned themselves with similar records, must have had their effect. A clerk could hardly be blamed for neglecting his registers when, in his view, he was merely doing his bit to eliminate duplication of effort.

Another problem was that the clerks had to live with their neighbors; no one could have been anxious to arouse antagonisms by prosecuting an individual for fail-

---

ordinarily — do servants." He observed, by comparison with other data, that "many are found to have disappeared in their old age without any record having been made of their deaths." Kenneth A. Lockridge, "The Population of Dedham, Massachusetts, 1636–1736," *Economic History Review*, 2nd ser., 19 (1966), 318–344, but esp. 318, 319, 325, 328, and 332–3.

28. I am indebted to Professor William McLoughlin for attempting to enlighten me about the knotty relationship between church, parish, and town. For published discussions of these relationships, see Emil Oberholzer, Jr., *Delinquent Saints* (New York: Columbia University Press, 1956), pp. 5–11; Ellen Bicknell Crane, *History of Worcester County, Massachusetts*, I (New York: Lewis Historical Publishing Co., 1924), 456–457; Susan M. Reed, *Church and State in Massachusetts, 1691–1740* (Urbana: University of Illinois Press, 1914), p. 52, n. 2, and p. 54, n. 7; Harold Field Worthley, "Pilgrim-Puritan Church Records," *Bulletin of the Congregational Library*, 13 (October 1961), 4–7; and J. M. Bumsted, "Revivalism and Separatism in New England: The First Society of Norwich, Connecticut, as a Case Study," *William and Mary Quarterly*, 3rd ser., 24 (October 1967), 589. See also Chapter V of the present study.

ure to report a birth or a death, in itself the pettiest sort of offense. In turn, few delinquent clerks or registrars were ever hailed into court. In 1674, however, several town clerks of York County, Maine, were tried for "Neglect in not giveing an Accompt unto the Clarke of the writts in their respective Towns of all births, deaths & marages in the say'd County." Their acquittal is less surprising than the fact that the case ever went to the courts.[29] For in Boston the Colony Secretary himself, Edward Rawson, seems to have been the most careless of recorders. Rawson is known to have neglected to transcribe many names on the General Court's lists of Freemen, but he was never prosecuted for these or other recording deficiencies.[30]

The difficulties of enforcing the registration laws were compounded by the fact that Massachusetts was far from a unified Puritan commonwealth. Antinomians, Quakers, and other dissenters were made so unwelcome that they felt little obligation to obey the colony's laws.[31] Many in the large group of socially or economically submerged persons, including those who could not or did not want to qualify for church membership, were in much the same situation. Consequently, the vital affairs of this latter group

29. Charles T. Libby, ed., *Province and Court Records of Maine,* vol. II: *York County Court Records* (Portland: Maine Historical Society, 1931), p. 291. Further studies are needed of the extent and effectiveness of enforcement of registration laws in all colonies. Colonial court records should be examined in detail in order to obtain a more accurate idea of the numbers of trials and nature of punishments, both of individual citizens and of clerks.

30. See Stephen Foster, "The Massachusetts Franchise in the Seventeenth Century," *William and Mary Quarterly,* 3rd ser., 24 (October 1967), 620–623.

31. Howard Mumford Jones has emphasized the "black legend of lawlessness" which grew up quickly in all of the new settlements of North America. See Jones, *O Strange New Yorld,* p. 278.

became increasingly difficult to control, despite harsh punishments meted out, say, for irregular sexual activities. The common-law marriages, casual breeding, and out-of-the-way deaths which occurred frequently in this fringe segment of the population must almost as frequently have gone unnoticed and unrecorded by the clerks.

Apart from legal and human inadequacies, there is no doubt that the course of official vital statistics registration in Massachusetts, as in Virginia, was impeded by factors of geography. Although New Englanders had a greater tendency than Virginians to cluster in groups close to their churches, there were always strays. The steady formation of new churches, parishes, and towns in itself often disrupted the mechanisms for recording the vital events of involved individuals. Meanwhile, the rapid push of population up the river valleys and into the New England interior from the mid-1630's to about 1675 increased the numbers of those who settled too far from the towns to be able to conform to town practices. A midwinter birth on a lonely farm might never be reported to the clerk. Likewise, burials in the family orchard could easily escape clerical notice.

A final difficulty in making civil registration work was the fact that not every citizen had equity in the registers. As organized in Massachusetts, registration was essentially the concern of the townships, which were both the effective units of government and the foci of life for the ordinary citizen. It was in the towns that such personal questions as those involving inheritance, legitimacy, or genealogy were settled by reference to vital records kept close at hand. Here the statistical mind served the Protestant Ethic directly. But there were many people who had no expectation of inheritances, who were in no position to benefit from the rules of primogeniture, and who cared little either about their ancestors or their own possible illegitimacy. Accordingly, only a certain segment of society in the towns had a stake in the public vital records before the nineteenth century. Only this segment was really interested in keeping the registers complete.

While the first generations of Massachusetts residents were far from being of a single mind about vital statistics registration, they had common misgivings about amassing population data. In this case the problem lay in the colony's ambiguous relationship with the mother country. In the early years this relationship was not demanding. Since virtually all the Puritan leaders of the Massachusetts Bay Company migrated to New England and took the Charter with them, the colony never had to make quantitative population or other reports to Company officials in London. More important, since social and religious difficulties were mounting in England itself during the 1630's, neither Crown nor church officials were in a position to inquire as closely as they might have into such matters as the government, religion, or demography of the colony's first years. Massachusetts leaders liked it that way. To help avoid such scrutiny, it was advantageous for some time for Massachusetts Bay and the other New England colonies to conceal, so far as possible, the numbers of their inhabitants. This secrecy about population became such a habit that there were no official censuses taken in New England during the seventeenth century. In the eighteenth century the habit was transformed into a deliberate effort to frustrate the wishes of the Crown.

Despite the lack of official censuses and despite the fact that neither church lists, tax lists, nor other lists ever included the whole population, New England officials knew fairly closely how many people there were in each colony. In fact, various enumerations of significant parts of the population were carried out during this period. Among the most extensive were those carried out under the Confederation of New England. The Confederation was organized primarily to coordinate the defense measures of Massachusetts Bay, Plymouth, Connecticut, and New Haven at a time when England could offer no help. Article 4 of the Articles of Confederation, which were adopted in May 1643, provided for enumerations in each member colony of all males between sixteen and sixty, in order to determine the colonies' respective shares of expenses and the number of troops to be furnished. Several enumerations, notably in Massachusetts, were carried out for this purpose during the next few decades.[32]

A population factor which was just as important to New England Puritans as the number of troops was that of the number of church members. Many people in the Puritan commonwealth kept an eye upon these figures. None compiled them in greater detail, however, than Edward Johnson. An early associate of Winthrop in Boston and subsequently a leading citizen of Woburn up to his death in 1672, Johnson at one time or another was selectman, captain of militia, and town clerk. As clerk he gained an acquaintance with the problems of keeping vital registers. Since he was something of a writer, Johnson began the first page of his town records in an unclerkly way, with a poem. Poetry, however, was not his forte. Johnson is best remembered today for his 1654 *History of New England,* usually known as *The Wonder-Working Provi-*

32. For further details, see Josiah H. Benton, Jr., *Early Census Making in Massachusetts 1643–1765* (Boston: Charles E. Goodspeed, 1905), chap. 1, passim.

dence of Sion's Saviour in New England. The work is an account of the growth of the Congregational churches of New England up to 1651 and of the towns which grew up around them. Like some other such accounts, Johnson's history is stronger in its propaganda for the "New England Way" than in its demographic accuracy. It is, nevertheless, notable for its descriptive and quantitative detail. "Water-Towne," for example, in 1651 had 450 cattle and sheep, 1800 acres under cultivation, 160 families in residence, and 250 souls in the church. In that same year, Johnson's survey of Charles Towne showed 150 houses, 1200 acres planted in corn, 400 cattle, and 400 sheep, while the church had "one pastor, and one Teacher, one Ruling Elder, and three Deacons, the number of Soules are about 160."

Johnson's over-all assessment of God's demographic providence for New England was jubilant in tone. Figuring from the establishment of the first feeble church in Salem in 1629, he saw that the entire population picture of New England had changed, and in only twenty-one years. During this span he found that the native Indian tribes, which had been "a populous Nation, consisting of 30,000 able men, [were] now brought to lesse than 300." Taking their place, "this poore Church of Christ consisting at their beginning, but of seven persons, [has] increased to forty-three Churches . . . and in those Churches about 7750 Soules." [33]

The number of non-church members in the population increased as rapidly during these decades as that of the church members. Meanwhile, the growth of all segments of the New England colonies was being affected by events.

33. *Johnson's Wonder Working Providence, 1628–1651,* J. Franklin Jameson, ed. (New York: Scribner's, 1910), pp. 48, 68, 74.

Most importantly, the English Civil War shut off the flow of emigrants to New England, and even induced a number of settlers to return to England. About this same time, moreover, Massachusetts Bay and other New England colonies were becoming increasingly selective about the kinds of immigrants they would accept. As if to help out in this situation, the leaders of Virginia and Maryland, as early as the mid-1640's, actively began to encourage New Englanders to move South. From this time on, through the rest of the colonial period, internal population movements affected virtually all the colonies.[34] Exchanges took place both among the mainland colonies and between them and the West Indies colonies. New England rarely gained from these internal movements.[35] Almost from the beginning, the region served in one degree or another both as a source of population supply for the rest of America, and as a source of religious, political, and cultural concepts. During the few decades following the Restoration, the planting and filling up of several new colonies greatly increased the competition for the available supply.

34. No special registers of immigration figures were kept in any of the colonies, but it was usually possible to obtain such data from passenger lists of incoming ships which were deposited with port authorities. For interesting analyses of some of these lists, see Charles E. Banks, *The Planters of the Commonwealth* (Boston, 1930); and John C. Hotten, *The Original Lists of Persons of Quality, Emigrants . . . who went from Great Britain to the American Plantations, 1600–1700* (New York, 1931).

35. See Hansen, *Atlantic Migration*, pp. 30ff. The large emigration from Barbados to the mainland colonies is pointed out in Richard S. Dunn, "The Barbados Census of 1680: Profile of the Richest Colony in English America," *William and Mary Quarterly*, 3rd ser. 26 (January 1969), 3–30.

Chapter III

Colonization and Political Arithmetic

1660–1700

The launching of new English colonies in North America during the last half of the seventeenth century took place not only in the changed political atmosphere which the Restoration brought to the home country, but in an intellectual climate that was more charged than ever with energy and innovation. If Virginia, with its elementary demographic concerns, began in the somewhat Olympian age of Shakespeare and Bacon, New York and New Jersey emerged with their own population problems in the empirical age of Pepys, Wren, and Boyle. If the registration system of Massachusetts was drawn up in the militant times of Milton and Cromwell, those of the Carolinas and Pennsylvania came into being in the more sparkling times of Sheridan and Petty. Statesmen not only took a new interest in colonies, but demanded up-to-date means of governing them. Scientists working in a variety of directions during these years not only laid the groundwork for statistical and population theory, but devised some of the quantitative methodology required by the administrators. Since it was an age of talent, in some cases the same person was both administrator and scientist.

In various corners of Europe, scholars had begun bringing quantitative data to bear upon their studies. By the 1660's one could point to a number of such applications. In Germany, for instance, the social scientist Hermann Conring was introducing a form of descriptive political studies into his university courses at Helmstadt. Within a century, in the hands of his followers, notably Gottfried Achenwall, these studies took on the name of "Statistik."

In France, a working theory of probability emerged in the mid-1650's when Pascal turned his attention momentarily from spiritual matters to games of chance. Christiaan Huygens of Holland and others developed the idea further during the next few years. Fortunately for the development of the colonies, no doubt, the theory did not extend far enough in the seventeenth century, at least in its application to probabilities of survivorship, to warn would-be migrants of the long odds against living more than a few months in a remote and dangerous New World. Actually, the reports which filtered back to Europe conveyed enough of an idea of these odds in any case to heighten the difficulties of recruiting new settlers.

Of greater immediate utility than probability theories for any countries during the 1660's was the improvement of parish registers and the development of other forms of quantitative official data. Jean Bodin and Sully had made early efforts at official data-gathering in France. Now Colbert sought to make such activities even more important parts of the administration of government, both at home and in the French colonies. From the beginning of New France, Champlain and Sagard, along with Jesuit missionaries, chronicled vital events in their personal journals, while vital registers came into being with the founding of the first church in Quebec. Colbert's administrative directives of the mid-1660's put the force of government authority behind the parish registers of France, though it was not fully effective in Quebec until 1678. His edict of 1666, however, did call for a precise enumeration of the population of the colony. Jean Talon, the Intendant, personally supervised the resulting house-to-house canvass of the area between Montreal and Quebec. In the next year and at varying intervals throughout French rule, other enumerations were made, even in scattered outposts such as those in the Illinois country.[1]

Dutch appreciation of quantification by no means stopped with mathematicians like Huygens. Well-kept parish mortality registers in the late 1660's, for instance, furnished the statesman Jan De Witt with data which served

1. For details of early French and Canadian vital statistics, see Paul Parrot, "History of Civil Registration in Quebec," *Canadian Public Health Journal,* 21 (November 1930), 529–540; and R. H. Coats, "Beginnings in Canadian Statistics," *The Canadian Historical Review,* 27 (June 1946), 109–130. For further details about France, see Fernand Faure, "The Development and Progress of Statistics in France," in Koren, *History of Statistics,* pp. 217–268; and P. Goubert, "Régistres paroissiaux et démographie dans la France du XVIe siècle," *Annales de démographie historique, 1965* (Paris: Société de Démographie Historique, 1966), pp. 43–48.

Similarly, the Spanish made periodic enumeration in areas which subsequently became parts of the United States. One of these was carried out as late as 1791–92 in the Natchez District of West Florida. See Laura D. S. Harrell, "Colonial Medical Practices in British West Florida, 1763–1781," *Bulletin of the History of Medicine,* 41 (November–December, 1967), 557.

as the base for his pioneer money-raising annuity. For all of this, somewhat oddly, colonial administrators of the Dutch West India Company made no provisions for collecting the vital data of their tiny settlements in New Netherlands. Such registers were left entirely to the initiative of Calvinist dominies of the Dutch Reformed churches. It is not surprising, given the vast area of the parishes and the often unsettled conditions in the colony, that these records left much to be desired. It is likely that more vital data were preserved in the family Bibles of the day than were entered in the church registers.

Late in the period of Dutch control, in 1657, the colony attempted (with little success) to establish official registers in connection with a somewhat feudal mode of classifying the inhabitants for civil and legal purposes. This provided for a "Great Burgherright" with four categories of leading citizens and a "Small Burgherright" with four categories of lesser folks. "In order that all this may be the better and more regularly practiced, observed, and obeyed," the ordinance specified, "the Burgomasters are ordered and authorized to make out . . . correct Lists of those who . . . are invested, qualified and favored, either with the Great or Small Burgherright . . . , and have a true Register thereof made." [2]

When the English seized New Netherlands in 1664 and changed its name to New York, they introduced tighter provisions for public administration than had existed under the Dutch, and they eliminated the intermediary of the trading company. The "Duke's Laws" of 1665 pro-

2. See *Guide to Public Vital Statistics Records in New York State,* 3 vols. (Albany, N. Y.: Historical Records Survey, 1942), I, vii; and Calhoun, *Social History,* I, 159ff. See also Jerrold Seymann, *Colonial Charters, Patents and Grants to the Communities Comprising the City of New York* (New York, City of New York, 1939), p. 192.

vided, among other details, for the recording of births, marriages, and deaths by the minister or clerk of every parish. The law made family heads or next of kin responsible for notifying the officials of such events and set penalties of five shillings for each failure to make the required notifications.[3] The effect of this law, however, was virtually nullified in several counties during the next century, largely because of failure to establish the Anglican Church in those parts of the state. This left such parts without any parish structure to carry out the desired registration.

The Duke's Laws marked an awareness in England of the need for greater administrative preplanning of colonial societies and governments. When Virginia, Plymouth, and Massachusetts Bay were founded, law and governmental systems had to be worked out empirically over the years. Accordingly, official provisions for recording vital events were made only when the leaders got around to it. From the period of the 1660's, the founders of new colonies left less to chance. They now attempted to prescribe in advance, or at an early stage of actual settlement, complete formulas for law and government. They made certain that provisions for vital statistics and other forms of registration were included in these formulas.[4] This new level of appreciation for advance planning for new settlements arose to a certain extent out of the mistakes, hardships,

---

3. See *Guide to Records in New York*, I, vii.
4. This was also true of the short-lived patent for the entire Virginia area which King Charles II in 1672 awarded to Lords Arlington and Culpeper. This document, among other things, granted the Proprietors full rights "to keep registers and records." See Sister Joan de Lourdes Leonard, "Operation Checkmate: The Birth and Death of a Virginia Blueprint for Progress 1660–1676," *William and Mary Quarterly*, 3rd ser., 24 (January 1967), 68–69.

and general confusion of the early years of the first English colonies. But it also reflected a newly critical view in administration at home. And, in the specific case of vital registration, it reflected important and widespread scientific advances in the quantification of data.

Although Francis Bacon had long since died, "Baconism" was at full tide during the 1660's. The founders of the Royal Society took conscious pride in having established the sort of mechanism for the systematic pursuit of scientific knowledge that Bacon had advocated. Robert Boyle and Robert Hooke, for instance, had made quantification an integral part of their approach to laboratory experimentation. For all of the members, inductive reasoning based upon accumulations of observed facts had become a way of life.[5]

When John Winthrop, Jr., left London in 1663 for his return to Connecticut, he offered to pass on to his fellow members in the Royal Society such scientific information as he could about America. The Secretary, Henry Oldenburg, reminded Winthrop that the members' thirst for such knowledge was well-nigh boundless, since the Society had "taken to taske the whole Universe." In any case, he knew that the Society would be interested in having a careful account of the geography and topography of Connecticut, a "history of all its productions," descriptive and numerical information about neighboring colonies, as well as accounts of Winthrop's method of salt-making and his

5. Letwin regards the Society's emphasis upon inductive reasoning and quantification to have been a "misplaced" faith. He feels that the "best minds of England squandered their talents" in "an absolute orgy of measurement." William Letwin, *The Origins of Scientific Economics* (Garden City: Doubleday, 1965), p. 106. See also Martha Ornstein, *The Role of Scientific Societies in the Seventeenth Century* (Hampden, Ct.: Archon Books, 1963).

other scientific activities.[6] Unfortunately, the busy Winthrop never found the time really to satisfy the curiosity of the Society's members, at least with respect to the quantitative aspects of America.

Perhaps the most inquisitive of all the members of the Royal Society — certainly about man in the aggregate — was Sir William Petty. Among other things, Petty was a physician, surveyor, mathematician, landowner, inventor, economist, and colonizer. In his pursuit of various of these interests, he also became a demographer and patron of John Graunt. Although Petty gathered and analyzed the vital statistics of his day extensively, he was something less than exact in using them. Accordingly, he never produced any work in statistical demography which came up to Graunt's great pioneering study of 1662, *Natural and Political Observations Made Upon the Bills of Mortality.*[7] Graunt's work — the first scientific study of vital data — earned him election to the Royal Society, but it had no discernible immediate impact in or upon the American colonies. Some of Petty's ideas, on the other hand, related directly to the colonization impulse.

More than a run-of-the mill "virtuoso," Petty elaborated a life-long Baconian passion for numbering, weighing, and measuring into an original and influential contribution to economics.[8] "Political Arithmetic," as he called his concept,

6. Henry Oldenburg to Winthrop, October 13, 1667 and August 5, 1663, in *The Correspondence of Henry Oldenburg,* ed. A. Rupert Hall and Marie Boas Hall, 3 vols. (Madison: University of Wisconsin Press, 1965–1966), III, 525–526, and I, 105.

7. For a discussion of Bacon's influence on Graunt and of the keen interest of the Royal Society in Graunt's statistical method, see Robert Kargon, "John Graunt, Francis Bacon, and the Royal Society: The Reception of Statistics," *Journal of the History of Medicine,* 18 (October 1963), 337–348.

8. For a general biography of Petty, see Eric Strauss, *Sir William*

extended the new quantitative methodologies to all the realm of political economy. He applied them with particular vigor to the subject of colonization as a demographic phenomenon.

Like Restoration mercantilists generally, Petty took a harder look at colonization than did earlier thinkers. He was only one of many who felt that "fewness of people is real poverty" for a nation.[9] In consequence, if England was to be supreme in seventeenth-century Europe, he thought, she could ill afford a substantial drain of population out of the country to the colonies. To offset this, Petty threw out various proposals, such as transplanting back to England some people from marginal lands and colonies such as Ireland and America, or at least stopping emigration to such places. But it is understandable that, as an interested colonizer and land-holder in Ireland, he did not want to

Petty: Portrait of a Genius (Glencoe, Ill.: The Free Press, 1954). One of the standard assessments of political arithmetic as well as a source of Petty's work is Charles Henry Hull, ed., _The Economic Writings of Sir William Petty,_ 2 vols. (Cambridge University Press [Eng.], 1899). For a provocative modern critique of Petty and political arithmetic, see Letwin, _Origins of Scientific Economics,_ pp. 107–157. Letwin observes that the arithmetic of political arithmetic was neither elaborate nor very original, and that Petty's _Treatise on Taxes_ was a far better economic work than anything he wrote on political arithmetic. Adam Smith, Letwin points out, wrote that he had "no great faith in political arithmetic," at least in the way Petty had used numbers. Nevertheless, although the term "political arithmetic" did not remain greatly in favor or use much beyond the lives of Petty's followers — Gregory King and Charles Davenant, for example — at least one of its basic principles, the quantitative approach to government activities and social science, was increasingly accepted and utilized. Moreover, even the term has tenaciously refused to die out, for it has kept cropping up right down to the present, used by men as widely separated as Richard Price in the late eighteenth century and Lancelot Hogben in the mid-twentieth.

9. Petty, "A Treatise on Taxes and Contributions" (1662) in Hull, _Economic Writings of Sir William Petty,_ I, 34.

stop completely the flow of Englishmen to Ireland. He had no such tenderness for the American colonies, since migration there diverted some potential English settlers from Ireland.

Mercantilist skepticism of colonization was so strong in early Restoration England that migration to the existing North American colonies fell off for some time. But the jaundiced view of the economists was directed particularly at New England. Even those who had no particular religious bias concluded that New England was more of a competitor than a contributor to the mother country. As such, it was, of course, a thorn in the flesh of mercantilist policy. Most agreed with Josiah Child, who regarded Virginia and the island colonies as assets, for, "with their great number of slaves, every Englishman in the plantations employs [i.e. makes work for] four at home [England]: whereas ten Englishmen sent to New England do not employ one man. Thus New England drains of population, whereas Virginia and the British West Indies make possible an increase of population in old England." [10]

Petty himself had no doubt that if the English population could be doubled, the country's foreign trade would be trebled and "the King will be the greatest in Christendom." This accomplished, he generously allowed that "at 25 yeares' end, above 600 heads . . . may be yearly sent to the American Colonyes." [11] But, a doubling of population evidently would call, not only for plugging the emigration to unproductive colonies, but for deliberate measures

10. Child, quoted in Joseph Dorfman, *The Economic Mind*, I, 53. For other statements of Child's views, see his *Discourse concerning Plantations* (1692), in *Select Tracts Relating to the Colonies* (London: J. Roberts, ca. 1760), pp. 31–40.

11. Petty, "On doubling the people 1687," in Marquis of Lansdowne, ed. *The Petty Papers*, 2 vols. (London: Constable, 1927), II, 57.

to stimulate the multiplication of Englishmen. James Harrington (in his *Oceana*, 1656) suggested levying double taxes on bachelors over twenty-five, and none for fathers with ten children. Petty went far beyond his friend and mentor in searching out means to encourage childbearing. He advocated the use of taxes to defray the costs of lying-in and nursing of children. He suggested public facilities to care for the children produced, and he proposed annual fines for women over eighteen who bore no children in any given year.[12]

Rapid natural increase obviously was also a desideratum in Ireland and the American colonies if they were to increase in value to England. In both places labor, "the Father and active principle of Wealth," was a critically scarce commodity. For Ireland, Petty at one time proposed introducing a type of mating covenant which was to be dissolved after six months if no pregnancy resulted. In the case of America, he once advocated that the English planters "buy Indian girls of under 7 yeares old and use them as wives." He was intrigued at another time by the possibilities of "California Marriages," a concept which may have come to him from some sea captain. This arrangement, by providing each individual with a scientifically predetermined number of selected partners, had the presumed advantage of ensuring that every fertile female would be impregnated quickly, thus increasing the population with dispatch.[13]

The task of measuring the results of such reproductive

12. Lansdowne, *Petty Papers*, II, 47, 49–51, and 54.
13. *Ibid.*, pp. 49–53, 113. Jonathan Swift spoofed some of Petty's proposals for Ireland with his satire, *A Modest Proposal, for preventing the children of poor people in Ireland from being a burden to their parents or country, and for making them beneficial to the public* (1729).

activity throughout the empire, as well as that of weighing the values of colonies, was among the concerns of political arithmetic as Petty thought of it. To collect data of all kinds for such tasks, Petty tried hard to get the establishment, in his time, of a central statistical office. He suggested to authorities that the post of Register General in such an office go at first to his friend John Aubrey, but he hoped that ultimately it would revert to himself.[14]

Although Petty could not get a central statistical office started in England, his blueprint was far more detailed than anything yet proposed. Such an office would carry out national population censuses and economic surveys, and would sponsor improvements in parish registers. It would naturally concern itself with data from the colonies as well as from the mother country. Petty had a clear idea of the kinds of human statistics which should be gathered from America: data on longevity, migrations, religious affiliations, occupations, fertility, militia enrollments, illegitimate births, the relations of vital events to the weather, and many others. In his own day, of course, he never obtained many such figures from the colonies. But, from scattered sources he collected odd bits which shed some light on the demography of America. In 1674, for instance, from conversations with a Mr. Frost and a Mr. Bartholomew, he was able to draw up tables giving the number of families in the towns of Massachusetts; the numbers of ships; the rivers, harbors, and islands; and the respective numbers of such community leaders as merchants, clergy, magistrates, and physicians. He also found out something about the incidence of crime. Several in the early 1670's had recently been executed for homicide, "especially wenches for killing Bastards . . . Adultery is [also] Death

14. *Petty Papers,* I, MSS 49, 51, and 52.

by the Law, but scarce ever executed." At other times, correspondents in Plymouth, Rhode Island, Connecticut, and New Hampshire, as well as Massachusetts, provided him with vital statistics, population figures of Whites and Negroes, data on imports, and numbers of the militia.[15] He obtained fewer data from Virginia than from New England, and none from Carolina, which was just starting out.

In keeping with the increased care of the 1660's, the colony of Carolina was launched only after considerable planning. In fact, it appears from the elaborate structure of the Fundamental Constitutions to have been over-planned. That curiously feudal document's provisions for registering vital events illustrate this problem of the confrontation of elaborate plans with the realities.[16]

A society which was to rest solidly upon feudal practices obviously needed accurate personal data. The mechanisms to obtain these in Carolina were spelled out in detail.

15. *Petty Papers,* II, 95, 105, and 108; also MSS nos. 107 and 108, passim.

16. The question of the authorship of the registration sections of the Fundamental Constitutions is as inadequately settled as that of the rest of that document. Many persons, of course, such as Petty, Graunt, Harrington, Aubrey, and Christopher Wren, or even lesser known individuals, could well have contributed advice on this subject. Not least among these was John Locke, Secretary to Lord Ashley and the proprietary board, who was at least a copyist of the Constitutions. Whether or not he was more than that, he was highly capable of designing a system of vital statistics registration. Like Petty, Locke avidly gathered and pondered the vital data of European cities. And, as a physician, he studied the weekly London Bills of Mortality closely and often commented upon them in his journal. For a résumé of opinions as to Locke's role in the Constitutions, see Mattie E. E. Parker, ed., *North Carolina Charters and Constitutions 1578–1698* (Raleigh, N. C.: Carolina Charter Tercentenary Commission, 1963), pp. 128ff. For Locke's statistical interests, see Kenneth Dewhurst, *John Locke, 1632–1704, Physician and Philosopher* (London: The Wellcome Historical Medical Library, 1963), pp. 149, 245, and 301.

Registries for deeds, land conveyances, and the like were to be opened in every precinct. There were to be registries of births, marriages, and burials for ordinary persons in "every Seignory, Barony, and Colony," and fines were prescribed for the negligent. Separate registers of the vital events of Lords Proprietors, Landgraves, and Caciques — the nobility — were to be maintained in the Chamberlain's Court. This body was evidently intended to be at the same time the central repository of vital data and the nerve center of the feudal activities which would rely upon such data. "The Chamberlain's Court . . . shall have the care of all Ceremonies, Precedency, Heraldry, reception of public Messengers, and Pedigrees; the Registries of all Births, Burials, and Marriages; legitimization and all cases concerning Matrimony or arising from it; and shall, also, have power to Regulate all Fashions, Habits, Badges, Games, and Sports." [17]

When the time came to put the Fundamental Constitutions into effect in Carolina, most of the feudal paraphernalia fell by the wayside. Unfortunately, the statistical apparatus did not fare much better. The only registry established under the document seems to have been in Charlestown, where the parish rector also served as register following his appointment in 1698.[18] Successive versions of the Constitutions which appeared in March 1670, January 1682, and August 1682 retained all of the original

17. See *North Carolina Charters*, pp. 141–162. Provision for registers to "keep exact entries in fair books of all public affairs" had also been made for the Carolinas in 1665 in the Concessions and Agreement Between the Lords Proprietors and Major William Yeamons and Others (*ibid.*, p. 112).

18. This individual was the Reverend Samuel Marshall. See Joseph I. Waring, *A History of Medicine in South Carolina, 1670–1825* (Charleston, S. C.: South Carolina Medical Association, 1964), p. 32.

provisions for records and registers. The April 11, 1698, version, however, said nothing about registering vital events, though precinct registers for deeds were retained. When, after 1700, the Church of England was established and the colony divided into parishes, the Constitutions' civil system of vital registration was transformed into an essentially ecclesiastical system similar to that of Virginia. An Act of 1704, which became the basic registration arrangement for South Carolina for the rest of the colonial period, required the vestries of each parish to designate someone as Register. The law provided for the parishes to register births, christenings, marriages, and burials of Whites, but not of Negroes, mulattoes, or Indian slaves. Upon division of the colony, North Carolina adopted its own somewhat similar Vestries Act in 1715. Among its provisions was one which permitted the civil registers of deeds in the precincts or counties to record betrothals, marriages, and other vital events as well until such time as parish clerks were selected.[19]

The founders of New Jersey also made early provision for collecting vital statistics, but here the registration remained civil throughout. In 1675 the General Assembly of the proprietary government instructed clerks in every town to record vital events, and the West Jersey General Assembly kept this arrangement in 1682. When the Proprietors drew up Fundamental Constitutions for East Jersey in 1683, they provided for each county to keep a registry of

19. See *ibid.*, passim. See also Edson L. Whitney, *Government of the Colony of South Carolina* (Baltimore, Md.: Johns Hopkins Press, 1895); *Guide to Vital Statistics Records in North Carolina*, vol. I: *Public Vital Statistics* (Raleigh: The North Carolina Public Records Survey, 1942), p. 1; Calhoun, *A Social History*, I, passim; and Howard, *Matrimonial Institutions*, II, 240ff.

vital events. Upon union of the two segments in 1702, the Crown ordered the governors of the new province to provide for such registers.[20]

Although Petty apparently had no immediate role in the founding and registration arrangements of either the Jerseys or the Carolinas, he was directly concerned with Pennsylvania. Petty met William Penn sometime before 1669. With similarly broad interests and utilitarian approach, they became good friends. Although Petty originally opposed Penn's proposal to launch a new American settlement, he eventually became interested to the extent of being enrolled on the original list of land purchasers. Both Lady Petty and he at one point even considered going to Pennsylvania for a time.[21]

While this never materialized, Petty was liberal with his advice to Penn on how to go about establishing, managing, and developing the new plantation. His statistical suggestions were explicit: "Enjoyne all men to keep Journalls of their receipts and payments . . . Keep an exact accompt of the people, their births, burialls, mariages, arrivals &c . . . Set up betimes a registry for contracts & obligations," and, a practical caution fundamental to all the rest, "Discourage the Learning of lattine & greek, and of University learning; but promote arithmetic & measuring & drawing."

Petty's hints for the demographic success of Pennsylvania were equally direct. It was a desideratum, for instance,

20. See *Guide to Vital Statistics Records in New Jersey*, vol. I: *Public Archives* (Newark: New Jersey Historical Records Survey, 1941), pp. 1–7.

21. Frederick B. Tolles, *Meeting House and Counting House* (Chapel Hill: University of North Carolina Press, 1948), p. 207. See also Lansdowne, *Petty Papers*, II, 109–112.

"that no youth of between 18 and 58 yeares old, nor woman of between 16 and 41 yeares old, bee unmaryed." Women in this age group were expected to be "teeming" most of the time, while all the "youths" were expected to contribute to the support of the children. As a means to increase the number of births, Petty made his suggestion that the colony "admit the Native women into freedome." [22]

After the founding of Pennsylvania, Petty maintained his interest in the colony and in its human data. Even though Penn and his successors did not undertake artificial or official measures to stimulate population, Petty was convinced as early as 1685, through some unexplained calculations, that the colony would be fully peopled in 124 years. Penn was delighted to hear this. Like many Europeans, Petty was as curious about the American Indians as about the Whites in the new colony. Before his death in 1689, he occasionally asked Penn and others to supply him with data pertaining to Indian population, longevity, numbers of children per family, the length of the nursing period, rules of marriage, heights and weights of individuals, colors of skin, and the numbers who had smallpox.[23]

Various of Petty's statistical suggestions for Pennsylvania were incorporated in the general system of laws which Penn and his associates drew up in England in 1682. These laws provided variously for a registry of deeds and land grants, a registry of servants, and a separate register of births, marriages, burials, wills, and letters of administration.[24] Registers-General were subsequently appointed to

22. *Ibid.*, 113–115.
23. *Ibid.*, MS no. 113; and Dorfman, *The Economic Mind*, I, 91.
24. William Penn, *The Frame of the Government of the Province of Pennsilvania in America: Together with certain Laws agreed upon in England by the Governour and Divers Free-Men of the aforesaid Province.* ([London] 1682).

handle these records.[25] These individuals, however, never had effective means to carry out the registration of the colony's vital data. Consequently, in 1700 the Assembly in effect tossed the whole matter back to the churches:

> *Be it enacted, etc.* That the Registry now kept, or which shall be hereafter kept by an Religious Society, in their respective Meeting Book or Books, of any Marriage, Birth or Burial, within this Province or Territories thereof, shall be held good and authentic, and shall be allowed of upon all occasions whatsoever.[26]

The Pennsylvania efforts at registering vital data did not produce any better results than the parish registers of Virginia and the Carolinas or the civil registers of New England and New Jersey. In every colony, restless people moving around on the edge of the wilderness often could not or would not record their vital events. As a result, the official registers were irregular, often incomplete, frequently inaccurate, and sometimes totally lacking, though to what extent is not known. If they sometimes fulfilled their legal purposes, they just as often had to be supplemented by other documents when such demands were made upon them. Similarly, when British officials needed demographic and other data in their efforts to administer

25. One of the earliest Registers-General was Captain John Blackwell, who filled the post several years before 1689. See J. Thomas Scharf and Thompson Westcott, *History of Philadelphia, 1609–1884*, 3 vols. (Philadelphia: L. H. Everts & Co., 1884), II, passim. See also Howard, *Matrimonial Institutions*, II, 318; and *The Laws of the Province of Pennsilvania* (Philadelphia: Andr. Bradford, 1714), pp. 158–159.

26. *Ibid.*, p. 21.

the colonies, they more often than not had to look elsewhere than to the official registers or records. The searches
of these mercantilists and public servants for relevant information were diligently pursued but not always successful.

Chapter IV

All the King's Men: Counting Souls

1660–1775

Information-gathering was a fundamental necessity for English mercantilists and political arithmeticians alike. If these men generally held similar views on the American colonies, they also shared a common respect for the quantitative approach to the information-gathering process, whether applied to colonial or to other economic matters.[1] The mercantilist Laws of Trade and Navigation (Navigation Acts) which passed Parliament between 1651 and 1696 brought forth a continuing official need for statistical data from America fully as extensive as the data Petty had hoped to obtain.[2] This need was intensified by require-

1. Joseph J. Spengler, "On the Progress of Quantification in Economics," *Isis*, 52 (June 1961), 260–261.
2. For a concise summary of mercantilism and of the scope and influence of the Navigation Acts, see John C. Miller, *Origins of the American Revolution* (Boston: Little, Brown, 1948), chap. 1.

ments of the long struggle with France for control of North America. The colonies' consistent inability, and occasional unwillingness, to provide as much vital and other data as the mother country wanted, was a frequent source of friction between the two sides.

Administrative responsibility within the English government for whatever supervision the colonies received fell originally upon the Privy Council. The Council's management efforts, like subsequent activities of the Lords of Trade, were decidedly spotty and ill-organized. Only after the organization in 1696 of the Board of Trade was there reasonably sustained and coordinated oversight of the colonies.[3] All of these bodies did what they could to gather information about the new appendages of empire. At the beginning they had to rely to a large extent on letters from people on the spot and on interviews with persons who had returned from the colonies. At an early date, however, English authorities began sporadic attempts to solicit particular kinds of information. In 1626, soon after Virginia was transformed into a royal colony, the Privy Council issued a clear mandate to Governor George Yeardley. Among other matters, he was "instructed to send by the first ship a particular account of the colony, the number of plantations, inhabitants, etc."[4] Later, as the colonies multiplied and became more complex, and as mercantilist ambitions soared, it sometimes became necessary to go after the needed information. During the 1660's, for instance, the Lords of Trade sent four Commissioners to New England to obtain aid in the war against the Dutch and to

3. For a résumé of the development of British colonial administration, see Max Savelle, *The Foundations of American Civilization* (New York: Henry Holt, 1942), pp. 191–202, 331–340.
4. *Calendar of State Papers, 1574–1660* (London, 1860), p. 79.

settle boundary disputes. They also looked into such matters as colonial governments and their compliance with the Navigation Acts. In 1676, as something of a follow-up, the Lords of Trade appointed Edward Randolph as special agent to New England to conduct a broad fact-finding mission.

Perhaps nobody ever did more to make English rule and statistical inquiries unpalatable to Americans than did Edward Randolph. A man who spent much time in the colonies after 1676, Randolph faithfully served the cause of mercantilism as well as his own career in a variety of posts. Since by temperament he was officious, petty, and overbearing, though doubtless well-meaning, he succeeded in alienating many of the colonists through his energetic and methodical interference in their affairs.

For his 1676 mission to New England, Randolph was commanded to "inform himself" on a wide range of subjects, such as the form of government, boundaries, Indian wars, relations to the French, imports, and public revenue. His inquiry included such touchy matters as the laws derogatory to England, shipping, attitudes toward England, church organization, and observance or nonobservance of the Navigation Acts. Demographically, he was to investigate the numbers of inhabitants, freemen, church members, planters, servants and slaves, members of the professions, and militia.

Although the Massachusetts authorities were evasive and uncooperative when confronted with these queries, Randolph managed to find some persons who furnished him with information. Back in London later that year, he submitted his report, which was highly unfavorable to the current governmental arrangement in New England. Subjective and one-sided as it was, the report was convincing to some, particularly insofar as it confirmed many of the suspicions of the Lords of Trade and provided the Lords with new ammunition against New England. Its statistical data were mostly rough guesses, but in the absence of anything more exact, they took on much authority back in England. For the population, he found that there were then "about 150,000" inhabitants, no servants but on hired wages, "not above 200 slaves," and but few members of the Anglican Church.[5] Some of the demographic data were not in themselves especially damaging to New England, but his population estimate for Massachusetts caused much resentment. Since the estimate was measurably higher than the colonists admitted, it provided England with a new base for taxation and served as a foundation for Randolph's critical general conclusions. These, along with other reports, helped lead ultimately to the tightening of imperial controls in New England as well as to the revocation of the Massachusetts charter. As a reward for his work, Randolph was shortly named Customs Surveyor for New England.

In 1684 Randolph persuaded the King to create for him the additional post of Secretary and Register of the New England Dominion. He had every expectation that from this post he could derive a good income from the various registration fees while collecting statistical data in the spirit of the Navigation Acts. However, as Randolph was by then anathema to the New Englanders, the merchants and officials did everything possible to frustrate his efforts

5. Randolph to Lords of Trade, October 12, 1676, *Calendar of State Papers, 1675–1676* (London, 1893), pp. 463–468. For an up-to-date discussion of Randolph's life and work, see Michael G. Hall's biography, *Edward Randolph and the American Colonies, 1676–1703* (Chapel Hill: University of North Carolina Press, 1960).

in this position. He wrote plaintively to William Blathwayt in 1686: "I am called Register, but no man comes and records their Deeds at my Office." To John Povey at about the same time he explained that he had even rented a special building in Boston in order to ward off possible objections against keeping the records in his own house. The fees he managed to collect, however, barely covered the rental of £60. "At present," he lamented, "I have little more than the troublesome title of Secry and Sole Register for they have placed the Register of Wills with the Clerkes of the County Courts, and the Record of Sales and Mortgages with them also: so that the Cheife end and publick benefitt of a Genll Register is quite destroyed." [6] He also failed in his aim to have a registry of persons over 16 established.

In the late 1690's the ubiquitous Randolph appeared several times in the Southern colonies. There, one of the chief objects of his attention was the population problem. Governor Andros and others had estimated that there were between 70,000 and 80,000 inhabitants in Virginia at the time. Randolph was shocked by this low figure, "considering what vast Numbers of Servants and others have yearly been transported thither." He went on to criticize the successive governments of the colony for not having done anything to stimulate larger families and otherwise increase the population. He assigned a large measure of blame for the past slow increase in population to the colony's land policy; since large tracts had been taken up by a few, comparatively little land was left to attract new

6. See Alfred T. S. Goodrick, ed., *Edward Randolph,* 7 vols. (Boston: The Prince Society, 1909), VI, 162–163, 181, 188, 255. Following Randolph, John West was Secretary and Register of New England for a time.

settlers.[7] In 1699 Randolph concluded the same thing about South Carolina, where he found "but few settled inhabitants" and not over 1500 white militia, while there were four slaves for every white man. He also sent the Board of Trade some figures on the French Huguenot refugees who had recently settled in South Carolina, 438 of them at that time located at four different sites.[8]

In general the principal foci of Randolph's North American inquiries were the tiny port cities. There he found the largest concentration of people and institutions and the main seats of political power. There also were the emerging centers of economic activity, wealth, and influence. In Boston, New York, Philadelphia, and ultimately other ports, an enterprising merchant class was emerging out of the seventeenth-century background of small shopkeepers. In the next few generations after Randolph, this class not only built up a complex and lucrative shipping and trading activity, but began to branch out into such profitable sidelines as land speculation, banking, insurance, candle or rope factories, and iron forges. With the increased size and complexity of these enterprises came the need for improved record-keeping and quantification of all kinds, including double-entry bookkeeping systems in their "Compting Rooms." And simultaneously, the increasing trade and commercial activity of the colonists gave ever larger labors to Randolph's eighteenth-century successors in the work of ferreting out statistical information for the Crown.[9]

7. Randolph, "Account of the Plantation of Virginia," Goodrick, *Randolph*, VII, 487; also *Calendar of State Papers, 15 May 1696–31 October 1697* (London, 1904), pp. 88–90.

8. Randolph to Council of Trade, March 16, 1699, *Calendar of State Papers, 1699* (London, 1908), pp. 104–107.

9. There are several good accounts of the development of particu-

Randolph himself was precisely the tireless, inquisitive, loyal, and methodical sort of person whom the Crown needed in America. His reports were conscientious and observant. His data were as good as anybody else's. The English government did not seem ever to have contemplated that Randolph's Register office should go much beyond the collection of commercial data and fees. Randolph's own concern for population data did not lead him beyond the point of rough estimates; he never involved himself in careful enumerations or in the registration of vital statistics. His total information-gathering efforts nevertheless were significant parts of the pragmatic English effort to organize its colonies. His death cut off a fertile source of descriptive and quantitative data on the economic, geographic, and social, as well as the political, aspects of the colonies. But the Crown needed more than one man to keep it informed about America.

Among the kinds of persons who could help in this were the customs officials. In fact, as early as 1660, the Navigation Act called for local customs officers in colonial ports to register all foreign-built vessels owned by Englishmen and to send returns back to London. An Act of 1696 ex-

lar business enterprises. Among these are William T. Baxter, *The House of Hancock: Business in Boston 1724–1775* (Cambridge, Mass.: Harvard University Press, 1945); and James B. Hedges, *The Browns of Providence Plantations; Colonial Years* (Cambridge, Mass.: Harvard University Press, 1952). Excellent general works on the subject include Virginia D. Harrington, *The New York Merchants on the Eve of the Revolution* (New York: Columbia University Press, 1935); Samuel Eliot Morison, *The Maritime History of Massachusetts 1783–1860* (Boston: Houghton Mifflin, 1925); and Tolles, *Meeting House and Counting House*. Hedges observes (p. 5) that by 1739 Americans were reading British accounting guides which gave descriptions of double-entry bookkeeping and accounting instructions for supercargoes on ships.

tended the registration to all vessels trading in the colonies. Registers which customs officers maintained during the rest of the colonial period included detailed information on the sizes of vessels, their types, owners, cargoes, home ports, ages, and places built.[10] Without doubt the persons who were normally best situated to assist the Crown were the colonial governors. As the numbers of colonies increased during the seventeenth century, the governors became the principal, though never the sole, foci of the English quest for colonial information. To them channeled the multitudinous instructions of the Privy Council, "Queries" of the Board of Trade, and other official communications. These included requests for information about every conceivable matter: boundaries, rivers and harbors, manufactures, imports and exports, agricultural and forest produce, mines, ships and shipbuilding, revenue, government organization and expenses, churches and church memberships, defense arrangements, and many others. Prominent among the queries were the frequent requests for such human data as the size and makeup of population, increases of population, amounts of immigration and naturalizations, numbers of slaves, servants, and Indians, neighboring French or Spanish populations, numbers of seafaring men, size of militia, and the numbers of births, marriages, and burials.

During the century and a half or so of English rule, large quantities of these kinds of data were sent by the respective governors. Officials in the home country analyzed the information, compiled it into reports, and used it as the basis of imperial policy. Here Political Arithmetic in its

10. See Bernard Bailyn and Lotte Bailyn, *Massachusetts Shipping, 1697–1714: A Statistical Study* (Cambridge, Mass.: Harvard University Press, 1959), p. 3.

broad sense — data describing the state — took on a role which Sir William Petty would have approved.[11] The fact that a colonial governor received a query for data was, of course, no guarantee that information would quickly flow back to the requesting office in England. The ocean trip was still so long and hazardous that dispatches were often lost or delayed. Governors were sometimes independent, often overworked, and occasionally procrastinating. Governors often had varying incentives to comply with requests, depending upon whether they represented royal, proprietary, or corporate colonies. Still, by the time of the Navigation Act of 1696, all governors were held responsible to the Crown and were expected to furnish the needed information.[12] While many governors made at least some effort to respond to queries for data, even their efforts were sporadic at best, while what they sent was never enough. Occasionally the reports sent in were intentionally misleading, as the Connecticut population figures of 1730 and 1749 were reported to be.[13]

11. For an example of a fairly comprehensive statistical account which was prepared in England from governors' and other reports, see the Report by the Council of Trade and Plantations to the King, dated September 8, 1721, on the "State of your Majesty's Plantations on the Continent of America," in *Calendar of State Papers, March 1720 to December 1721* (London, 1933), pp. 408–449. Although the compilers had to confess having virtually no information on Connecticut and Rhode Island, they included varying quantities from all other colonies and most from the Carolinas. Besides extensive narrative information, the report was of particular statistical note for its tabular summaries of such commercial data as numbers and tonnages of ships cleared in various ports, together with imports and exports.

12. See Savelle, *Foundations*, p. 200.

13. Dexter, "Estimates of Population . . . ," in *Proceedings*, American Antiquarian Society, 5 (1888), n.s., pt. 1, 22, 32ff. Greene concludes that "on the whole this duty of informing the home govern-

Those governors who tried conscientiously to satisfy the demands of the Board of Trade or of other London offices ran into endless difficulties. Nowhere were these more apparent than in their efforts to conduct population enumerations. Populations were widely dispersed and often hard to reach. Frontier hostilities sometimes cut off whole areas.[14] Many independent souls were scornful of officialdom and evasive of the law, particularly when they understood that the results of enumerations were for use in military requisitions or tax assessments. The sheriffs, justices, assessors, and other local officials who actually were called upon to carry out the enumerations often had few qualifications and smaller enthusiasm for the task. Governor Nicholson in 1698 and Governor Blakiston in 1700 found so many of the constables of Maryland to be illiterate that they could not obtain adequate enumerations. Moreover, the arguments of such officials that census-taking was not a part of their legally defined duties were hard to answer; there were no appropriations to pay them for such extra labors. Governor Wentworth's inability to obtain an enumeration in New Hampshire in 1767 was only one of the cases where censuses were impossible due to lack of appropriations and authority. Although some colonial governors were known to have gone to substantial personal expense to induce settlers to come to their colonies, there is no record of any

ment was very much neglected" by colonial governors. Evarts B. Greene, *The Provincial Governor in the English Colonies of North America* (Gloucester, Mass.: Peter Smith, 1966), pp. 65–67.

14. The 1746 census of New York, for instance, had to be sent incomplete, since the French and Indian wars prevented enumeration of Albany County (Rossiter, *Population Growth*, p. 6). Similarly, Governor Bernard of Massachusetts apologized for delays in his reports in the early 1760's, and promised to send a population enumeration as soon as peace came (Benton, *Early Census Making*, pp. 30–50, passim).

of them using their own funds to pay census enumerators to count the people who were already there.[15]

Another potent obstacle to some colonial population enumerations arose out of popular recollection of the Old Testament sin of David. God-fearing churchgoers knew full well the account of the disastrous pestilence which had struck the Israelites in the wake of the census which King David, disregarding ancient taboos, had ordered.[16] These people had no wish to risk God's wrath again. Governor Hunter of New York felt the force of this fear in 1712 when he attempted a head-count of his colony for the Board of Trade. He reported:

> I have issued out orders to the several Counties and cities for an account, of the numbers of their inhabitants and slaves, but have never been able to obtain it compleat, the people being deterr'd by a simple superstition and observation, that the sickness follow'd upon the last numbering of the people.[17]

15. Names of the sheriffs who conducted the 1731 enumeration in New York are listed in Rossiter, *Population Growth,* pp. 2–3, 6, and 181. See also Dexter, "Estimates of Population . . . ," *Proceedings, American Antiquarian Society,* 5 (1888), n.s., pt. 1, 36, 41; Sutherland, *Population Distribution,* pp. 186ff; J. Potter, "Growth of Population in America," in D. V. Glass and D. E. C. Eversley, ed., *Population in History* (Chicago, Ill.: Aldine Publishing Co., 1965), p. 655; *Calendar of State Papers, 1700* (London, 1910), p. 121; *Calendar of State Papers, 27 Oct. 1697–31 Dec. 1698* (London, 1905), p. 389; and Jeremy Belknap, *The History of New Hampshire,* 2d. ed., 3 vols. (Boston: Bradford & Read, 1813), III, 175. The first edition was published between 1784 and 1791.

16. See Samuel 2: 24, and Chronicles 1: 21. See also George A. Buttrick, ed., *The Interpreters' Dictionary of the Bible,* 4 vols. (New York: Abingdon Press, 1962), I, 547 and 780.

17. E. B. O'Callaghan, ed., *Documents Relative to the Colonial History of the State of New York,* V (Albany, N. Y.: Weed, Parsons and Co., 1855), 339.

This same reason dissuaded Governor Burnet of New Jersey from ordering a census in 1726. Burnet concluded that enumeration would "make the people uneasy, they being generally of a New England extraction, and thereby [religious] enthusiasts." [18]

New York governors were not permanently frustrated by this objection, for that colony ultimately conducted more censuses than any other.[19] Political factors were probably more decisive than the religious in most colonies in causing opposition to censuses. Still, it is a fact that literalists or conservatives kept bringing up the Sin of David throughout the colonial period. As late as the Constitutional Convention of 1787 it was cited in opposition to the proposal for a regular national census. And the same argument helped defeat all proposals for an English census until after 1800.[20]

18. Quoted by Rossiter, *Population Growth*, pp. 3ff; see also Potter, "Growth of Population in America," Glass & Eversley, *Population in History*, p. 637.

19. Out of the thirty-eight "official" censuses which Rossiter identified as having been accomplished before 1789, 11 were in New York, 7 in Rhode Island, 4 in New Hampshire, 4 in Connecticut, 3 in New Jersey, 2 each in Maine, Maryland, Massachusetts, and Virginia, and 1 in Vermont. Of these, only two were taken before 1700 (in Virginia in 1635 and in New York in 1698), while 14 occurred 1700–1749, 11 between 1750 and 1773, and 11 between 1774 and 1789. Rossiter found no "official" counts in Pennsylvania, North Carolina, South Carolina, or Georgia. No general enumeration of the colonies as a whole was ever attempted. For details, see Rossiter, *Population Growth*, pp. 3–6.

20. John Graunt was well aware of the tradition when he attempted to obtain population data for his study of 1662. See Graunt, *Natural and Political Observations*, p. 67. Nearly a hundred years later, in 1754, when a bill went to Parliament for the enumeration of the British population, politicians succeeded in stirring up enough people in opposition so that "nothing but the *sin of David* was heard of, 'till the bill was laid aside." John Fothergill, *The Works of John Fothergill, M. D.*, 3 vols. (London: Charles Dilly, 1783–1784), II, 110. See also Rossiter, *Population Growth*, passim.

The counts which the colonies actually took were usually, but not always, in response to instructions from England. They naturally varied widely in sophistication. Board of Trade population inquiries sometimes asked only the simple question: "What is the number of Inhabitants?", so the answer was a simple count of heads. Often, however, the Board wanted a breakdown, as by race and sex. Some enumerations, therefore, like those of Rhode Island in 1748 and Connecticut in 1756, gave breakdowns of Whites, Negroes, and Indians. Maryland's census of 1755, by contrast, had thirty-eight categories, for such factors as sex, color, and age, along with numbers of convicts, servants, slaves, and clergy. Most censuses fell somewhere in between, with perhaps ten or twelve different categories of population figures. At the same time, some provided information of special or local interest: the Massachusetts census in 1764 revealed the number of its French Neutrals (about 570); that of New Jersey in 1745 had a column for "Quakers or reputed Quakers"; and New Hampshire in 1775 foresightedly made a count of firearms and powder along with that of its people.[21]

In some colonies, as in Massachusetts in 1755 and 1764, separate or supplementary counts of families, houses, or slaves were made. Occasionally, enumerations of people or houses in particular cities were undertaken. "Inquisitors" made several local counts in Boston, New York, Baltimore, Philadelphia, and Charlestown. A 1749 enumeration of houses in Philadelphia, in fact, "was made by citizens of the first respectability"; Joseph Shippen in Dock Ward, Benjamin Franklin in Mulberry Ward, William Allen in Lower Delaware, Thomas Hopkinson in Upper Delaware,

21. For details of pre-1790 censuses, see the valuable tabular summaries in Rossiter, *Population Growth*, pp. 149–185. The first federal census, 1790–91, had six different categories of information.

and six others.[22] Even small places like Bristol, Rhode Island (1689), and the Delaware River settlement (1680) sometimes conducted formal population counts. Far out on the frontier, a census of the tiny settlement of Pittsburgh in the mid-1760's showed 305 settlers (including squatters), plus 79 nearby soldiers.[23] Occasionally, the division of community lands as in Dedham, Massachusetts, in 1644-45, necessitated a count of land-owners.[24]

Colonial governors looking for data frequently were unable to obtain precise population figures. Accordingly, they often had to resort to estimates in order to satisfy the Board of Trade. To be sure, population estimation was a perfectly respectable procedure in England throughout the seventeenth and eighteenth centuries and later. Political Arithmetic, in fact, in the hands of men like Petty, Gregory King, and Charles Davenant, rested substantially upon an elaborate fabric of educated guesses. To deduce the numbers of people, these men employed a variety of tax returns, such as those upon chimneys, hearths, or later (after 1696) on windows.[25] None of these particular taxes were imposed in the American colonies. The governors relied, therefore, for purposes of estimates, on such documents as

22. James Pease, quoted in *ibid.*, p. 13.

23. See Sutherland, *Population Distribution,* passim; Greene & Harrington, *American Population,* pp. 121 and 174; Rossiter, *Population Growth,* pp. 2-3 and 10-20; and "Records of Church of Christ of Bristol (Congregational)," *New England Historical and Genealogical Register,* 34 (October 1880), 404-405.

24. B. Katherine Brown, "Puritan Democracy in Dedham, Massachusetts: Another Case Study," *William and Mary Quarterly,* 3rd ser., 24 (July 1967), 387. For the Dedham division, 82 men and 1 woman were listed.

25. For the work of Gregory King and a brief biography, see George E. Barnett, ed., *Two Tracts by Gregory King* (Baltimore, Md.: Johns Hopkins Press, 1936).

land records, militia muster rolls, polling lists, and general lists of titheables.

One of the most conscientious and elaborate efforts on record to calculate population from such sources is Governor Bernard's three-way estimate for Massachusetts in 1763. He made his first estimate from the 1761 return to the General Court of "rateable polls" (males over 16 eligible to vote). To this number (57,000), he added an estimate of those males who were too poor to pay the poll tax (19,000), and finally added like numbers of females for each category, for a total of 152,000. Another estimate was made by multiplying the militia returns (41,000) by four, which gave 164,000. For his third estimate, which he made from the number of houses (calculated at about 32,000 in 1761), Bernard provided a choice of two factors. Since many persons of his day figured an average of five inhabitants per house and many others preferred five and a half, Bernard used both figures. These multiplications totaled 160,000 and 176,000, respectively. Having given the Board of Trade several choices, Bernard then concluded that the actual population was none of these figures. Rather, it was probably close to 200,000. Since all of the returns used in the estimates had been made for tax purposes, it was understood that they would be well on the low side.[26]

Requests from the Board of Trade or other agencies for information about vital events were somewhat simpler for the colonial governors to fill than those for numbers of inhabitants. They found that either they could provide them or they could not. There was little attempt at making

26. This paragraph is drawn from the discussion in Benton, *Early Census Making,* pp. 45–60.

estimates. Instructions upon this subject usually called for governors to see that the colonies kept adequate records of births (or baptisms), marriages, and deaths. In addition, it was clearly specified that "you shall yearly send fair abstracts thereof to His Majesty and to his Commissioners for Trade and Plantations." [27]

Governors sometimes managed to obtain such data from their local registrars and clerks. Governor Dudley, for instance, in November 1705 sent the Board a register of births in Massachusetts towns for the period between April 1704 and April 1705. Again, in 1713, the Board received from Lieutenant Governor Spotswood an account of births and burials in Virginia for the period of April through September 1712.[28] No governors, however, could furnish such data at all regularly, while some of them sent frankly negative replies in answer to requests for this information. In New York, in 1678, Governor Andros replied that "ministers have been so scarce and religions so many that no acct cann be given of children's births or christenings . . . Scarcity of ministers and [the] law admitting marriages by justices no acct cann be given of the number married." More than thirty years later, Governor Hunter had to report that a similar condition still prevailed in the colony: "As to births and burials has never been any Register kept that I can hear of neither is there any possibility of doing it until such time as the Countys are subdivided into Parishes,

27. The example given is the instruction from the Board of Trade to Governor Shirley of Massachusetts, September 8, 1741, in Benton, *Early Census Making*, p. 9. See also *Vital Statistics Records in New Jersey*, I, 2 and 7.

28. *Journal of the Commissioners for Trade and Plantations* (London: His Majesty's Stationery Office, 1920 and 1925), I (1920), 209; II (1925), 457.

great numbers remaining unchristen'd for want of ministers."[29] Governors of Connecticut in 1680 and North Carolina in 1767 were among those who reported similarly that there were just no data available on vital events. Governor Franklin of New Jersey could not send a report on vital statistics in 1772 since most of the county officials to whom he had sent forms refused to complete them.[30] Many other governors similarly found it difficult if not impossible to extract vital data from the local officials in their territories. And the reasons were similar: political resistance to royal authority, loss or unavailability of the records, religious diversity, or the disruptions caused by frontier hostilities.

Detrimental as it was to the gathering of vital statistics and to the carrying out of census enumerations, the grimly recurrent factor of warfare actually stimulated the gathering and reporting of two special kinds of colonial human data. These were the figures on the population of the Indians, and those on the strength of the colonial militia forces.

Colonial governors often pointed out to the Board of Trade how markedly the population of their colonies was kept down by the various French and Indian wars. Governors Bernard and Hutchinson of Massachusetts, for instance, in the mid-eighteenth century emphasized how the deaths of thousands of young men in these conflicts materially diminished the numbers of children born in that

29. Andros quoted in Calhoun, *A Social History*, I, 158; Hunter quoted in O'Callaghan, *New York State Documents*, V, 340.
30. See *Calendar of State Papers, 1677–1680* (London, 1896), p. 577; and *Vital Statistics in North Carolina*, I, 1. See also Potter, "Growth of Population in America," Glass & Eversley, *Population in History*, p. 655.

colony.[31] Well before that, King Philip's War alone caused the death of an estimated one out of every ten New England men of fighting age. In that war the Indians pushed the settlers of the interior parts of New England so far back toward the sea that it was some forty years before the frontier line again reached its earlier point of furthest advance.[32] In the battle for survival, the English showed themselves to be fully as ruthless in killing as were the Indians. In the Pequot War of 1637 a slaughter of Indian men, women, and children went on at Mystic until the colonists grew weary. And when King Philip was killed in 1676 it seemed quite natural for the settlers to place his head upon a pole in Plymouth, where it served as a grim reminder for the next few decades.[33] Even larger numbers of Indians, of course, were destroyed by disease than by the English.[34] Yet, regardless of how the extermination went on, as long as the neighboring Indian populations appeared as a menace, the colonists had a vital need to know their numbers.

31. See Benton, *Early Census-Making*, pp. 40–60, passim; and Thomas Hutchinson, *The History of the Colony and Province of Massachusetts Bay*, ed. Lawrence S. Mayo (Cambridge, Mass.: Harvard University Press, 1936), II, 150, and III, 62. See also Lemuel Shattuck, *Report to the Committee of the City Council Appointed to Obtain the Census of Boston for the Year 1845* (Boston: John H. Eastburn, 1846), p. 5; and further discussion of this subject in Chapter VII of the present work. Deaths in colonial battles were sometimes entered either in militia records or in town and parish registers or both, but occasionally they were never recorded anywhere.

32. See, for example, Morison, *Intellectual Life of Colonial New England*, pp. 55ff.

33. See Jones, *O Strange New World*, p. 59; and Ray A. Billington, *Westward Expansion* (New York: Macmillan, 1949), p. 78.

34. For one account of this, see E. Wagner Stearn and Allen E. Stearn, *The Effect of Smallpox on the Destiny of the Amerindian* (Boston: Bruce Humphries, Inc., 1945).

The settlers along the American frontier never had a completely clear idea of the strength of the adversary. In their own minds they "seemed to be perpetually contesting with enormous, shadowy forces, always untrustworthy, always irresponsible, always cruel." As a result of the fear engendered by this image, many of them "forever exaggerated" the Indian population.[35] In a somewhat similar reaction, Englishmen in the Southern colonies during the eighteenth century sometimes had only vague impressions of the numbers of Negroes, rather than any precise figure.[36] Yet, just as many attempts were made in the individual colonies to enumerate or estimate the Negro population, so there were many efforts to pin down the size of the elusive Indian population.[37]

Throughout much of the seventeenth century and even later, some Indians remained in their villages close to the English settlements. These could be easily counted.[38] So

35. Jones, *O Strange New World*, p. 153. According to Cotton Mather, early New Englanders felt themselves "assaulted by unknown numbers of devils in flesh on every side." Quoted by Daniel Boorstin, *The Americans, The Colonial Experience* (New York: Random House, 1958), p. 348.

36. Hugh Jones, *The Present State of Virginia* (1724), quoted in Abbot Smith, *Colonists in Bondage*, p. 330.

37. Slaves generally were enumerated at the same time as the white population. Occasionally, however, separate counts were made, like the Massachusetts enumeration of 1754. In that year, Governor Shirley asked and obtained from the General Court a count of all Negro slaves over 16 years of age, by sex. This count was desired apparently as a means to ensure the colony equitable tax assessments by England in the pursuit of the French and Indian wars. See Benton, *Early Census Making*, pp. 15–21, passim.

38. The nearby, somewhat "domesticated," Indians as individuals frequently became thoroughly degenerate. Colonial Whites not only contributed to this all too often but exploited and kept the Indians in a servile condition. In this state the latter were sometimes lumped together with Negroes in the census enumerations.

could the "Praying Indians" in their Massachusetts towns and such Indians as came into the communities of the Whites or were pushed onto reservations. Governor Hinckley of Plymouth in 1685 had no particular trouble enumerating 1439 Indians over twelve years of age in fourteen locations in that colony.[39] Likewise, in 1697, Governor Andros had about as good demographic information about the nineteen small Indian tribes of tidewater Virginia as about the Whites.[40] The New York census of 1786 had separate figures for "Indians who pay taxes."[41] Other censuses throughout the period similarly included by and large just the more or less peaceful Indians who were easily accessible. The Connecticut census of 1774 was precise not only as to the numbers of these Indians but as to their condition. When the Board of Trade asked, "What number of Indians have you; and how are they inclined?", the Connecticut reporters succinctly replied:

> There is Thirteen Hundred and Sixty three; many of them dwell in English Families; the rest in small tribes in various Places; — they are in Peace, good Order, and inclined to Idleness.[42]

Counting the unbroken Indians in their frequently distant villages was another matter.[43] The census enumerator

39. Hutchinson, *History of Massachusetts Bay*, I, 296. Those under 12 were estimated at well over 4000.

40. Andros to Board of Trade, April 22, 1697, *Calendar of State Papers, 15 May 1696–31 October 1697* (London, 1904), p. 455.

41. See Rossiter, *Population Growth*, pp. 181–184.

42. *Heads of Inquiry Relative to the Present State and Condition of his Majesty's Colony of Connecticut* (New London: T. Green, 1775), p. 7.

43. For a résumé of many counts or estimates which were made, see Greene and Harrington, *American Population*, pp. 194–206.

usually never reached these sites. In place of exact numbers, there often were only the round figures, estimates, or rumors obtained from hunters, trappers, traders, or soldiers. An attempt of the Virginia Assembly in 1669 to obtain such an enumeration of Indians was virtually fruitless for the western parts of the colony and far from complete for the eastern tribes. Lord Culpeper could only make the broadest of guesses about the situation there in 1681: "None of our neighbouring Indan tribes can make above two hundred fighting men, except the Occanagees, about three hundred; the Tuscarorees, towards Carolina, six or eight thousand, but these are peaceable; and the Senacas, a fierce and dangerous race, about four thousand." Lord Baltimore simply reported to the Lords of Trade in 1678 that, in the case of Maryland, it seemed certain that "the more remote Indians [are] more numerous, but their strength cannot be guessed." [44]

Sometimes, however, fairly accurate information could be obtained both of friendly and of hostile tribes. An enumeration of southern tribes in 1715 listed some 28,000 fighting men. The English enumerated the fighting men of the Iroquois several times during the colonial period, and estimates of certain other northern tribes were made. The Commissary at Oswego in 1749 provided Governor Clinton of New York with a "return of the far-off Indians,

44. *Calendar of State Papers, 1681–1685,* p. 157; and *Calendar of State Papers, 1677–1680,* p. 226. See also Thomas Jefferson, *Notes on the State of Virginia,* ed. William Peden (Chapel Hill: University of North Carolina Press, 1955), pp. 93–96. David Ramsay, writing in 1792, commented that around 1725 "there were Indians in almost every direction but their distinguishing names, numbers & geographical residence were not then nor at any time since particularly recorded." Ramsay to B. Trumbull, March 7, 1792, in Robert L. Brunhouse, ed., *David Ramsay, 1749–1815,* in *Transactions of the American Philosophical Society,* n.s., vol. 55, pt. 4 (1965), p. 131.

the number of canoes, the number of people, &c." [45] William Douglass, preparing his history of British North America at about the same time, dug out figures on the fighting men of most of the principal northern tribes, and was surprised at the small total. Colonel Henry Bouquet, in the course of his 1764 campaign against the Indians, obtained from a French trader population figures for twenty-four tribes generally west of the Mississippi and for twenty-three to the east. The engineer and geographer Captain Thomas Hutchins was sent out to visit Indian tribes in 1768 expressly to learn their numbers. His inquiry provided information on thirty-one tribes east of the Mississippi and six further west. In 1778 William Wilson attempted to assemble population information for all tribes east of the Mississippi. The following year, the trader John Dodge supplied figures for fourteen tribes in that area.[46]

Meanwhile, the French in North America continued gathering similar information. In 1730, as one example, the Commandant General of Louisiana, Perier, undertook a census of forty-five Choctaw villages. His agents found 3010 fighting men.[47] But Jesuit missionaries, pursuing their lonely and dangerous lives in the wilderness, had always

45. Clinton to Board of Trade, November 26, 1749, *Journal of the Commissioners for Trade and Plantations, from January 1749/50 to December 1753* (London: His Majesty's Stationery Office, 1932), p. 46.

46. For a summary of the lists of Bouquet, Hutchins, and Dodge, see Jefferson, *Notes on Virginia*, pp. 102–106. Hutchins published his data in his book, *A Topographical Description of Virginia, Pennsylvania, Maryland and North Carolina* (London: J. Almon, 1778), pp. 65–67. Hutchins's short book also gave detailed information about the Whites in the tiny towns along the Ohio and its tributaries between Fort Pitt and St. Louis. This included such specific demographic information as numbers of houses, French inhabitants, Negroes, and fencible men.

47. Greene and Harrington, *American Population*, p. 203.

sent back reports on the numbers of the Indians among whom they labored and prayed. And, similarly, Anglican missionaries of the Society for the Propagation of the Gospel in Foreign Parts often did the same in the areas of the English colonies.

In mid-eighteenth century, the agents for Indian affairs, Sir William Johnson and George Croghan, were knowledgeable sources of information about the Indian population. Croghan, for instance, in 1759 furnished General John Stanwix with a list which gave rough population figures for fifteen different tribes, all but two of them east of the Mississippi.[48] Among other royal officials, few knew more about the Indians than Cadwallader Colden, scientist and Lieutenant Governor of New York. In his official capacity, Colden was often preoccupied with the logistics of waging the brutal war in his colony; that is, obtaining militia or regular troops, supplying them, and helping coordinate their movements. Colden also found time to gather the data about the Iroquois which went into his *History of the Five Indian Nations*. Surprisingly, he made no attempt therein to examine systematically or report upon the demographic condition of the Iroquois, even though others showed, as early as 1698, that the Federation was losing appalling numbers of its men in the French wars and through disease.[49] It was only in passing that Colden briefly described for posterity how the Iroquois sometimes num-

48. Jefferson, *Notes on Virginia*, pp. 102–106.

49. Governor Bellomont of New York had sent a special table to the Board of Trade in 1698 showing the disastrous decrease of the Iroquois during the current phase of the French conflict. From 2800 before that year, it had dropped to an estimated 1324. The Whites in Albany County had also dropped from 662 men, 342 women, and 1014 children to 382 men, 272 women, and 805 children. *Calendar of State Papers, 1697–98*, p. 531.

bered their people. The method was used while the Indians were negotiating the numbers of warriors to be furnished for a projected joint expedition with the English against Canada. Colden recorded how the Iroquois "told the numbers by laying down bundles of little sticks for each Nation adding that they were obliged to keep a good force in their own Countries to defend their Wives & children from their enemies as they find the Christians likewise do." [50]

Colden's frequent preoccupation with troops — whether English, French, Indian, or colonial — was symptomatic of his times. With the first appearance of colonial newspapers in the early eighteenth century, no news items held more sustained interest for colonial readers than the regular dispatches from London or the Continent on the British Empire's current military fortunes. These included details about military campaigns, numbers of troops in encampments or on the move, engagements, assignments of officers, and numerical summaries of casualties. Not only was the political fate of the colonies wrapped up in these events, but many individuals had acquaintances participating in them. Further, up to a point anyway, many colonists thought of themselves as comrades-in-arms of the British forces against the common enemy, the French; the colonists held the lines in America, while the British did so in Europe.

During the colonial period just as now, military service was a fact of life with which most men had to reckon at one time or another. As a fighting body, the colonial militia was sometimes as shadowy and hard to pin down as were the Indian forces. Since it did not ordinarily maintain a ready professional force, after a given engagement it dissolved overnight. Nevertheless, almost every able male from soon after puberty to the age of sixty, except Quakers and Anabaptists, was likely to be on the rolls of the local militia body, ready for call at any time.[51] County militia commanders had the duty of ascertaining all men in their areas who were eligible for service, and of providing annual lists of these eligibles to the governors.[52] The muster rolls of actual or potential militia service usually included such information as names, dates and places of birth, and occupations for each individual.

Colonial governors were under standing orders from the English authorities to supply the fullest possible data both on potential militia manpower and on existing organized militia forces, in order "that the King may know what force can, in case of need, be brought together." [53] Reports which streamed constantly back to England on this subject characteristically gave numbers of foot soldiers and horse troops, the numbers in the population able to bear arms, names of officers, quantities of muskets available, the state of training of the various bodies, and occasionally the numbers of seamen. Massachusetts was reported to have three regiments of militia in 1656, six in 1671, and twelve in 1706. Such figures may have been sometimes taken at face value in London. But some English sources before King Philip's War maintained that in New England "not above three of their military men [officers?] have been actual

51. For a good summary of the nature and role of the militia, see Boorstin, *The Americans*, pp. 352–357. The effect of the Pennsylvania Quakers' refusal, as a matter of conscience, to bear arms or vote money for defense, has been discussed in many studies.

52. The 1680 requirement in Virginia is given in *Calendar of State Papers, 1677–1680*, p. 634. See also Bruce, *Social Life of Virginia*, pp. 14ff.

53. "Journal of Lords of Trade," November 26, 1681, *Calendar of State Papers, 1681–1685*, p. 145.

soldiers, but many such soldiers as the artillery men at London." [54]

Almost as important as their defense connotations, the militia returns provided keys for estimating total populations. Like tax lists and other bases of estimation, these returns had their drawbacks in use. A serious source of confusion, for example, was the lack of uniformity in the formulas used. In Massachusetts in 1751, Governor Shirley, from a figure of 20,000 militia, used a 1 for 6 ratio to estimate the population at 120,000 Whites. Only a dozen years later, however, in the same state, Governor Bernard figured the militia at "1/4th part of the Souls," a ratio which left him with an estimate of 164,000.[55] William Douglass estimated that New England in 1742 had a population of about 354,000, a figure arrived at in some unexplained way from the region's total of some 90,000 "fencible men," of which only 70,000, however, were regarded as "fencible marching men." Pennsylvania, in contrast, provided virtually no reliable basis for population estimation. As Douglass complained, "No regular Estimate can be made of the Inhabitants, because there is no Poll Tax, nor any Militia List allowed for Alarums, or common Trainings, as in the other Colonies, to form Estimates by." [56]

Just as important as estimates of militia and Indians to many Whites, especially in the South, were the figures on

54. "Copy of a Curious Paper Concerning the Inhabitants of this Government," Massachusetts Historical Society, *Collections*, ser. 1, IV (1795), 217. This comment refers evidently to various military groups of London which, over the years, had evolved into largely social or honorary organizations.

55. See Benton, *Early Census-Making*, pp. 22–60, passim.

56. William Douglass, *A Summary, Historical and Political, of the First Planting, progressive Improvements, and present State of the British Settlements in North-America*, 2 vols. (Boston: Rogers and Fowle, 1749), II, 324 and passim.

the Negro population. As the slave trade accelerated, the Negro appeared almost everywhere, perhaps just an occasional house servant in rural New England, but outnumbering Whites ten to one in some districts of South Carolina. By the end of the seventeenth century, many Whites in the South were apprehensive as they looked out on "the vast *Shoals* of Negroes" everywhere around them. Officials in the Carolinas thus early sought ways to maintain a "safe" racial balance. Like their counterparts in Jamaica, Barbados, and other settlements which had large slave populations, they passed legislation to encourage white immigration. Acts of 1698, 1712, and 1716 offered bounties for bringing in white servants, and required planters to buy at least one white servant for each six Negro slaves they owned. These Acts were also said to have been motivated by the desire to build up the white militia for defense against the French and Indians, as well as by the fear of possible slave uprisings.[57]

In some of the other southern colonies a slightly different reaction arose out of the combined influx of slaves and indentured servants. When in 1698 the white planter class of Maryland was decimated by deaths from fever, Governor Nicholson feared that the resulting population imbalance was close to critical proportions. "If next year, or within two or three years, the like number of inhabitants should die and as many Irish and Negroes be imported (especially the first, who are most if not all papists) it may be of dan-

---

57. See Abbot Smith, *Colonists in Bondage*, pp. 32–34 and 330. See also the brilliant study by Winthrop D. Jordan, *White Over Black: American Attitudes toward the Negro, 1550–1812* (Chapel Hill: University of North Carolina Press, 1968). That work is filled with demographic insights essential to an understanding of the period before 1800. See especially, in the present connection, pp. 102–103, 315, 320, 546ff and 575.

gerous consequence to Maryland, and also to Virginia, which, I hear, is in the same circumstances." [58]

Although Nicholson's fears about a deluge of papists in Maryland and Virginia proved groundless, the problem of population balance remained an extremely sensitive one for whites throughout the South. Some observers, like George Milligen of South Carolina, eventually even came to feel that the Indians were the key in maintaining a safe equilibrium:

[The Negroes] are in this Climate necessary, but very dangerous Domestics, their Number so much exceeding the Whites; a natural Dislike and Antipathy, that subsists between them and our *Indian* neighbours, is a very lucky Circumstance, and for this Reason: In our Quarrels with the *Indians* . . . it can never be our Interest to extirpate them, or to force them from their Lands; their Ground would be soon taken up by runaway *Negroes* from our Settlements, whose Numbers would daily increase, and quickly become more formidable Enemies than *Indians* can ever be, as they speak our Language, and would never be at a Loss for Intelligence.[59]

During the early eighteenth century, few Southerners were more closely involved in the area's population development than the Virginians, Robert Beverley and William Byrd. As large landowners, they were also large importers

58. Nicholson to Council of Trade, August 20, 1698, *Calendar of State Papers, 27 October 1697–31 December 1698*, p. 390.

59. George Milligen, *A Short Description of the Province of South-Carolina, with an Account of The Air, Weather, and Diseases, at Charles-Town.* Written 1763 (London: J. Hinton, 1770), p. 26. (In later years Milligen took the name Milligen-Johnston.)

of slaves and indentured servants. With such considerable human and material property, both found practical values in keeping good records, including those of vital events. But they were also concerned with the demographic situation of the colony as a whole.

Beverley, in 1705, published his *History and Present State of Virginia*, a descriptive survey of the colony and its institutions. Beverley's population chart for 1703 was compiled from the best sources. He provided data on the "number of souls" (60,606), "Titheables" (25,023), women and children (35,583), number of militia (9,522), number of horse (2,363), and number of foot and dragoons (7,159). "The French refugees are not accounted within this list." [60]

Both Beverley and Byrd felt that an enlightened policy on the part of the colony's founders could have averted some of its population problems, particularly those brought on by Indian warfare. Beverley, doubtless thinking somewhat of Randolph's criticisms of Virginia, discussed some of the problems in his *History*. A large part of the difficulty, he thought, was the refusal of the early Englishmen to intermarry with the Indians. "Had they embraced this Proposal . . . the Colony, instead of all these Losses of Men on both sides, would have been encreasing in Children to its Advantage; the country wou'd have escaped the *Odium* which undeservedly fell upon it, by the Errors and Convulsions in its first Management; and in all Likelihood, many, if not most, of the *Indians* would have been converted to Christianity by this Method; the Country would have been full of People." [61]

Byrd, who well knew what Englishmen like Petty had

60. Robert Beverley, *The History and Present State of Virginia* (Chapel Hill: University of North Carolina Press, 1947), p. 253.
61. *Ibid.*, p. 38.

written on the subject, pushed this point even further. Writing in 1728, in his *History of the Dividing Line*, Byrd declared: "Had the English consulted their own Security and the good of the Colony . . . they would have brought their Stomachs to embrace this prudent Alliance." After all, Byrd thought, the Indians were probably no greater heathen than most of the early white settlers.

Besides, the poor Indian would have had less reason to complain that the English took away their land, if [the latter] had received it by way of Portion with [the Indians'] Daughters. Had such Affinities been contracted in the Beginning, how much Bloodshed had been prevented, and how populous would the Country have been, and consequently, how considerable? Nor would the Shade of the Skin have been any reproach at this day, for if a Moor may be washt white in three Generations, Surely an Indian might have been blancht in two.

Finally, it seemed to Byrd that "The Indian Women would have made altogether as Honest Wives for the first Planters, as the Damsels they used to purchase from aboard the Ships." [62]

During his travels along the frontier, Byrd gathered what numerical data he could about the Indians. The Cherokee of South Carolina and Georgia, he discovered, numbered "more than 4,000 Fighting Men" living in 62 towns. In North Carolina, on the other hand, Byrd noticed that the once-populous Usheree Indians had been reduced by 1728

62. *The Writings of "Colonel William Byrd of Westover in Virginia Esqr.",* ed. John Spencer Basset (New York: Doubleday, Page, 1901), pp. 8–10, 101–102; see also p. xliii and Appendix A.

to about 400 fighting men. The causes of this, he thought, were liquor, white men's diseases, and wars with Northern Indians. In Virginia the reduction was even more marked; he found that a town of some 200 Nothaways were, in fact, "the only Indians of any consequence remaining in Virginia." [63] The decline in Indian population which Byrd noticed in Virginia and the Carolinas was consistent with observations made in other colonies. Bishop Berkeley found, for instance, from a 1730 census, that there were only 985 Indians left in Rhode Island.[64] In 1751 Governor Shirley of Massachusetts reported about three thousand friendly Indians living in or near the English settlements; but by 1763 Governor Bernard found only a few hundred.[65] The Reverend Ezra Stiles of Newport compared a 1698 census of Cape Cod Indians with his own enumeration of 1762. In only sixty-four years, that group had declined from 4168 to 1573.[66] Over-all, it appeared that by the mid-1760's "there were not forty thousand souls, Indians, from the

63. *Ibid.*, pp. 98, 185, 237, and 247.
64. Berkeley used these figures in 1731 to help persuade the Society for the Propagation of the Gospel that the Rhode Island Indians and Negroes offered a promising missionary field. He found that there were half again as many Negroes as Indians in Rhode Island, while "both together scarce amount to a seventh part of the whole colony." Berkeley was of the same mind as Beverley and Byrd, that the early English would have been well-advised demographically not only to try to convert the Indians and Negroes but to intermarry with them, See *The Works of George Berkeley, D.D.*, 2. vols. (Dublin: John Exshaw, 1784), II, 456–457.
65. See Benton, *Early Census-Making*, pp. 22–60.
66. See Franklin B. Dexter, ed., *Extracts from the Itineraries and other Miscellanies of Ezra Stiles, D.D., LL.D., 1755–1794* (New Haven, Ct.: Yale University Press, 1916), p. 59. See also Edmund S. Morgan, *The Gentle Puritan, A Life of Ezra Stiles, 1727–1795* (New Haven, Ct.: Yale University Press, 1962), p. 139.

Mississippi to the Atlantic, and from Florida to the Pole." [67] William Douglass, writing in 1749, attributed some of the decline to the practice of the colonists of sending large numbers of domestic male Indians out on the many military and naval expeditions.[68] He thought that intemperance was another prominent cause. Most observers, in fact, agreed generally with Jefferson's diagnosis of 1782, that the reduction in numbers was due to "spirituous liquors, the small-pox, war, and an abridgment of territory," generally in that order.[69] The quantitative data of the day well reflected the inexorable population pressures which were exerted on the Indians by the aggressive white newcomers from across the sea. Many devout persons among these newcomers thought that the data also marked the wise operation of God's demographic plan for the New World.

67. Ezra Stiles, *The United States Elevated to Glory and Honor* (New Haven: Thomas & Samuel Green, 1783), p. 13. In other places Stiles estimated other figures, but never more than 100,000. Stiles thought that early sexual promiscuity was a factor in the decline of Indian populations. But he was also aware that the steady increase of the English had a close relationship to the Indians' decrease.

68. William Douglass, *Summary, Historical and Political*, II, see chapter on Rhode Island. The general practice of impressment of colonial men, white and black, off the streets for service in the Royal Navy is thought to have noticeably affected the population of coastal cities such as Boston and New York during the 1740's and 1750's. A "press" in New York in 1751 took away some 800 men, about a fourth of the male adults. See Jesse Lemisch, "Jack Tar in the Streets: Merchant Seamen in the Politics of Revolutionary America," *William and Mary Quarterly*, 3rd ser., 25 (1968), 383–384.

69. Jefferson, *Notes on Virginia*, p. 96.

Chapter V

Divine Order and Vital Human Events

The enumeration of population and vital human events was one thing to the colonial governors, agents, constables, justices, and militia commanders who scurried around for data to send to the king. It was quite another thing to the clergymen, elders, and sextons of the colonial churches. If the building of a terrestrial empire required human statistics, pursuit of a celestial domain needed them not a bit less. Ministers of every denomination bore witness to the baptisms, marriages, and burials which occurred among their congregations, and often to the sicknesses as well. After such events many of these men went back to their parsonages, recorded the facts they had witnessed, and sometimes pondered their significance. Among the various denominations, the special circumstances of the New England Congregational churches seemed to afford particularly favorable opportunities both for the collection of such data and for generalizing from them.

Although colonial church groups differed about many matters, there was virtual unanimity as to the importance of keeping church records, including registers of vital events. For the Anglicans it was not only a matter of well-established church policy but one of civil law wherever Acts of Establishment were passed, as in Virginia, the Carolinas, Maryland, New York, and Georgia. Actually, wherever stable parishes were established, with more or less compact populations, strong vestries, and an uninterrupted supply of ministers, good registers were often maintained. At Christ Church in Philadelphia, parish registers of a high standard were kept up throughout most of the eighteenth century. In many places, on the other hand, the keeping of such registers was a sporadic matter at best.[1]

The registers suffered noticeably whenever some parish ingredient was missing; no ingredient was more crucial than the minister. Even such an out-of-the-way spot as Pensacola, West Florida, had regular registers of christenings and burials among the town and garrison personnel between 1768 and 1771. But these terminated abruptly when the Anglican rector, Nathaniel Cotton, himself died and was not replaced for some time.[2] On a larger scale, Maryland, in 1676, was said to have a population of some 20,000 but only three Anglican ministers to serve them.[3]

1. This spotty maintenance of registers is indicated by occasional calls for registers to be completed retrospectively. In 1742, for instance, a notice was posted upon the doors of the churches in All Saints Parish, Maryland, requiring parishioners "to have all former and future baptisms, marriages, and burials put on the parish records or they will be prosecuted as the law directs." Quoted in Calhoun, *A Social History,* I, p. 261.

2. See Laura D. S. Harrell, "Colonial Medical Practices in British West Florida, 1763–1781," *Bulletin of the History of Medicine,* 41 (November–December 1967), 547.

3. See *Calendar of State Papers, 1675–1676,* p. 435.

This situation caused as widespread a lack of parish registers there as in New York, Virginia, and the Carolinas, throughout the century. Despite subsequent strenuous efforts, the Society for the Propagation of the Gospel in Foreign Parts never was able to obtain ministers for many of the parishes of these colonies. Authorities in England frequently called upon the colonial governors for quantitative data on religion. They were chiefly interested in knowing how many parishes had been established, what the number of ministers was, and what the strength of the Dissenters was. None of these data were particularly hard to come by so long as the numbers of each were small. In 1681 Governor Culpeper assured the Lords of Trade that in all Virginia there was but a single Papist and only about 150 Dissenters who called themselves "Sweet Singers." [4] But even in Virginia the Anglicans could not boast such dominance for long. Dissenters were both increasingly hard to count and hard to manage in the colonies in which the Church of England was established.

The proliferation of dissenting sects in such colonies was an ever-growing source of frustration to authorities who tried to register vital events in the parishes. As each sect grew, it naturally had no wish for Anglican priests to baptize or bury its members. In consequence, increasing numbers of such events were not recorded in parish registers. Even the marriages of Dissenters, which were supposed to be performed under Anglican sanction in order to be legal, disappeared increasingly from Church of England registers as local magistrates agreed to perform civil ceremonies or blinked at ceremonies performed by dissenting clergy.[5] As dissenting churches began to appear, each body

4. *Calendar of State Papers, 1681–1685,* p. 145.
5. For comment on the limited success of the parish system even

ultimately kept its own vital records. Since these had no legal standing, dissenting churches did not report their data as parishes were required to do. There was thus no effective way of knowing the full extent of vital human occurrences in such colonies. The registration of the vital events of slaves was not required of the parish system. Accordingly, any recording of these events that was done in the Southern colonies usually fell to the plantations. While it was by no means a universal practice, some plantations, at least those of substantial size, kept track of the births, deaths, and diseases of their slaves, along with their other business records.[6]

Among the Quakers, William Penn was by no means alone in seeking good and complete records. Back in England, George Fox himself "not only instructed the people in the value of making their wills . . . but he admonished them to keep a number of other records in addition to those of a vital statistic nature."[7] In America, Quaker Yearly Meetings made it their business to see that the Monthly Meetings kept adequate registers of the births, deaths, and marriages of their members. The latter usually did this faithfully, except when persecution or small numbers hampered formal organization of the local Friends groups. In 1750 Peter Kalm reported that the Quakers

in Virginia, see Winthrop S. Hudson, *Religion in America* (New York: Scribner's, 1965), p. 15. A comparable situation, of course, prevailed in England, where vital events of Dissenters and Papists did not appear in parish registers, except for their marriages.

6. For a discussion of some such surviving plantation records, though chiefly those of the nineteenth century, see Guion G. Johnson, *A Social History of the Sea Islands* (Chapel Hill: University of North Carolina Press, 1930).

7. E. Kay Kirkham, *A Survey of American Church Records*, 2 vols. (Salt Lake City, Utah: Deseret Book Company, 1959–60), I, 30.

"never baptize their children, though they keep a pretty exact account of all who are born among them." [8]

Similarly, members of the various Dutch, German, and Swedish Protestant groups made every effort to continue in the American colonies the careful record-keeping practices they had followed as a matter of course in Europe. More often than not it was the pastors who actually did the job, either in formal registers or in the diaries they kept. Henry Muhlenberg's journal rivals even Judge Sewall's in the numbers of deaths that it records. The journal of the Swedish preacher, Nicholas Collin, on the other hand, records as many baptisms and marriages as deaths for his successive pastorates in New Jersey and Pennsylvania. Collin found that his official church registers were sometimes useful in holding wayward members within his flock.[9]

Although the word "Papist" remained a dirty word in English America throughout the colonial period, wherever Catholic churches were organized vital registers were begun as a matter of course. Parishes in French and Spanish settlements which later were absorbed within the United States had registers at an early date, St. Augustine continuously since 1594. Similarly, priests of the French churches at such outposts as Mobile (established 1701), New Orleans (1718), and Sainte Genevieve, Missouri (in the 1750's) began keeping registers soon after the settlements began.[10]

8. *The America of 1750: Peter Kalm's Travels in North America*, 2 vols. (New York: Wilson-Erickson, 1937), I, 32.

9. Amandus Johnson, *The Journal and Biography of Nicholas Collin, 1746–1831* (Philadelphia: The New Jersey Society of Pennsylvania, 1936), p. 254.

10. See *Guide to Public Vital Statistics Records in Louisiana* (New Orleans: The Louisiana State Board of Health, 1942); *Guide to Public Vital Statistics Records in Missouri* (St. Louis: Missouri Historical

Vital record-keeping among the colonial Baptists, Presbyterians, and Methodists is not as simply described. The rugged autonomy of the individual Baptist churches, if nothing else, may have made for variations in their records. Some Baptist congregations in relatively stable population areas had as good registers as almost any Anglican or Lutheran church. In southern New England, the Baptist preacher Isaac Backus, between 1749 and 1805, kept a private "account of Deaths both comon & untimely" — he called it a "Bill of Mortality" — which, in this respect went far beyond most of the journals kept by preachers of other faiths. But most of the Baptist congregations in New England were not served by Backuses. And most were neither stable nor well-off by worldly standards. In no New England colony except Rhode Island did this sect enjoy any civil or social status before the Revolution. Elsewhere in New England, the seventeenth-century suppression and persecution of Baptists, and their subsequent general harassment, taxation, and ostracism in the eighteenth, made for a chronic situation of insecurity and instability in which vital registers of their churches suffered badly.[11]

In principle, both the Presbyterians and the Methodists inclined toward the careful keeping of their vital church records. The Presbyterians in this were true to their Puritan heritage, while the Methodists merely followed their Anglican upbringing. Still, the circumstances in the devel-

---

Records Survey, 1941); *Guide to Public Vital Statistics Records in Florida* (Jacksonville: Florida Historical Records Survey, 1941); and Calhoun, *A Social History*, I, passim.

11. Modern genealogists looking for colonial Baptist vital data have sometimes, in the absence of preserved church registers, had to fall back upon records of oaths required of Baptists in some New England colonies. See Kirkham, *Survey of American Church Records*, I, 9ff.

opment of these two denominations in America did not always permit them to follow their inclinations. In the cities, it is true, where the Presbyterian congregations were often not only well organized but supplied both with educated clergy and intelligent parishioners, the registers tended to be well kept. Yet, much of the strength of the Presbyterians, and later of the Methodists and other sects, was outside the older, settled areas. Throughout this and subsequent periods, their growth was largely among dispersed rural populations or among uprooted people along the routes of migration into frontier areas. In consequence, as long as the congregations themselves remained unstable, their early church registers were often as incomplete or nonexistent as those of the Baptists.

Between the 1720's and the 1750's, virtually every American denomination was caught up in that revivalist phenomenon known as the Great Awakening. The unsettled state of many congregations during this time was anything but favorable to the maintenance of church registers.[12] "New Light" (revivalist) or other groups which split off from established (Old Light) congregations in settled areas often had to start from scratch in their physical arrangements, from buildings to church records. The tiny and scarcely organized groups of enthusiasts who met in the

12. The Anglican preacher Timothy Cutter characterized the Great Awakening as a time when "Our presses are forever teeming with books and our women with bastards." William Douglass and the Reverend Charles Chauncy were among contemporaries who agreed with this assessment. A twentieth-century scholar, however, does not think the Awakening was "an orgiastic interlude." Rather, he believes that the greater sense of sin and increased church discipline of that era caused increased publicizing of sexual irregularities, through church confessions of fornication. See Cedric B. Cowing, "Sex and Preaching in the Great Awakening," *American Quarterly,* 20 (Fall 1968), 624–644.

members' poor cabins in backwoods areas, moreover, often had little concept of the values of record-keeping. The frequently unlearned clergymen who preached to these latter widely scattered groups sometimes had little more appreciation than their congregations. These men held back the establishment of vital church registers just as illiterate constables made a farce out of some population enumerations.[13] More important, probably, itinerant clergymen could hardly know about the vital occurrences in all of their far-flung congregations, much less find circumstances favorable to record them in register or journal. Similar conditions, of course, prevailed in large areas of America long after the Great Awakening. The continuing combination of itinerant preachers (whether learned or not) and uneducated congregations throughout many rural areas as well as along the frontier regions generally held back the development both of church registers and civil vital statistics in the United States far up into the nineteenth century.[14]

The emotionalism of the revival in itself was to some extent unconducive to record-keeping activities. Nevertheless, the participants in the Great Awakening did not necessarily repudiate the notion that churches should keep the

13. Nicholas Collin, newly arrived in America in the 1770's, had repeated encounters with roaming Anabaptist preachers who served the "wild" unchurched people of the back country of New Jersey. He found them insolent, conceited, and "without the slightest education." Johnson, *Journal of Nicholas Collin,* p. 264.

14. Professor Richard Vann observes (in a personal communication) that the relative learning of the clergy was of less relevance to the adequacy of church registers than the actual presence of ministers. In the case of seventeenth- and eighteenth-century Episcopal parishes, the registers remained in the uncertain hands of the parish clerks, since clergymen often resided away from parishes which they served.

vital statistics of their members. In fact, many revivalist preachers followed their church records with more than usual interest during these noteworthy times. Peter Thacher, of Middleborough, Massachusetts, for instance, noted that the Awakening had the extraordinary effect of bringing more males to church membership then females, the reverse of the usual condition.[15] At the Northampton church, one of the high priests of the Awakening, Jonathan Edwards himself, faithfully maintained his baptismal and other church registers throughout the movement's greatest periods of stress. Thomas Prince of Boston, another confirmed revivalist, was equally devoted to such record-keeping. But Edwards and Prince were both Congregationalists; and Puritans, we recall, had a special incentive for keeping vital records.

Congregational ministers, as the spiritual shepherds of the members, usually kept the religious (as opposed to the legal) records of their churches. These were kept sometimes as virtually private documents, though often they passed from one pastor to another as part of the permanent heritage of the church. It is hardly an exaggeration to say that the church parsonage in colonial New England, fully as much as the market or the merchant's office, deserved the title of "counting house." For there the ministers numbered the church members as well as the non-members, added up baptisms, burials, and marriages, and often wondered about the heavenly demography of the elect and the damned. Account had to be kept of days of thanksgiving and days of humiliation or fast. After 1662, the ministers' lists had to distinguish between those who had made a full confession of faith and those who remained only halfway

15. Cowing, "Sex and Preaching in Great Awakening," *American Quarterly*, 20, 632.

(birthright) members.[16] And there were all the records to keep of disciplinary actions — excommunications in the case of heresy, perhaps only public reprimands in the case of members who owned up to fornication before marriage. The New England Churchmen often wrote down the causes of death among their flocks: deaths from diseases known and unknown, from epidemics which struck whole congregations, from lightning and tragic accidents of every description, deaths "at sea," from "old age," or "perished in the cold." Pity the poor infant who was "buryed unbaptized." And pity the whole community when "melancholy tidings" came in from the French or Indian wars of sons and neighbors who "died at Cape Breton" or some other far-off place.[17] Sometimes, though rarely, the registers noted a burial "in the way by John Emmersson's House," or another over "in the lower Syde of the Calves pasture." These were good New England places in which to be buried. But it was comforting to pastor and congregation alike to think that most would end up together in the burial place at the side of the meetinghouse. That was the orderly way.[18]

16. For examples, see Bumsted, "Revivalism and Separatism in New England . . . ," *William and Mary Quarterly*, 3rd ser., 24 (1967), 590–596.

17. For typical entries in journals and church records, see John W. Lane, "Deaths in Hampton, N. H., 1727–1755," *New England Historical and Genealogical Register*, 58 (1904), 29–36 and 136–140; and "Scituate and Barnstable Church Records," *ibid.*, 9 (1855), 279–287, and 10 (1856), 37–43.

18. There is a vivid and intimate history of New England Congregationalism in Ola Elizabeth Winslow, *Meetinghouse Hill* (New York: Macmillan, 1952). In New England (as elsewhere), gravestones, while including much vital information about the dead, revealed also much about New Englanders' attitudes toward death. These views, together with Puritan artistic symbolism of death, are discussed and richly illustrated in the recent book by Allen I. Ludwig, *Graven*

In the tiny towns of New England, the Congregational minister did not often (any more than the town clerk), have the special parchment paper for his records that English law had long since required for official registers. Sometimes he was lucky to have any paper. Hence there was much improvising. The Reverend Jeremiah Barnard in Amherst, New Hampshire, kept his marriage records over a fifty-year period on the blank leaves of a book from his library. William Williams of Weston, Massachusetts, had proper record books for his own members, but listed out-of-town baptisms on the flyleaves of those books. And Seaborn Cotton, after he became minister in the Hampton, New Hampshire, church, used the blank leaves of the commonplace book he had kept as a Harvard student for his church records. Posterity finds his sober record of births and marriages "following a highly erotic extract from Sir Philip Sidney's *Arcadia*." [19]

In some cases, of course, despite good intentions the colonial minister did not manage to get the records down on paper. For, likely as not, he had to work as hard for a material living for his family as did anyone else, with all that meant of clearing woods, building fences or houses, draining swamps, tending livestock, planting and harvesting crops, and so on. Not every minister was as fortunate as Thomas Clap at Windham, Connecticut, who received enough from his parish to spare him some of the physical tasks. This left Clap with enough energy for keeping the

---

Images: New England Stonecarving and its Symbols, 1650–1815 (Middletown, Ct.: Wesleyan University Press, 1966).

19. Morison, *Intellectual Life of Colonial New England*, p. 49. See also *New England Historical and Genealogical Register*, 61 (1907), 235; and Mary F. Peirce, ed., *Town of Weston: Births, Deaths, and Marriages 1707–1850* (Boston: McIndoe Bros., 1901), pp. ivff and 324.

records properly and otherwise instilling administrative order into his church.[20]

In filling their church registers, some of the clergymen, like some clerks, obviously had no higher thought in mind than in following precedent, law, or tradition. For them, the keeping of vital records was merely an exercise in order for its own sake, an example of the bookkeeping mind. But some found utility or meaning, or both, in the various records of people and human events. For devout Puritans, the measure of utility for such demographic data was clear. What did they tell about the progress of the New England Congregational church-community toward the special destiny which they knew God had planned for it?

Puritans often thought of this destiny in terms of an already written record, one which was unworldly but was of a vividly personal and immediate sort. This record contained the most crucial vital statistics of all — the unknowable demography of God's chosen and the damned. In 1670 William Stoughton preached directly to this record: "Consider and remember always," he cautioned, "that the *Books* that shall be opened at the last day will contain *Genealogies* in them. There shall then be brought forth a *Register of the Genealogies of New Englands' sons and daughters.*" [21]

While God's will was hidden from human understanding, worldly records could be compiled and studied for signs which might suggest something about it. The text, as Simon Bradstreet pointed out, was in Psalms 107, 43: "Whoso is wise and will observe these things, even they

20. See Louis L. Tucker, *Puritan Protagonist, President Thomas Clap of Yale College* (Chapel Hill: University of North Carolina Press, 1962), p. 39.
21. William Stoughton, *New Englands True Interest, Not to Lie* (Cambridge, 1670), p. 33, quoted in Edmund S. Morgan, *The Puritan Family* (Boston: Boston Public Library, 1944), p. 99.

shall understand the kindnesse of the Lord." [22] The diaries and church records of New Englanders from John Winthrop and Bradstreet onward were accordingly filled with notations of observed incidents, of providences ordinary and special.[23] While the portent of comets, earthquakes, and certain other strange events could only be guessed at, the deducible message from demographic occurrences was generally fairly clear. To Edward Johnson, for instance, the population changes in Massachusetts between 1630 and 1650 had been certain signs of God's favor toward New England. They were part of the "wonderous worke of the great Jehovah." [24] Calamities such as wars or epidemics, on the other hand, left no doubt as to God's displeasure.

22. Bradstreet's own journal recorded a wide variety of such events. Over a period of several months in 1664, for instance, he watched a great blazing star which had no observable effect either for good or evil in New England. But he afterwards felt that this occurrence had led to such calamitous judgments of God in England as the great fire of London and another visit of the plague. "Bradstreet's Journal, 1664–83," *New England Historical and Genealogical Register,* 9 (1855), 43–44.

23. The recording of special providences was by no means confined to Puritans. The Baptist preacher Isaac Backus, for example, carefully listed "special providences" along with his lists of "untimely deaths," "remarkable deaths," and ordinary deaths. Following the death of some 150 persons in Norwich, Connecticut, in 1753 from "camp distemper," Backus commented: "Terrible indeed have been God's dispensations to this Town! May the Inhabitants awake and learn Righteousness." Isaac Backus, "Bills of Mortality," unpub. manuscript (1749–1805), at Andover Newton Theological School. Professor William McLoughlin kindly drew my attention to this manuscript.

24. *Johnson's Wonder-Working Providence,* p. 48. See also my discussion of Johnson in Chapter II. Some 135 years after Johnson wrote, Jedidiah Morse echoed Johnson's sense of religious wonder over the decline of the Indians: "The hand of Providence," Morse wrote, "is noticeable in these surprising instances of mortality, among the Indians, to make way for the English. Comparatively few have

Possibly none of God's providences was less comprehensible than the terrible throat epidemic (diphtheria) which attacked New England children during the mid-1730's. Nearly a thousand died in New Hampshire alone. Jabez Fitch, the Congregational Minister at Hampton, gathered together the frightful death totals for each town and tried to analyze them. In Hampton alone, he found, "Nigh Twenty Families lost all their Children, Twenty-two lost all their Sons, most of them being only Sons," and some twenty-five other families lost three or more children. But why was it mostly children who were the victims? Fitch could not explain this. He merely pointed out that "The Grave is a Land of Darkness without any Order [by age] . . . Yet every one may be said to die in his own order, in respect of God's appointment, who has determined the Time of every one's Death." In going on to point up the moral, however, Fitch had no doubt as to the ultimate cause of the epidemic. Such a *"strange* unusual Distemper" as this, he felt, was the "Fruit of *strange* Sins," of which increasing worldliness seemed to be one of the gravest. Whatever they were, the sins were such that they had remained unatoned for by the usual days of fasting. Accordingly, "God has answer'd us by terrible things in righteousness." In any case, Fitch saw the epidemic as a setback to God's religio-demographic plan for New England:

> The Loss of so many Children, whom if it had pleas'd God that they had liv'd, might have built up many Families, will be a great Prevention of the Growth and Increase of the Country; and ought therefore to

---

perished by wars. They waste and moulder away — they, in a manner unaccountable, disappear." — Jedidiah Morse, *The American Geography*, 2nd ed. (London: John Stockwell, 1792), p. 159.

be lookt upon as a Frown of Providence upon the Land in general, as well as a sore Affliction to the Parents in particular.[25]

The idea that God's demographic providence worked in very immediate ways remained strong throughout the eighteenth century. Nevertheless, some people were beginning to believe that God only rarely made such arbitrary direct interventions. Rather, it increasingly appeared that he governed the universe in an orderly manner by well-established laws. Science, in fact, was beginning to reveal some of these laws. Physical scientists like Galileo and Newton showed how celestial bodies moved in regular, predictable paths. Similarly, observers who followed John Graunt began to point out that the vital events of men's lives also occurred in orderly discernible patterns.

The English physician, mathematician, and satirist, John Arbuthnot, adapted Graunt's ideas to several of his own writings which appeared soon after 1710. He argued essentially, that "all the visible works of God Almighty are made in number, weight, and measure; therefore to consider them we ought to understand arithmetic, geometry, and statics." So far as Arbuthnot was concerned, colonial Americans were in no position to know much about God. For, as he concluded, those nations that lack arithmetic are "altogether barbarous, as some Americans, who can hardly reckon above twenty." [26]

25. Jabez Fitch, *An Account of the Numbers that have died of the Distemper in the Throat, Within the Province of New Hampshire, with some Reflections Thereon* (Boston: Eleazer Russel, 1736), pp. 4, 7, 12, 13.

26. John Arbuthnot, "An Essay on the Usefulness of Mathematical Learning," in George A. Aitken, *The Life and Works of John Arbuthnot* (Oxford: Clarendon Press, 1892), pp. 413, 421. See also Lester M. Beattie, *John Arbuthnot, Mathematician and Satirist* (Cambridge, Mass.: Harvard University Press, 1935).

Arbuthnot's point about proficiency in mathematics was well taken. Even if mathematics had been assumed to be entirely irrelevant to the search for divinity, it was still central to the development of demography and vital statistics as sciences, at least after their collection phases. During the seventeenth century, knowledge of mathematics in the American colonies was indeed scant and did not extend beyond a few almanac makers, land surveyors, and occasional scholars. Even in the eighteenth century, it remained elementary and chiefly practical; but instruction was gradually beginning to improve in the colleges, while individuals increasingly were teaching themselves enough advanced mathematics to read Huygens, Newton, Halley, DeMoivre, and D'Alembert, as well as Arbuthnot. Just as the increasing colonial interest in astronomy and navigation required more mathematical knowledge, so the gradually broadening applications of statistical methods also helped create a need for better mathematics. But the fundamentally practical motivations of colonial users militated against original contributions to mathematical theory for many years.[27] For the time being, a fund of mathematical knowledge which contributed to a simple appreciation of God's plan of the universe was all that many people asked.

A more elaborate English argument from design than Arbuthnot's came from Canon William Derham of Windsor, whose Boyle lectures were published in 1713 under the title, *Physico-Theology*.[28] One chapter of this

27. A concise review of early American mathematics can be found in David Eugene Smith and Jekuthiel Ginsburg, *A History of Mathematics in America before 1900* (Chicago: Mathematical Association of America, 1934), pp. 1–64.

28. The scientist Robert Boyle, long President of the Society for the Propagation of the Gospel, provided in his will for annual lectures which would provide proof of the Christian religion against atheism.

work, which drew heavily from John Graunt's book as well as from later political arithmeticians, discussed such matters as human longevity, the proportions of the sexes, and ratios of births to deaths. Derham concluded that all these matters were worked out in God's laws for the universe: "I say, there is a certain rate and proportion in the propagation of mankind: such a number marry, so many are born, such a number die: in proportion to the number of persons in every nation, county, or parish." [29] Colonial thinkers ultimately became familiar with the demographic writings of Arbuthnot and Derham. In fact, by 1731 the Anglican clergyman Samuel Johnson was recommending Derham's *Physico-Theology* to students of philosophy on both sides of the Atlantic. He subsequently came to believe that the statistical approach generally was a desirable one in the ordering of mid-eighteenth century society. When he opened Kings College in New York in 1754, therefore, he proposed to instruct his students, among other subjects, "in the Arts of *numbering and measuring; of Surveying and Navigation."* [30] In New England, Cotton Mather of Boston drew heavily

29. Derham, *Physico-Theology*, 3rd Scots ed. (Glasgow: Robert Urie, 1758), p. 212. To be sure, the mathematical approach to God was not new with Arbuthnot and Derham, only further developed. Two and a half centuries earlier, Nicholas Cusanus, and before him the Greeks and Roger Bacon, among others, declared that God created "all things in number, weight and measure." He further considered that both "mundane and divine truth may only be had through a knowledge of numbers." Allen E. Debus, "Mathematics and Nature in Chemical Texts of the Renaissance," *Ambix*, 15 (February 1968), 3–7.

30. Quoted in Theodore Hornberger, *Scientific Thought in the American Colleges, 1638–1800* (Austin: University of Texas Press, 1945), p. 30. See also Herbert and Carol Schneider, *Samuel Johnson*, 4 vols. (New York: Columbia University Press, 1929), passim, but esp. II, 318.

from "the inquisitive Mr. Derham" in preparing his own 1721 work, *The Christian Philosopher*. Here Mather summarized at some length the current scientific information which demonstrated God's orderly plan for the physical universe. By this time there was no longer much argument about such a concept, at least among serious thinkers, for Mather reported that "the *Virtuosos,* and all the *Genuine Philosophers* of our Age, have approved." [31]

Although Mather did not, in this volume, present the evidence of God's design which could be found in patterns of vital human events, there is no doubt that he assumed there was such order. Not content with the mere mechanics of keeping church records, in fact, he had long since tried to identify regular patterns in the records. Few other colonists of his day were inquisitive about these regularities. Mather, however, as early as 1691, took note of such demographic matters as the sex ratio of Boston churchgoers: "I have seen it without going a Mile from home," he wrote, "that in a Church of between Three and Four Hundred Communicants, there are but few more than One Hundred Men; all the rest are Women." [32] A few years later, in 1700, he observed somewhat more generally, that Boston was filled with widows and orphans. "In the church whereof I am the servant, I have counted the widows make about a sixth part of the communicants, and no doubt in the

31. Cotton Mather, *The Christian Philosopher* (London: Eman. Matthews, 1721), pp. 3–4. Mather's book also drew heavily from John Ray's *The Wisdom of God Manifested in the Creation,* though this latter work did not use demographic illustrations in its argument.

32. Cotton Mather, *Ornaments of the Daughters of Zion* (Boston, 1691), quoted in Herbert Moller, "Sex Composition and Correlated Culture Patterns of Colonial America," *William and Mary Quarterly,* 3rd ser., 2 (April 1945), 153.

whole town the proportion differs not very much." [33] If, in works like his commentary, the *Biblia Americana,* his discussions of human longevity, fruitfulness, population, and other demographic matters, were largely antiquarian or Old Testament in viewpoint, he never lost sight of the realities and problems of the demography of the present in New England.[34]

Another Puritan clergyman who increasingly viewed the world as a place governed by God's laws rather than by his impulses, was Thomas Prince. By the late 1720's, Prince was not only in accord with the Newtonian concepts of a well-ordered physical universe, but was aware that the phenomena of birth and death similarly exhibited patterns of regularity. In a 1736 sermon Prince contemplated with rather grisly satisfaction the fact that, as part of this law, God subjects mankind to a constant assault of death through disease and other regular causes. Marshaling data from Graunt, Petty, Davenant, and Edmund Halley, among his authorities, he went on to illustrate details of this assault:

> For as by the latest Computations, there are near a *Thousand Million* People on the Face of the Globe, and about a *Thirtieth Part* as many Dye in a Year; one Day with another then there must be near a

33. Mather, quoted by Lemuel Shattuck, *Report on the Boston Census, 1845,* p. 62.

34. See Otho T. Beall, Jr., and Richard H. Shryock, *Cotton Mather, First Significant Figure in American Medicine* (Baltimore, Md.: Johns Hopkins Press, 1954); and Otho T. Beall, Jr., "Cotton Mather's Early 'Curiosa Americana' and the Boston Philosophical Society of 1683," *William and Mary Quarterly,* 3rd ser., 28 (July 1961), 371. See also my discussion of Mather in another context, in Chapter VI below.

Hundred Thousand now a Dying, near *Seven hundred thousand* in one Week, near *Three Millions* in one Month, and near *Thirty six Millions* in one Year. And all these by the meer Course of Nature: tho' there shou'd not one be murthered, executed, drowned, or kill'd by Plague or Battles.[35]

As transitional figures, Mather and Prince, like Derham, helped to fit the new demography, one part of the new science, into the prevailing religious frame of reference. Somewhat in the way that certain of the more effective proponents of evolutionary theory, a century and a half later, were clergymen, so, in the early eighteenth century leading clergy did much not only to introduce demography but to have it accepted. The most ambitious European contribution to this end was made by the Prussian pastor, Johann Peter Süssmilch, in 1742. An exhaustive analysis of vital data from church registers, Süssmilch's *Die Göttliche Ordnung* of that year became the ultimate scientific demonstration of the regularity of God's demographic laws.[36] In America, the outstanding eighteenth-century clerical contributor to demography and vital statistics was Ezra Stiles.

35. Thomas Prince, *A Sermon Occasioned by the Death of the Honourable Mary Belcher* (Boston: D. Henchman, 1736), pp. 12, 32–33. See also Theodore Hornberger, "The Science of Thomas Prince," *New England Quarterly*, 9 (1936), 20–42.

36. Johann Peter Süssmilch, *Die Göttliche Ordnung in den Veränderungen des Menschlichen Geschlects, aus der Geburt, dem Tode, und der Fortpflanzung desselben erwiesen*, 1st ed. (Berlin: J. C. Spenser, 1741). No English translation of this classic exists. A short analysis of the work and biography of Süssmilch is available in English, but the man and his work deserve further study. See Frederick S. Crum, "The Statistical Work of Süssmilch," American Statistical Association, *Publications*, n.s., 7, no. 55 (September 1901), 1–46.

By training, inclination, and accomplishment, Stiles as much as anyone, was the epitome of the statistical mind in mid-eighteenth century America.[37] He was, to start with, one of those broad-gauged colonial clerics who not only read (and appreciated) what Newton wrote on the prophecies of the Old Testament, but also read (and understood) what Newton wrote on astronomy and mathematics.[38] Along with such interests, throughout his life Stiles avidly sought figures, particularly those having to do with human life and death. By the time he was twenty, he was aware of the work of Graunt and Petty and had begun to read certain treatises on demography and vital statistics. Among others, he read Edward Halley's two well-known papers on human mortality.[39] These papers showed how the vital registers of a community could be used mathematically to predict the life expectancies at different ages of the members of that community. Stiles was also considerably influenced by, among others, the demographic observations of Benjamin Franklin.[40]

Most, although not all, of Stiles's demographic contributions were made during the first half of his career, during his pastorate at the Second Congregational Church in New-

37. Many of Stiles's statistical activities and demographic views are discussed in the excellent biography by Edmund S. Morgan, *The Gentle Puritan: A Life of Ezra Stiles, 1727–1795* (New Haven, Ct.: Yale University Press, 1962). My treatment owes much to that study.

38. Isabel M. Calder, ed., *Letters and Papers of Ezra Stiles* (New Haven, Ct.: Yale University Library, 1933), pp. 5–8.

39. Halley's papers appeared originally in 1693 in the *Philosophical Transactions* of the Royal Society. They have been edited by Lowell Reed and issued in a separate modern publication under the title *Degrees of Mortality of Mankind* (Baltimore, Md.: Johns Hopkins Press, 1942).

40. See further discussion of this in Chapter VII, below.

port, Rhode Island.[41] There, along with his regular church and civic duties and a wide range of other scientific interests, he carried his record-keeping propensity to extraordinary lengths. The birth, marriage, death, and other registers which he kept for his congregation were outstanding in completeness, at least for that time. Outside his congregation, he tried to collect current vital data for all of Newport, besides whatever he could glean by correspondence for New England as a whole.[42] In addition to such material, Stiles crammed his notebooks with every sort of statistical detail: numbers of houses; lists of ships and mills; exports and imports. But his prime interests were always the figures having to do with people and religion: immigration data, college enrollments, militia figures, lists of professional people and officials, data on the Indians, lists of churches and church members, notes on long-lived people, lines of descent of prominent people, and epitaphs from gravestones.[43]

Stiles gathered his data from many sources: books and newspapers, town clerks and tax officials, midwives and visitors. When he traveled around New England he was a virtually compulsive counter of people, houses, and other objects. He took full advantage of these trips to inquire into the records that had been preserved at local churches. Sometimes he importuned the pastors to allow him to make verbatim copies or extracts of the registers he found. In

41. After 1777 Stiles was President of Yale College.

42. For a sample of Stiles's registers, see "Births and Deaths in Newport, R. I., 1760–1764," *New England Historical and Genealogical Register*, 62 (1908), 283–291 and 352–363; and *ibid.*, 63 (1909), 51–58.

43. For some of Stiles's interests in Indian populations, see Morgan, *Gentle Puritan*, pp. 139 and 141. See also, *The Literary Diary of Ezra Stiles*, ed. Franklin B. Dexter, 3 vols. (New York: Scribner's, 1901), passim, but esp. I, 416.

such ways, over the course of many years, Stiles accumulated vital statistics of congregations from Cape Cod to the Berkshires and all over New England.[44] The statistics and laws of population held a continuing fascination for Stiles. He digested every enumeration or census he could lay his hands on and compared their figures with his own totals. He was quick to note discrepancies, such as that between the official Connecticut census of 1756 (121,000 Whites, 3,900 Negroes, and 685 Indians) and the figures sent that same year by Governor Fitch to the Board of Trade (128,218 Whites and 3,587 Negroes).[45] As early as the 1760's, in his private schemes for an Academy of Sciences in America, Stiles was looking ahead to the possibility of obtaining vital data from every colony on a regular basis. He wanted such an academy to conduct regular intercolonial census counts, to register immigrants, and to obtain regular vital statistics reports from all sections of America. He also advocated regular population surveys, studies of the effects of race mixing, and broad collections of facts about the American colonization experience which could serve as bases for a scientific study of the laws of population in the American setting.[46]

In the final analysis, the most crucial population segment, in Stiles's eyes, was that of the New England Con-

44. Owing to subsequent losses of the records of some of these churches, the transcripts in Stiles's notebooks remain in some cases the only source of data for certain periods.

45. The official census was done with "great care and exactness," according to Jonathan Trumbull. See Trumbull to Stiles, July 14, 1762, Calder, *Letters and Papers of Ezra Stiles*, pp. 9–10.

46. Special aspects of Stiles's theories of population will be discussed in Chapter VII. For a further account of Stiles's Academy, see Morgan, *Gentle Puritan*. See also Brooke Hindle, *The Pursuit of Science in Revolutionary America* (Chapel Hill: University of North Carolina Press, 1956), pp. 120–121.

gregational Church membership. And in considering this population Stiles took up the same theme which concerned so many of his predecessors among the Puritan clergy of New England, that of the region's ecclesiastical destiny. In 1760, as in 1650, Puritans still felt that God had special and wonderful things in mind for New England, albeit the predictable laws of science had, for some, replaced special providences as the guideposts to the plan.

Like many another Puritan divine before him, Stiles had a vivid awareness, when he spoke of the numbers of souls in a locality, that souls were immortal. He even speculated upon the numbers of souls that would have accumulated since the Creation by the time the Judgment Day came around.[47] When he thought about such matters, he relied upon the familiar Old Testament framework of beliefs. That was certainly the appropriate point of reference for an address which he delivered in 1760 at a convention of the Congregational clergy of Rhode Island. This address, "A Discourse on the Christian Union," was essentially an appeal for greater harmony and cooperation among all of the New England Congregational churches, in order that the denomination might attain a yet greater growth and destiny. It stands out from many other such sermons by the statistical detail which reinforces some of its key arguments. In fact, it was largely this material which brought Stiles to the attention of European writers on demographic matters during the next half-century or so.[48]

The text of Stiles's address consisted in two quotations. These provided, in numerical terms, a striking parallel

47. Morgan, *Gentle Puritan,* p. 141.
48. Among the writers who used and quoted from the demographic sections of Stiles's address were such personalities as Thomas Short, Richard Price, and Thomas Malthus.

between the demographic flourishing of the two chosen
peoples of God, the Israelites and the New England Puritans:

> Thy Fathers went down into Egypt with three-score
> and ten Persons, and now the Lord thy God hath
> made thee as the Stars of Heaven for Multitude.
> Deut. 10:22

> Four thousand British planters settled New-Eng-
> land, and in 120 years their Posterity are increased to
> five hundred thousand Souls.

In making this parallel, Stiles studied the New England
record carefully. He drew upon earlier observers and historians from Bradford, Winthrop, and Johnson, to Mather,
Thomas Brattle, Prince, and Douglass. The statistical record showed that, in this multiplication, New England had
surpassed both the Spanish and French colonies in America.
It was thus natural for him to conclude that "God has
great things in design . . . he purposes to make of us a
great people and a pure and glorious church."

Stiles went on to give the numerical strength of all of
the main denominations in New England as of 1760. Then
he projected the data of each denomination forward a
hundred years, using a twenty-five-year doubling period
for his calculations (see table).

	1760	1860
Episcopalians	11,000	185,000
Friends	16,000	256,000
Baptists	22,000	352,000
Congregationalists	440,000	7,000,000

The result was an ecstatic demographic prospect for the believer in the way of New England Congregationalism. And Stiles was a very firm believer.

We transport ourselves to a distance of 100 years forward, look over this wide spread wilderness, see it blossom like the rose, and behold it planted with 123 churches and temples consecrate to the pure worship of the most High . . . when divinely resplendent truth shall triumph, and our brethren of the congregational communion may form a Body of Seven Millions! A glorious and respectable body this, for Truth and Liberty! Well might our fathers die with pleasure.[49]

The religious uses of demographic data reached a new height in the American colonies with Stiles. Given the way of thinking in the seventeenth and eighteenth centuries, these uses were no less important for Americans than were the economic, political, and civil uses to which people were also putting such data. It was not surprising that, as the scientific interest in demography and vital statistics spread among the clergy and other learned men, still other potentialities for the use of these data began to be evident. Principal among these was what may be called broadly the public health dimension of vital statistics. Applications in this dimension began to emerge around 1700 in such forms as bills of mortality and medical statistics. Modest at first, these health uses only gradually approached in extent the religious uses of vital records.

49. Ezra Stiles, *A Discourse on the Christian Union* (Boston: Edes and Gill, 1761), pp. 102–103.

Chapter VI

Colonial Bills of Mortality
1700–1775

Although many colonial preachers kept their church records assiduously, few if any, at least in the seventeenth century, thought about publishing them as potential bases for public health action in their small communities. Neither did town or parish clerks. For many years there were no provisions anywhere in the colonies for anything comparable to the London Bills of Mortality. This mattered little in tiny communities where everyone knew everything about their neighbors. But as towns grew, public awareness of the aggregate numbers of births and deaths became a hazy impression shaped much by rumor or hearsay. With the beginning of newspapers in British America around 1700, a means emerged for remedying this situation to some degree. Some editors, realizing that the data of human life and death had both public interest and news value, went to the trouble of digging what figures they could out of the local church and town records. In the journalistic process the long lists or raw registers of data were transformed into summaries which were loosely termed "bills of mortality." [1] Accumulated and published in tabular form, the data took on new social and scientific significance. Issued in a variety of publications, the published bills became the earliest relatively systematic American health reports.

Amidst the seventeenth-century upheavals of war, changes of rulers, and shifts of economic and religious fortunes, the London Bills of Mortality remained among the eternal verities for Englishmen. Londoners could count on finding the printed bills on sale in each parish every week; bills with lists of diseases printed on the back were priced at twice the ordinary bills. Persons returning to London after years in the colonies found the bills being issued as before. Those who remained in America sometimes received copies from relatives or friends. Just as John Graunt had found the English doing, the early Americans used the bills as grist for conversation if for nothing else.

It is unlikely that more than a few persons in America knew of Graunt's analysis of the London Bills of Mortality for years after its publication in 1662.[2] But many colonists

1. There has been some confusion as a result of differing uses of the term "bill of mortality." Originally, as noted above (Chapter I), the term was precise in representing the published broadsides of the Company of Parish Clerks which gave the totals of plague deaths in the City of London (later expanded to include all deaths, plus births or baptisms). Subsequently, authors have often included in the term all the vital statistics of a given community, among them the raw records found in parish registers, whether published or not. In this chapter, I use the term to include only published compilations in one form or another.

2. See Chapter III. By the middle of the eighteenth century,

knew within a few months what the Bills revealed about the twin disasters of plague and fire that struck London in 1665 and 1666. Thomas Vincent's vivid account of these events, *God's Terrible Voice in the City*, was one of the means by which this came about.[3] Published in London in 1667, Vincent's book drew liberally from the 1665 bill of mortality to illustrate the grim effects of God's judgment upon London. New Englanders were so impressed with the message of the book that two American editions were reprinted at Cambridge by 1668. Still, the colonists did not take steps to publish their own bills of mortality for several decades after that time.

The fact that no colonial bills of mortality were published in the seventeenth century seems to have been partly a matter of printing priorities, partly an absence of legislative requirements. While a printing press began operation in Cambridge, Massachusetts, as early as 1638, there were still no more than five in the colonies over half a century later. These few presses were essentially official in nature and were generally kept busy printing governmental documents.[4] (The Cambridge press naturally served reli-

---

Graunt's book was in several large private colonial libraries. By 1756 it was in circulation in the Charlestown, S. C., library. (Waring, *History of Medicine in South Carolina*, p. 373.)

3. Thomas Vincent, *God's Terrible Voice in the City* (London, 1666). Defoe's famous history of the plague of 1665 also drew heavily upon the London Bills. It became well known in the colonies soon after its publication in 1722. Daniel Defoe, *The History of the Great Plague in London in the Year 1665*, new ed. (London: Renshaw and Rush, 1832).

4. In 1693 there were presses in Cambridge, Boston, St. Mary's (Maryland), New York, and Philadelphia. Although Virginia, except for one abortive effort, had no operational press until 1730 and only one up to 1766, by the mid-1760's the colonies as a whole contained about forty. For a short discussion of colonial printing, see Boorstin, *The Americans*, pp. 319–340.

gious objectives as well.) Again, although the law in every colony required the registration of vital statistics, it did not require their processing or publication. Thus, it remained for private enterprise to furnish the earliest public accounts of such data.

The first regularly published colonial newspaper was *The Boston News Letter*. In its eleventh number, the issue for June 26–July 3, 1704, the paper printed a simple chart of the numbers of Whites buried in Boston each month of 1701, 1702, and 1703. The printer-editor, John Campbell, explained that the chart did not include the many deaths at sea of Boston's large seafaring population. He speculated upon his data only to the extent of inquiring rhetorically how the percentage of the Boston population which died annually in normal times compared with the 1 in 50 which he had read somewhere prevailed in certain European communities. (Actually, eighteenth-century estimates of this ratio ranged from 1 in 60 to 1 in 25. Petty's figure of 1 in 30 for London and Edmund Halley's figure of 1 in 35 for Breslau became the most generally accepted.)[5] Campbell hoped that persons from other Massachusetts towns would compile similar mortality data and send them to him to be published.[6] The *News Letter* went on to print simple annual mortality notices, or bills, usually in March, almost every year. Most of the subsequent bills included figures on Negroes and Indians as well as of Whites, while

5. In 1750 Benjamin Franklin reported as follows: "In a healthy country (as this is) political Arithmeticians compute, there dies yearly One in Thirty-Five." See *Poor Richard Improved* (Philadelphia: Benjamin Franklin, 1749). But in 1787 Ezra Stiles was claiming an annual death ratio for New Haven as low as 1 in 60. See Ezra Stiles, *A Funeral Sermon, Delivered Thursday, July 26, 1787* (New Haven, Ct.: T. and S. Green, 1787), p. 37.

6. *The Boston News Letter,* no. 11, June 26–July 3, 1704.

in 1721 the paper presented a twenty-year summary of Boston burials.

As other newspapers appeared in Boston, most of them included annual notices of the mortality totals, while some also had weekly lists.[7] Some occasionally printed reports of deaths in other colonial cities or, just as often, summaries of the London bills. Virtually every printer considered smallpox and other epidemics as newsworthy and often published mortality for particular epidemics. From time to time compilations appeared of mortality by age or of mortality totals for series of years. Beginning in the early 1730's a few papers expanded their bills to include figures on baptisms in the Boston churches.

Newspapers in most other colonial communities had by no means the early or consistent coverage of vital statistics which the Boston newspapers provided. Of course, few places had as many newspapers. What did appear was usually irregular in the extreme, often composed of second-hand data, or otherwise unsatisfactory, even in its news value. There were some exceptions to this condition. Occasionally, and unpredictably, editor-printers put in their columns general British articles discussing vital statistics or demography. William Bradford, publisher of *The New York Gazette,* for instance, in the summer of 1731, reprinted from the *Political State* (London) an article which analyzed the latest London Bills of Mortality in the light of Halley's longevity calculations.[8] Later the same summer Bradford covered a smallpox epidemic which broke out in

7. See John B. Blake, *Public Health in the Town of Boston, 1630–1822* (Cambridge, Mass.: Harvard University Press, 1959), p. 106.

8. Similarly, the *Maryland Gazette* for Feb. 4, 1762 included an anonymous article entitled, "Observations on the Importance of Bills of Mortality with Computations of the Number of People in the Known Parts of the Globe."

New York. As part of this, he published brief weekly bills which gave total burials in each cemetery as well as those of which the deaths were due to smallpox. After the epidemic disappeared in November, Bradford recapitulated the mortality (burials) for the whole period since August. These are shown in the table.

Church of England	229
Dutch Church	212
French Church	15
Lutheran Church	1
Presbyterians	16
Quakers	2
Baptists	1
Jews	2
Whites in all	478
Blacks in all	71
Whites and blacks, in all	549[9]

Even with the termination of the epidemic, Bradford continued to print brief burial notices almost every week during the following year. But in 1733 he discontinued the weekly notices and never resumed any kind of regular vital statistics, even annual bills.

In Charlestown, *The South Carolina Gazette* was not especially regular in publishing bills of mortality, but for a time in 1733 it provided its readers with a short series of weekly mortality totals. In Salem, Massachusetts, *The Essex Gazette,* between 1769 and 1774, published a series of annual vital statistics reports which were as sophisticated as any issued in colonial American papers. These included

9. *The New-York Gazette,* no. 316, Nov. 8–15, 1731.

not only the total burials and baptisms, but usually breakdowns as well of deaths by age, sex, race, and principal diseases.[10]

In the fall of 1729, Benjamin Franklin became printer-editor of *The Pennsylvania Gazette*. In November he published a small chart of the interments in Philadelphia burial grounds during the previous week. From this time on, and regularly for well over three years, Franklin published weekly bills. If he occasionally missed a week, he carefully included the data in the following issue. It was a matter of journalistic pride to him that the data were complete. As he swore to his public early in 1730: "The country may depend upon it, that there are not more Burials in a Week in this City than we give an Account of." [11]

Like his fellow printers, Franklin occasionally slipped into his paper yearly bills from other cities, special figures on smallpox, and other demographic data or news. In August 1731 he reprinted the same long article on the London Bills which William Bradford in New York had taken from the *Political State*. Presumably, the two editors chose the article independently of each other.[12]

Printed usually among the notices of ship arrivals or departures, the lists of food prices, and the advertisements

10. Guerra has summarized some of the vital statistics reports in colonial newspapers. While these are suggestive, they are not exhaustive. The important series of weekly bills in *The Pennsylvania Gazette*, for instance, is not mentioned, while only a small portion of the series of notices in *The New-York Gazette* is cited. For many others, however, see Francisco Guerra, *American Medical Bibliography 1639–1783* (New York: Lathrop C. Harper, Inc., 1962), pp. 435–688.

11. *The Pennsylvania Gazette*, no. 120, Feb. 23–March 4, 1730/31.

12. See *The Pennsylvania Gazette*, nos. 143, 144, and 145 (Aug. 5–12, Aug. 12–19, and Aug. 19–26, 1731).

of various commodities, Franklin's burial lists reported the city's demographic business alongside its commercial business. It was logical enough. But it may well have been this very juxtaposition of death statistics with business matters which led Franklin to give up publication of the weekly bills permanently at the beginning of 1733. Although Franklin himself did not give any reason, it is possible that the bills became victims of advertising pressures of intercity trade rivalries. It was no secret that large quantities of death and disease discouraged trade. It was common practice for colonial printer-editors to minimize, distort, or suppress these kinds of local data in hopes of promoting the economic well-being of their communities. Conversely, they were happy enough to print the death figures of other cities.[13]

The fact that Franklin stopped printing the weekly Philadephia bills in the *Gazette* did not mean that he had lost interest in such things. On the contrary, his concern for demographic matters was just beginning in 1733. From his multiple vantage point as printer, postmaster, scientist, and public official, he continued not only to gather local vital data but to absorb the European literature on the subject. During the 1750's he forwarded Philadelphia bills of mortality to Peter Collinson. The latter not only found a London publisher for these, but in return sent Franklin a copy of Thomas Short's important *Observations . . . on*

13. An analyst of the mortality statistics which were published in Charleston, S. C., papers from 1732 to 1800 reported: "Indeed the editors of all the papers were jealously and persistently reticent with regard to the number of deaths, especially *during* an epidemic, and all such information is correspondingly meagre." William H. Bailey to Joseph M. Toner, Sept. 2, 1880, Box 99, Toner Collection, Library of Congress. The point is made for the colonial press generally by John Duffy, *Epidemics in Colonial America* (Baton Rouge: Louisiana State University Press, 1953), p. 53.

Bills of Mortality.[14] Again, Franklin saw to it that a proper statistical account was prepared for the admissions, diseases, cures, deaths, and other matters at the new Pennsylvania Hospital.[15] He even mixed journalism and vital statistics again, notably in his 1750 almanac, *Poor Richard Improved,* in which he devoted several pages to tabular demographic data and analyses. These included summaries of the 1737 and 1748 enumerations of New Jersey population; Philadelphia mortality tables for 1738 to 1744; counts of houses and immigrants in Philadelphia, 1748–50; and figures of Massachusetts taxables for 1735 and 1742. Included also were results of the 1742 enumerations in Boston of houses, warehouses, widows (1200, of whom 1000 were poor), persons in the almshouse (111) and workhouse (36), Negroes (1514), horses (418), and cows (141), as well as some notes on Halley's uses of the Breslau birth and burial data. In the aggregate this formed one of the largest and most important published colonial collections of demographic statistics.[16] However, the 1750 issue of *Poor Richard* was exceptional in this respect. Franklin did not often fill his almanacs with bills of mortality or other vital data. Rather, he preferred lighter touches, such as his own special variety of mortuary humor:

My sickly Spouse, with many a Sigh
Once told me, — Dicky I shall die:

14. Thomas Short, *New Observations, Natural, Moral, Civil, Political, and Medical on City, Town and Country Bills of Mortality* (London: Longman and Miller, 1750).

15. B. Franklin, "Some Account of the Pennsylvania Hospital," in *The Papers of Benjamin Franklin,* ed. Leonard W. Labaree et al. (New Haven, Ct.: Yale University Press, 1959–), V, 324.

16. *Poor Richard Improved, for 1750* (Philadelphia: Franklin, 1749).

> I griv'd; but recollected straight,
> 'Twas bootless to contend with Fate;
> So Resignation to Heav'ns Will
> Prepar'd me for succeeding Ill;
> 'Twas well it did; for, on my life;
> 'Twas Heav'ns Will to spare my Wife.[17]

Stimulated by the example of the newspaper bills of mortality, or perhaps by their lack, a handful of colonial churches undertook to publish their own bills. In Charlestown, South Carolina, several annual bills of mortality of St. Philips Church were published during the mid-1750's in broadside form. Known as "Sheed's Bills of Mortality," these took their name from the Sexton of the church, George Sheed (1725–1799), who was also a schoolmaster and subsequently a city and state official.[18]

Beginning even earlier and continuing far longer were the annual broadside bills of Christ-Church Parish in Philadelphia. Perhaps in an effort to continue in some form the bills of the *Gazette*, the Parish issued a bill in 1738 for the period December 24, 1736, to December 24, 1737. Apparently there was then a publishing gap of about ten years. But, beginning in 1748 the Parish managed to issue its one-page bills almost every year until the outbreak of the Revolution and then again after the war.[19]

17. *Poor Richard, 1740,* by Richard Saunders, pseud. (Philadelphia: Franklin, 1739).
18. *The South-Carolina Gazette* of June 19, 1775 (no. 1095), refers to Sheed's bills for 1753 and 1754. Joseph I. Waring, *History of Medicine in South Carolina,* p. 64, has a photograph of the bill for Dec. 25, 1755–Dec. 25, 1756. The format and contents of Sheed's bills were essentially the same as those of Christ-Church Parish, described below, and may have been inspired by them.
19. Although Guerra and some other authors "assume" that bills

The bills attempted to provide statistical coverage of the entire Philadelphia community. The 1736–37 bill thus, in addition to the report of the parish's own christenings and burials by sex and an elementary chart of causes of death, included burials among the Presbyterians, the Baptists, and "The People called Quakers." For the Strangers Burying-Ground, there had been "no account kept." The 1746–47 bill was much more sophisticated than its predecessor: the list of causes of death included 29 instead of only 8 names; deaths were classified in 13 age groups; increases or decreases in christenings and burials from the previous year were indicated; and data were included for burials among the Swedes, Lutherans, Dutch Calvinists, and "in the Negroes Ground," as well as those in previously listed burial grounds.

This pattern continued substantially the same for the rest of the Parish's eighteenth-century bills. To be sure, the data from each Philadelphia church was by no means equally full. The Swedish visitor Peter Kalm, scientist colleague of Linnaeus and Per Wargentin, reported in 1750 that "the lists of mortality . . . are not kept regularly in all the churches of Philadelphia." Similarly, he found that "the number of births cannot be determined since in many churches no order is observed with regard to this affair." Kalm found no good basis for estimating the Philadelphia population, particularly since immigration was so great at the time. He settled by printing what little he could find of mortality figures in old Philadelphia

---

were printed during the revolutionary years, none have been located for that period nor for all of the 1780's, though they are complete for the decade of the 1790's. Beginning in the mid-1760's, the bills were issued in the name of St. Peters as well as of Christ-Church, while beginning in 1809 St. James was also a sponsor.

newspapers, together with extracts from the Christ-Church broadsides.[20]

The Christ-Church bills always appeared under the names of church officers. This first bill, the one for 1736–37, was by Charles Hughes, Sexton. From 1747 through 1772, the bills were prepared jointly by the Clerk, Caleb Cash, and a succession of sextons. Cash was succeeded as clerk and part author by Matthew Whitehead, who served for over thirty years, from 1773 to 1805.[21]

Although a few other churches, both in Philadelphia and elsewhere, occasionally published similar broadside bills of mortality, none produced a continuous series which could in any way rival that of Christ-Church, whether for coverage, longevity, or influence. The Christ-Church bills which Franklin sent to Collinson in England provided the best idea some foreigners had of colonial mortality. In Philadelphia they came to be about as durable and indispensable an institution as were the London Bills for that city. They were, in fact, the direct antecedents of the official vital statistics reports which the city of Philadelphia began to publish beginning in 1807.[22]

Despite the spread of colonial newspapers and the exist-

20. [Peter Kalm], *The America of 1750: Peter Kalm's Travels in North America,* 2 vols., English version of 1770, rev. and ed. Adolph B. Benson (New York: Wilson-Erickson, 1937), I, 32, and II, 662.

21. Clerks of St. Peters who contributed between 1768 and 1800 included William Young, John Ormond, and John Cook. Christ-Church sextons before 1800, in addition to Hughes, included Samuel Kirke, William Davis, James Weyley, Jacob Digle, and Joseph Dolby. St. Peters sextons were George Stokes and James Barker. Most of the Christ-Church bills are preserved at the Library Company of Philadelphia, although the 1736–37 bill is at the Henry Huntington Library.

22. For further comment of the beginnings of official vital statistics reports see Chapter XI.

ence of a few church bills of mortality, British publications remained among the colonists' best sources of vital statistics information. For the tiny number of intellectuals who had access to them, The *Philosophical Transactions* of the Royal Society provided enlightenment in demography and vital statistics as well as in other fields of science. There could be found some of the pioneer demographic articles of Petty, Halley, and Arbuthnot, together with others by such writers as the English physician Charles Maitland and the Dutch demographer William Kersseboom. And regularly through the eighteenth century, the *Transactions* contained bills of mortality sent in by members or correspondents: résumés of data from the old registers of Freyberg, Dresden, or Augsburg; more contemporary bills from the Barbados, Madeira, or tiny English parishes.

For each of the few Americans who saw the *Philosophical Transactions,* many read one or more of the English literary or popular magazines. Readers of the *Spectator* presumably were not only familiar with the bills of mortality themselves but were able to cope with the early scientific analyses of the bills. Such sophisticates could well appreciate Joseph Addison's allegorical work, "The Vision of Mirza," which appeared in the *Spectator* in 1711, and which is said to have been inspired by Halley's analysis of data on expectation of life.[23] More modestly, beginning

23. "The Vision of Mirza" appeared in Number 159 of the *Spectator.* William Farr, the nineteenth-century English demographer, is usually credited with noting the relationship between Addison's poem and Halley's calculations. Beattie comments that the *Spectator* of Jan. 31, 1712 (no. 289) must have owed directly or indirectly to John Arbuthnot its contention that a bill of mortality is "an unanswerable argument for a Providence." A similar paper, in *The Guardian,* no. 136 (Aug. 17, 1713) dwelt upon the greater mortality among men than women and the providential allowance for this waste "by a suitable redundancy in the male sex," and used figures

in the 1730's and continuing with few omissions, both *The London Magazine* and *The Gentleman's Magazine* published data of the annual London Bills of Mortality. *The Scots Magazine*, and possibly others, published the bills sporadically.[24] In *The Gentleman's Magazine*, particularly, American readers also found occasional statistical accounts of epidemics, articles discussing population trends in English or American communities, and even bills of mortality sent in by American correspondents. Thomas Prince, for example, in 1753 furnished a tabular bill of Boston mortality for the period 1701 through 1752. Compiled from Boston newspapers, the bill includes mortality data on Whites beginning in 1701 and Blacks from 1704, with baptisms from 1731.[25] In 1754 the magazine reprinted from *Poor Richard* a discussion of trends in the population of New Jersey. The next year, probably through the efforts of Peter Collinson, it published Franklin's paper, "Observations Concerning the Increase of Mankind," thus assuring wide notice to that important work.[26]

No vital statistics of the eighteenth century were of more interest or concern to readers on both sides of the Atlantic than those for smallpox mortality. With the disappearance

which are "traceable to Derham rather than Graunt." Both papers were attributed to Addison. — L. M. Beattie, *John Arbuthnot*, p. 343.

24. For an analysis of this coverage, see J. A. R. Seguin, *The London Annual Bill of Christenings and Burials (1732–1799) in Ten Tables* (Jersey City: Ross Paxton, 1964). Publication of the London Bills in these magazines beginning 1732 may have been a factor in the discontinuance of local weekly burial notices after 1732 by both Franklin in Philadelphia and Bradford in New York.

25. *Gentleman's Magazine*, 23 (September 1753), 413.

26. The item on New Jersey appeared in vol. 23 (1754), p. 271. Franklin's paper appeared in vol. 25 (1755). For a discussion of that paper and of Franklin's general demographic views, see the next chapter.

of the plague, the London Bills began to reflect smallpox more than any other disease.[27] Similarly, in colonial communities, smallpox was so serious that it called forth new efforts to quantify the incidence of and mortality from the disease.

The young Cotton Mather, only fifteen but precocious, sought in 1678 to chart for his uncle the course of a smallpox epidemic in Boston. At the height of the epidemic, so many people were dying in the city, he wrote, that "to attempt a Bill of Mortality, and number the very spires of grass in a Burying Place seem to have a parity of difficulty and in accomplishment." After he became a minister, Mather found himself equally frustrated in his efforts to keep records during smallpox and other epidemics. In 1702 he barely found time to record in his diary that several of his own children had died (of smallpox) and that his wife had succumbed to another disease after a long illness. For all of Boston he noted that "more than four score people, were in this black month of *December,* carried from this Town to their long Home." [28]

Like many pastors, Mather frequently attempted to care for the bodily health of his flock as well as its spiritual health. He was immensely more learned about medicine than most clergymen, and indeed much more than most physicians of his time. From his readings of iatrophysical authors, Mather was convinced that the quantitative ap-

27. In 1751 John Fothergill declared smallpox to be the only disease mentioned in the weekly Bills for which there was a "tolerably exact account." Fothergill, "Essays on Weather and Diseases," *Works,* I, 159–160.

28. Mather to John Cotton, November 1678, *Collections of the Massachusetts Historical Society,* 4th ser., VIII (Boston: Wiggin and Lunt, 1868), 384; and *Diary of Cotton Mather,* in *Collections of the Massachusetts Historical Society,* 7th ser., VII, 445–451.

proach offered considerable promise for the future of medicine. "How much would the Art of Medicine be improved, if our Physicians more generally had the mathematical skill of a Dr. Mead or a Dr. Morgan, and would go his Way to work, mathematically, and by the Laws of Matter and Motion, to find out the Cause and Cure of Diseases." [29]

By the time of the Boston smallpox outbreak of 1721, Mather had devised a simple arithmetical means of following the course of the epidemic among his flock, and he had also heard of a measure which he thought might prevent the disease. At the outset of the epidemic he made arrangements in his Old North Church for prayers to be said for those who were ill of the disease. Requests for such prayers were made by notes deposited at the church. After he had collected the notes and said the prayers, Mather confided the numerical totals to his diary. On October 7 he wrote: "The Number of the Sick that had Prayers asked for them in the Bills at the Old North Church, on the last Lord's-Day, was two hundred and two." On October 15 the number of prayers soared to 322, but on the 22nd it fell back to 180. By November 5 only about 50 were reported sick.[30]

Keeping records was one thing; managing smallpox was another. It is entirely possible that during the fall of 1721 some of Mather's parishioners were offering up their own prayers — for protection from the consequences of their pastor's ideas about smallpox. For Mather was deeply engaged in his famous campaign to introduce inoculation.

29. From Mather's opus, "The Angel of Bethesda," published in part in Beall and Shryock, *Cotton Mather,* p. 154. The physicians mentioned are Richard Mead and Thomas Morgan.

30. *Diary of Cotton Mather,* in *Collections of the Massachusetts Historical Society,* 7th ser., VIII, 652–656.

Here he showed his willingness to compromise the scientific — and statistical — method in order to attempt a shortcut to medical progress. It was as rash as it was bold; but unlike many poorly founded medical ventures, this one succeeded.

The Turkish practice of inoculation, which had been reported in *The Philosophical Transactions* in 1714 and 1716, intrigued Mather, and he tried unsuccessfully to stimulate interest in it in England. When the 1721 smallpox outbreak began, he tried in turn to persuade Boston physicians to adopt the practice. Only Dr. Zabdiel Boylston, backed by most of the clergy and by a few other prominent men, agreed to undertake the experiment. Most other physicians, led by William Douglass and strongly backed by public opinion in general, violently opposed inoculation. The argument of the opposing sides over the practice went on throughout the epidemic and was not really settled until many years had passed.[31] In presenting their cases for and against inoculation, the respective sides argued variously from religion, medical ethics, and science. But they both also argued ultimately from the quantitative evidence at hand. This phase of the argument furnishes one of the first instances of the use of statistical analysis in a given medical or epidemiological problem.

Both Mather and Boylston realized that the future of inoculation depended upon the results of a statistical comparison of the mortality among non-inoculated persons

31. Much has been written about the inoculation controversy. Among the best accounts are those of Beall and Shryock, *Cotton Mather*, pp. 93–122; John B. Blake, *Public Health in the Town of Boston 1630–1822*, pp. 52–73; and Perry Miller, *The New England Mind: From Colony to Province* (Cambridge, Mass.: Harvard University Press, 1953), pp. 345–366.

with that among the inoculated (either from the disease itself or from faulty inoculation techniques).[32] Boylston, in a summary of his inoculation activities, reported that during 1721 and 1722 he and two other doctors inoculated 286 persons, of whom only 6 died, or 1 out of 46. In contrast, out of 5759 persons who had smallpox the natural way, 844 died, or 1 out of 6. Boylston's published account included a statistical table of ages, reactions, deaths, and other data on those inoculated. He hoped that his account would encourage others to be inoculated, "seeing, from time to time, in the weekly bills, numbers who have died of smallpox." [33]

Mather, too, reported upon the outcome of inoculation in Boston in numerical terms. Among his correspondents on this subject was James Jurin, Secretary of the Royal Society. In a letter to Jurin, Mather gave 300 as the number of inoculations, which was a somewhat higher figure than Boylston's, as it covered a slightly different period. Since he reported the same number of deaths where inoculation was given as Boylston, the death ratio then became 1 out of 50.[34]

32. Beall and Shryock, *Cotton Mather*, p. 108.

33. Zabdiel Boylston, *An Historical Account of the Smallpox Inoculated in New England upon all Sorts of Persons, Whites, Blacks, and of all Ages and Constitutions*, 2nd ed., corr. (London: S. Chandler, 1726; reprinted Boston: S. Gerrish, 1730). At the time of the 1730 smallpox epidemic in Boston, Boylston, upon public demand, published a list of all those he had inoculated in the month of March. This included a statistical summary which showed 72 inoculations and 2 deaths (57 whites and 15 blacks inoculated, and 1 death among each of the races). *The New England Weekly Journal*, no. 161, April 20, 1730.

34. Cotton Mather, "The Way of Proceeding in the Smallpox Inoculated in New England," Royal Society, *Philosophical Transactions*, no. 370, 32 (January–March 1722), 33–35.

So far as the statistics of the epidemic were concerned, there was little room for disagreement. The Boston Selectmen, *The Boston News Letter,* and Douglass had to rely largely upon the inoculators for figures of the inoculated persons. The total number of smallpox deaths, moreover, was accepted by all of the parties. There turned out, however, to be four different sets of figures for the total numbers of smallpox cases (see table). The differences were not great, but they were sufficient to keep the argument going.

	No. of Cases	Deaths
Selectmen's Report (1722)	5980	844
Boylston (1722 and 1726)	5759	844
Douglass (1730)	5989	844 [a]
Boston News-Letter (Feb. 19–26, 1722)	5889	844

[a] Douglass at one time was reported to have claimed a death total of 899 out of a total of "about 6,000" cases, but the 899 may have been a misprint since he used the figure of 844 upon at least two occasions.

Douglass's criticisms of Mather and Boylston at first centered upon his contention that inoculation was untested scientifically. Arguing from a properly conservative scientific position, he was at the beginning more interested in repressing than in measuring a process whose introduction was accompanied by many extravagant claims and which had no basis of proof. Thus, at the height of the controversy, in 1722, he rejected such claims out of hand. Like many others, he attributed most of the mortality of the epidemic to its having been gratuitously spread by inoculation itself. He compared this, though without providing any statistics, to the smaller mortality of epidemics during which there had not been any inoculation.[35]

About the same time as the Massachusetts experiment, a number of English investigators began inoculating and collecting data upon results of the practice. James Jurin, one of the most systematic of these, obtained an independent account of the results of inoculation in Boston.[36] He also examined the record of smallpox mortality shown in the London Bills going back to 1667, as well as of a large number of contemporary cases which occurred during the 1720's. By 1724 he had drawn together a record of successful results from a number of inoculators in different parts of England as well as in various colonies. He concluded that the chances of dying of natural smallpox were 1 out of 6, while the chances from carefully administered inoculation were only about 1 in 50 — figures that were close to the Boston results.[37] Although controversy over the practice continued in England for many years, as it did in the colonies, Jurin's conclusions were substantially borne out by a variety of later investigators.[38]

As the experimental results of inoculation unfolded in the journals of the day, Douglass eventually brought him-

35. William Douglass, *The Abuses and Scandals of some late Pamphlets in favour of Inoculation of the Smallpox Modestly Obviated* (Boston: J. Franklin, 1722).

36. This account was procured at Jurin's request by "Dr. Nesbitt, from Capt. John Osborne," who was living in Boston. James Jurin, "A Comparison Between the Danger of the Natural Smallpox, and that Given by Inoculation," Royal Society, *Philosophical Transactions*, no. 374, 32 (1722), 213ff.

37. See James Jurin, *An Account of the Success of Inoculating the Smallpox in Great Britain* (London: J. Peele, 1724); J. G. Scheuchzer, *Dr. Scheuchzer's Account of the Success of Inoculating the Smallpox, for the Years 1727 and 1728* (London: J. Peele, 1729); Beall and Shryock, *Cotton Mather*, pp. 118–120.

38. There is a thorough account of European inoculation in Gene-

self to accept inoculation, if properly done.[39] But he did not condone any more than before the intuitive approach to medical discovery. He continued to criticize Boylston and Mather, though by 1730 his criticism was leveled principally at their methods.

Not the least among their defects, he felt, were their inadequate statistics. Essentially, he charged both of his antagonists with manipulation of their data. Mather, he said, had been misleading in his inoculation reports through his excessive rounding off of numbers. In other words, by merely stating generally that out of "something more than 5,000" people who contracted smallpox, "near 900" died, Mather was able to say that the mortality was 18 percent, or 1 out of 5.5. Using his own figures, 844 deaths out of 5989 cases, Douglass claimed the actual rate was 14 percent, or 1 in 7. Boylston, Douglass asserted, "makes use of round numbers to a pitch much exceeding" that of Mather.[40]

vieve Miller, *The Adoption of Inoculation for Smallpox in England and France* (Philadelphia: University of Pennsylvania Press, 1957). Dr. Miller has an excellent section on European statistical and mathematical evaluations of inoculation between 1722 and 1730, as well as on later statistical studies. See especially pp. 111–123. For a more technical analysis of and commentary upon eighteenth-century inoculation statistics, see M. Noel Karn, "An Inquiry into Various Death-Rates and the Comparative Influence of Certain Diseases on the Duration of Life," *Annals of Eugenics*, 4 (1931), 279–302.

39. Douglass deserves a high place among colonial physicians. He was not the reactionary obstructionist to medical progress that he has often been painted, and he was not merely the "compleat snarler" that Dr. Alexander Hamilton made him out to be. A brief account of Douglass's work is given in George H. Weaver, "Life and Writings of William Douglass, M.D.," *Bulletin of the Society of Medical History of Chicago*, 11 (April 1921), 229–259.

40. William Douglass, *A Dissertation Concerning Inoculation of the Smallpox* (Boston: D. Henchman & T. Hancock, 1730).

One of the most damaging statistical criticisms which could be made of the Boston inoculation experiment was that of the inadequacy of the sample. Although Douglass did not make this criticism directly at the time, in later years he came to realize the importance of this factor. In 1751 he concluded: "In making of medium Estimates, we ought to take large Numbers in a long series of Time, but not the cases of singular Families." [41] This is the earliest known American statement, at least in a medical application, of the law of large numbers, a statistical principle which had been expressed by James Bernoulli in 1713 (in his *Ars Conjectandi*), and subsequently in a vital statistics context by Süssmilch.[42]

Douglass's comment upon statistical method appeared, not in *Philosophical Transactions* or in some medical or mathematical treatise, but in a chapter of the author's ambitious history of the British colonies in North America. Even more than such earlier historians as Winthrop and Beverley, Douglass made his work a compendium of fact and numerical data. In a manner somewhat like that of the German universitarians who followed Hermann Conring in Europe, he attempted a more or less systematic factual description of each of the colonies in its totality. Like a nineteenth- or twentieth-century almanac-maker, he

41. Douglass, *Summary, Historical and Political*, II, pt. I, p. 412.
42. Dr. William Black is usually regarded as the earliest writer in English to express this principle in connection with medical statistics. Black's work, however, *Observations Medical and Political on the Smallpox . . . and on the Mortality of Mankind at every Age in City and Country*, did not appear until the 1780's, thirty years after Douglass's book. For comment on Black see Major Greenwood, *Medical Statistics from Graunt to Farr* (Cambridge University Press [Eng.], 1948), p. 64; and George Rosen, "Problems in the Application of Statistical Analysis to Questions of Health, 1700–1880," *Bulletin of the History of Medicine*, 29 (1955), 34.

brought together a remarkable array of miscellaneous information: mileages, taxes, laws, troops, government posts and officials, commerce, crops, rivers, resources, and Indian tribes.

Douglass's history also includes one of the most extensive eighteenth-century collections of population and vital statistics for the various colonies. Here Douglass shows capacity as a collector. He also shows a somewhat uneasy familiarity with the writings of Halley and other "Philosophical and Political Arithmeticians." To estimate the pre-1721 population of Boston, Douglass started with the 1722 post-epidemic count of 10,670 made by Aeneas Salter upon the order of the Boston Selectmen. To this he added the 844 persons who died and the 850 who fled from the epidemic, and arrived at 12,364. He then checked this estimate by use of Halley's 1 in 35 ratio of mortality to population in healthy years. Using this ratio with the 345 Boston burials of the previous healthy year, he calculated a population of 12,075. Later in his book Douglass somewhat inconsistently attempted precisely the reverse sort of calculation. Assuming a Boston population of only 11,000 in 1720, and taking an annual average of 350 burials, he concluded that Boston's mortality: population ratio was 1 in 31.[43]

One section of Douglass's book was obviously intended to serve as the ultimate justification of his position in the inoculation controversy. It was also something of a review of the status of inoculation at mid-century. Here he summarized the epidemiological data on smallpox which had gathered over long years in Great Britain. He provided a detailed numerical account of mortality from every smallpox epidemic in Boston since 1702, with comparative

43. Douglass, *Summary, Historical and Political,* I, 530–531, and II, 399–405.

figures for inoculation since 1721. In addition, he introduced statistical data, chiefly from Boston and Charlestown, South Carolina, to compare smallpox mortality among Whites and Negroes. He concluded that "Smallpox in cold Countries is more fatal to Blacks than to Whites," while for hot countries he found the reverse to be true.[44]

Even more than his antagonists in the smallpox controversy, Douglass contributed to the advancement of the statistical method in America as a means of studying disease. In addition to his writings on smallpox, he studied other New England epidemics. He wrote, for example, an important account of the 1735–36 scarlet fever attack in Boston. In it he stressed the need for "many repeated observations and experiments" in order to gain a true idea of the disease.[45] And, to dispel unfounded rumors as to the extent of the scarlet fever, he and other physicians of the city invited anyone interested to consult the actual facts in the "Boston Weekly Journal of Burials." [46]

Despite his appreciation of the statistical approach, Douglass knew little mathematics, had no concept of controls, and, like most of his contemporaries, used statistics

44. *Ibid.*, II, 398–399.
45. Douglass, *The Practical History of a New Epidemical Eruptive Miliary Fever, with an Angina Ulcusculosa which Prevailed in Boston New-England in the Years 1735 and 1736* (Boston: Thomas Fleet, 1736). Douglass's description of scarlet fever is said to have preceded Fothergill's better-known account by ten years. In fact, Cadwallader Colden "sent to Dr. Fothergill studies on throat distemper which had originally been supplied by Douglass." Michael Kraus, *The Atlantic Civilization* (Ithaca, N. Y.: Cornell University Press, 1949), p. 199.
46. Cited in Ernest Caulfield, *A True History of the Terrible Epidemic Vulgarly Called the Throat Distemper which Occurred in his Majesty's Colonies Between the Years 1735 and 1740* (New Haven, Ct.: Beaumont Medical Club, 1939), p. 38. Presumably they referred to the weekly accounts published in Boston newspapers.

in an elementary way. Nor was he always entirely innocent of some of the same statistical shortcomings of which he accused Cotton Mather. At the end of the eighteenth century an anonymous commentator who noted Douglass's own use of rounded figures concluded that Douglass was "*always* positive, and *sometimes* accurate." [47] Perhaps, in the final analysis, however, his principal statistical weakness for his own day lay in the general inadequacy of the American data upon which he had to rely. Caulfield has shown how Douglass was misled about the nature of the New Hampshire throat distemper of 1735–36 because of his reliance upon the faulty diagnoses and accounts of others.[48] The wide-ranging statistics which correspondents sent him for his history were equally open to question.

It must be granted that statistically minded observers with even Douglass's minimal qualifications were exceptions in America. In many seventeenth- and eighteenth-century communities, quantitative reports upon the results of epidemics were arrived at only by a rough consensus. In such a manner, after a season of severe fevers, Governor Nicholson of Maryland wrote the Board of Trade "that by common computation eight or nine hundred people have died." Similarly, Lord Cornbury in New York could only speak of "upwards of five-hundred dead." [49] Still, through the eighteenth century there were many who wanted more precision; and some tried to supply it, in the occasional

47. "Account of Burials and Baptisms in Boston, from the Year 1701 to 1774," Massachusetts Historical Society, *Collections*, ser. 1, IV (1795), 215.

48. Caulfield, *True History*, p. 42. Douglass thus mistakenly called the throat distemper scarlet fever rather than diphtheria.

49. F. Nicholson to Council of Trade, May 28, 1698, *Calendar of State Papers, 27 Oct. 1697–31 Dec. 1698* (London, 1905), p. 250; and *Documents Relative to the Colonial History of New York*, IV, 972.

newspaper bills, broadsides, or private publications. Thus, in Charlestown, South Carolina, occasional statistics on yellow fever and other fevers were published.[50] In New York City, the city government itself issued an official bill of mortality following an onslaught of "bilious plague" (yellow fever) in 1743.[51] In New England towns, broadside poems of lamentation with appended lists of the dead were occasionally printed following some unusually heavy epidemic mortality, such as that in Hartford (1724–25) and East Guilford, Connecticut (1751).[52]

A variety of newspaper reports and other statistical accounts appeared in New England in connection with the great throat distemper epidemic of 1735–40.[53] Among the

50. For a discussion of the vital statistics of the Charlestown physicians, Lining, Chalmers, and Ramsay, see Chapter XI, below.

51. Packard calls this the "first official report of the city's mortality." Francis R. Packard, *History of Medicine in the United States,* 2 vols. (New York: Hafner, 1963), I, p. 114. He quotes the report as follows:

New York, October 24, 1743. By the Mayor of the City.

An account of persons buried in the City of New York:

From July 25 to Sept. 25, 1743		From Sept. 25 to Oct. 22	
Grown persons	115	Children	16
Children	51	Grown persons	36
	165 [sic]		52
			165
			217

And I do find, by the best information I have from the doctors, &c., of this city, that the late distemper is now over.

John Cruger, Mayor.

52. See Guerra, *American Medical Bibliography,* plate nos. 44 and 89 (following p. 688). A detailed study, from contemporary records, of the epidemics of this period is found in Duffy, *Epidemics.*

53. See especially Caulfield, *A True History.* Caulfield has painstakingly reconstructed the nature and course of this epidemic, as well as of the simultaneous attack of scarlet fever in some towns,

fullest of these statistics were those originating with clergymen like Jabez Fitch for essentially religious purposes. A
Boston bookseller, Daniel Henchman, impressed by the appeal of Fitch's data for New Hampshire, proposed to
prepare similar figures for all of New England. Accordingly,
in 1737, by means of a printed circular, he asked ministers
to send in mortality data on the distemper in their towns.
He requested exact accounts, by various age groups, for
three periods between June 1735 and May 1737. Apparently Henchman did not receive enough replies to make
the publication worthwhile. The Reverend John Brown,
however, did prepare such an account for Haverhill, Massachusetts, which Henchman published. Like Fitch, Brown
presented several pages of statistical material, followed
by a tract upon the religious significance of the epidemic.[54]

Whatever published statistics there were for other epidemic diseases throughout the colonial period, the bills and
records kept for smallpox exceeded those for all others.
This was particularly true of quantitative accounts by
colonial physicians. James Kilpatrick in 1743 published
figures on the success of inoculation in a 1738 epidemic in
Charlestown, South Carolina, and thereby helped the cause

---

from every conceivable record: town and church records, diaries,
newspaper accounts, medical writings, sermons, gravestones, and
others. His comments upon the frequently fragmentary nature of
these records show the difficulty of his synthesis (p. 100). See also
Duffy, *Epidemics*, pp. 116–129; and Fitch, *An Account of the Distemper*.

54. Caulfield prints a photograph of Henchman's questionnaire
and comments upon Brown's pamphlet. Caulfield, *A True History*,
pp. 63–66. Brown's pamphlet was entitled *A Relation of some remarkable deaths among the Children of Haverhill, under the late
Distemper in the Throat: with an address to the bereaved* (Boston:
S. Kneeland and T. Green for D. Henchman, 1737). The work was
popular enough to require a second edition in 1738.

of inoculation both in the colonies and in England. Lauchlin Macleane of Philadelphia in 1756 published tables on fifty-five years of smallpox mortality in that city and on inoculation since its start there. Benjamin Gale's extensive account of the Boston smallpox epidemics of 1764 and earlier was published in the *Philosophical Transactions*.[55]

Laymen also continued to observe the disease closely. In 1753 Thomas Prince sent the *Gentleman's Magazine* an analysis of the occurrence of smallpox in Boston the previous year. From data gathered by the City Overseers, Prince prepared statistical tables of monthly numbers of cases during the epidemic, and of persons who either had previously had the disease or who had moved out of town.[56] Of central importance was his chart of comparative deaths from inoculation and natural smallpox (see table).

	Cases of natural smallpox	Died	Inoculated cases	Died
Whites	5060	470	1985	24
Blacks	485	69	139	6
Totals	5545	539	2124	30

55. J. Kilpatrick, *An Essay on Inoculation* (London: J. Huggonson, 1743); Lauchlin Macleane, *An essay on the expediency of inoculation and the seasons most proper for it* (Philadelphia: William Bradford, 1756); and Benjamin Gale to Dr. John Huxham, May 23, 1765, *Philosophical Transactions*, 55 (1765), 193–204. John Blake provides a résumé of Boston inoculation statistics for the period 1721–1792 as well as total Boston mortality statistics, 1701–1774, Blake, *Public Health in Boston*, App. I and II (pp. 243–249). See also Duffy, *Epidemics*, pp. 26–27, 35.

56. Prince noted that if the few uninoculated persons who stayed in the city but did not get the disease were inoculated, and if all those who left town during the epidemic remained away, the disease could be easily controlled henceforth, since only young children would then be susceptible, and they could easily be inoculated.

Prince was impressed by a comparison of these Boston figures with contemporary data for London. He saw that the Boston mortality from natural smallpox, which was only about 1 in 10, was lower than ever before in either city (London usually had a rate of 1 in 6). Through inoculation, on the other hand, Boston had 1 death out of 71 cases, while in London the rate was 1 in 150. Why, Prince asked, did statistical analysis show such difference in the inoculation experience of the two cities? The answer was much what one might expect of a Puritan clergyman who was impressed by Enlightenment science. It was, he thought, because of the operation of God's comprehensive scheme of orderly government for the universe. Specifically, he observed that inoculation had greater success in London because physicians there had fewer patients to take care of, because there were more and better nurses, and because inoculated people in London took more care to avoid being infected in the natural way. Even these activities were "under the superintendency of the highest intelligent cause." Prince had no doubt that man is expected, under God's plan, to exercise all his wisdom and faculties in the fight against smallpox. Not least among these resources, he was sure, were inoculation and the statistical method of inquiry.[57]

Benjamin Franklin's concern with smallpox was no less than Prince's. Having been among the first to support inoculation in Philadelphia, Franklin went to some pains over the years to gather statistics on the practice not only in that city but in other towns. As data accumulated, he passed the figures on in his letters to physicians (including

57. Thomas Prince, "Observations on the State of the Small Pox at Boston, in 1752," *Gentleman's Magazine,* 23 (September 1753), 414–415.

Douglass) and other correspondents.[58] In 1759, in order to obtain wider dissemination among the public of William Heberden, Sr.'s account of inoculation, Franklin had the latter's pamphlet republished, with additions. In the preface Franklin argued on his own behalf for the furtherance of inoculation. Citing statistics on its use in Boston and Philadelphia, as well as in London hospitals, he argued that inoculation had become a tested and proved public health measure. During the 1753–54 epidemic, he related, Boston magistrates had taken special pains to obtain correct inoculation data by requiring certified returns from the enquiring constables. Still, whether or not such precautions were adopted, the statistical results invariably showed that it was an overwhelming advantage for persons to be inoculated. Franklin closed by emphasizing just how much this advantage really was:

> On the whole, if the chance were only as *two* to *one* in favour of the practice among children, would it not be sufficient to induce a tender parent to lay hold of the advantage? But when it is so much greater, as it appears to be by these accounts (in some even as *thirty* to *one*), surely parents will no longer refuse to accept [this practice].[59]

58. Whitfield J. Bell, Jr., "Benjamin Franklin and the Practice of Medicine," *Bulletin of the Cleveland Medical Library,* n.s. 10 (July 1962), 53.

59. Franklin's Preface to [William Heberden], *Some Account of the Success of Inoculation for Smallpox in England and America, Together with plain instruction by which any person may be enabled to perform the Operation, and conduct the patient through the distemper* (London: W. Strahan, 1759), in I. Bernard Cohen, *Benjamin Franklin* (Indianapolis: Bobbs-Merrill, 1953), pp. 193–199.

In such ways, Franklin, Douglass, and others in the colonies, already using a simple calculus of probabilities, participated in the widespread mid-eighteenth-century statistical examination of the incidence of smallpox and the use of inoculation.[60] But these individuals knew full well that disease and mortality represented only one side of the demographic coin. Some of them, with other observers, were at the same time looking at the birth statistics of eighteenth-century America. And some even ventured to generalize about the astounding rate of the population growth which was taking place around them.

60. In France, for instance, scholars like La Condamine, Voltaire, Daniel Bernoulli, and D'Alembert utilized virtually the entire range of mathematics in their studies. In England, men like Sir William Watson and John Haygarth joined Heberden in promoting the extension of inoculation, while John Fothergill used the London Bills of Mortality extensively in his 1751 and 1752 studies of smallpox. See Creighton, *Epidemics in Britain,* II, 385–390 and 628; and Stearn, *Effect of Smallpox on the Amerindian,* pp. 38–42.

Chapter VII

Virgin Land, Teeming Women

The grim colonial concern with mortality went hand in hand with an often earthy interest in fertility. While the demographic scale at first was generally painfully weighted on the side of mortality, at some point in time, which varied from colony to colony, this precarious imbalance righted itself. Operating with little restraint in an exceedingly favorable natural environment, human reproduction ultimately was sufficient to ensure a steady rise in population. By mid-eighteenth century, with assistance from immigration, this growth had achieved what seemed to be an astonishing rate. Although their data were far too imperfect to allow definitive generalizations about the phenomenon, a few American observers studied it with whatever statistics they had. Their findings proved to be of more than merely provincial interest.

The factors which held down the colonial population in the early decades were well-recognized, although by no means everyone agreed as to their order of importance. The more common reasons included deaths from disease, malnutrition, accidents, and frontier warfare, along with those from the hard work or general hardships of the "seasoning" process. A shortage of women which long existed in most colonies outside New England was one obvious drawback.[1] Costs of passage kept many away. The shipment of convicts to certain colonies sometimes deterred the migration of solid citizens. Restrictions on land distribution, moreover, were strong bars to marriage and child-raising.[2]

Yet another deterrent was the adverse image which many Europeans had of the New World. The image of America as a fearsome wilderness filled with every imaginable terror kept away many potential settlers, and the concept was long dying in Europe. The harrowing early reports of epidemic disease and death which filtered back to Europe from one colony after another did nothing to modify that adverse impression.

Yet, from the earliest times, other imaginative Europeans

1. See discussion in Herbert Moller, "Sex Composition and Correlated Culture Patterns of Colonial America," *William and Mary Quarterly,* 3rd ser, 2 (1945), 113–129; and Morison, *Intellectual Life in Colonial New England,* p. 10. The large numbers of widows in Boston and some other communities were not, presumably, exportable.

2. In seventeenth-century New England (as elsewhere) land availability had a direct effect upon marriages. This was reflected in the frequently advanced age of marrying and in the difference in average ages at marriage of eldest and younger sons in a family. This is pointed out, among other places, by Philip J. Greven, Jr., "Family Structure in Seventeenth-Century Andover, Massachusetts," *William and Mary Quarterly,* 3rd ser., 23 (April 1966), 234–256. Kenneth A. Lockridge, "The Population of Dedham, Massachusetts, 1636–1736," *Economic History Review,* 2nd ser., 19 (1966), 330, also notes the high age of marriage and attributes it to economic reasons.

thought of America as an idyllic, lovely garden, rich and fruitful in the produce of the earth. And it would have been surprising if abundant fecundity did not extend to the human inhabitants of such a place. Common experience, buttressed by the vital human record, soon made it clear that such was indeed the case. In fact, the abundance of fertile land, when available, was the most potent of possible population lures.[3] It drew people inexorably to America from abroad, and for those who came, it made large families not only easy but desirable. If the European literary pastoral ideal of the eighteenth century demanded that the New World garden be inhabited and cultivated, this posed no particular problem. While the frontier American has often been characterized by his resourcefulness and individualism, none of his traits was more typical than his prolificacy. Since most persons who came to America were already willingly guided by the Biblical injunction, to "increase and multiply," it was probably no surprise to anyone that fertility surpassed mortality well before the end of the colonial period. And, in the process, what had been a general fear of or excessive preoccupation with death steadily abated.[4]

3. Differing land policies of the colonies modified the strength of the land lure in varying degrees. As noted earlier (Chapter IV), the distribution of large land parcels for plantations in southern colonies was a considerable damper on immigration to those areas.

4. There are discussions of the pastoral ideal and of the image of America as a garden in *Jones, O Strange New World*, pp. 1–200, passim; Henry Nash Smith, *Virgin Land* (Cambridge, Mass.: Harvard University Press, 1950), pp. 1–125, passim; and Leo Marx, *The Machine in the Garden* (New York: Oxford University Press, 1967), pp. 3–144. Odell Shepard, describing the iconographic symbolism on New England gravestones, found that over the years "the death's head acquires more and more the look of a cherub and the crossbones give place to wings. By the middle of the eighteenth century

Every colony had its own turning point at which births began to be sufficient to maintain and increase the population, although no one could have said just when this occurred.[5] The demographic data of the day revealed something of the story to those who dug into it. Fortunately, there were eighteenth-century Americans who were not too fastidious to use what they had. Later statisticians might well have despaired of finding any pattern or order in the data.

Marriage data were admittedly incomplete wherever there were shortages of ministers. There were no counts of the common-law marriages which occurred in remote or frontier areas,[6] and the records for adjoining colonies were distorted when the marriage laws of one were less stringent than those of another. Maryland, as early as the 1670's,

the horror of death is so far subordinated that portraits of the deceased not unlike those to be seen on the tombstones of the ancient world occur frequently." Quoted in Kraus, *The Atlantic Civilization*, p. 299. Some scholars, on the other hand, assert that death was more frightening for some Enlightenment people than for their fathers since the former no longer regarded death as the desirable door to paradise which their ancestors had considered it. Erwin H. Ackerknecht, "Death in the History of Medicine," *Bulletin of the History of Medicine*, 42 (1968), 20–21.

5. Dr. George Milligen, however, wrote as follows for Charlestown, S. C., in 1763: "I have examined a pretty exact register of the baptisms and burials for fifteen years, and find them, except when the smallpox prevailed, nearly equal." Milligen estimated the mortality of South Carolina Whites at 1 in 37. George Milligen, *A Short Description of the Province of South Carolina, with an Account of The Air, Weather, and Diseases at Charles-Town* (London: John Hinton, 1770), p. 32.

6. Some colonies, like Rhode Island in 1665, however, passed legislation to legalize common-law marriages which had been entered into during earlier, unsettled periods. See *Guide to the Public Vital Statistics Records*, pp. 79–80. See also Paul and Pauline Jacobson, *American Marriage and Divorce* (New York: Rinehart, 1959).

already had something of a "Gretna Green" reputation among eloping couples from Virginia.[7] Colonial governments from time to time tightened their laws, not only to cope with such problems as fornication, adultery, and bastardy, but to prevent clandestine marriages and those involving servants or minors. And they periodically passed the laws which they hoped would ensure that marriages and other vital events were properly registered. Miscegenation, though banned in most colonies, was extensive anyway. Just how widespread it was no one could say, but the numbers of mulatto offspring were very considerable.[8]

Divorce was not unknown, at least in New England and the middle colonies. The total numbers of divorces granted by colonial governors or legislatures, however, were so small that they apparently never became sources of statistical concern to anyone.[9] Colonies which were under the

7. Bruce, *Social Life of Virginia*, p. 233.

8. A New Jersey act of 1718 required minors to have certificates of parental consent. *Guide to Vital Statistics Records in New Jersey*, I, 2. Thanks to the churches, at least in New England, some data were kept of the numbers of couples who had premarital sexual relationships. The records of the Congregational Church in Groton, Connecticut, for instance, reveal that between 1761 and 1775, some 66 public confessions of such occurrences were made. Calhoun, *A Social History*, I, 106ff. "The dynamics of interracial sex" are discussed in considerable detail by Jordan, *White Over Black*, pp. 136–178. He points out that while Negroes were widely regarded as more ardent sexually than Whites, it was the white masters who had the opportunities for sexual aggression against their slaves.

9. Around 40 divorce cases are known to have come before Massachusetts authorities between 1639 and 1692 and another 96 between 1760 and 1786, though no separate registers were kept of these events. Nelson Blake, *Road to Reno*, pp. 35ff; and Jacobson, *American Marriage and Divorce*, passim. A few divorces were granted in New York before 1675 but none during the rest of the colonial period. Matteo Spalletta, "Divorce in Colonial New York," *The New York Historical Society Quarterly Bulletin*, 39 (October 1955), 422–440.

blanket of English ecclesiastical law, of course, had no provision for divorce.

The number of babies added to the population in any one year was the most uncertain of all demographic data throughout the colonial period, as it remained later. What happened along the frontier, out of reach of counting mechanisms, was anybody's guess. Even in organized communities, as interested persons realized, the records of baptisms gave by no means the full record of births.[10] In many communities, however, these were the only such data to be had throughout the seventeenth and eighteenth centuries.

As was to be expected, various observers had their own sources of data about births and population trends, and some had original ideas. William Byrd, down-to-earth as well as inquisitive, roguishly reported that, despite the general depopulation of Indian tribes, few Indian women were barren. An Indian of his acquaintance, he wrote, "informed me with a Broad grin upon his Face that, if any Indian woman did not prove with child at a decent time after Marriage, the Husband, to save his Reputation with the women, forthwith entered into a Bear-dyet for Six Weeks, which in that time makes him so vigorous that he grows exceedingly impertinent to his poor wife and 'tis great odds but he makes her a Mother in Nine Months." [11]

Writers on population matters were not usually as frivolous as Byrd. William Douglass, invariably serious, noticed

10. Lionel Chalmers, writing about South Carolina in 1776, made a common observation: "Births cannot be ascertained from the Christenings; for Children are not always Baptized the same year in which they are born; but it is certain, they far exceed the deaths of the settled inhabitants." Lionel Chalmers, *An Account of the Weather and Diseases of South Carolina* (London: Edward and Charles Dilly, 1776), I, 37.

11. Byrd, "History of the Dividing Line," *Writings,* p. 190.

before 1749 that although the Indians occupied large areas of territory the land did not encourage a large population among them. Since Indians made little or no effort to cut down the woods and left fallow most of the year the little agricultural land there was, the country could not support many people. Besides, the Indians were "not so lascivious as Europeans." As for the Whites in America, Douglass concluded, from the data he obtained for his History, only that "the Virility of the Men, and Fecundity of their Women . . . are much the same as in *Great Britain,* their Mother Country, [but] Their Longevity falls much shorter." [12]

Contemporaries who were less restrained than Douglass generally played up the demographic contrasts between America and Europe rather than the similarities. By mid-eighteenth century, the predominant difference appeared to be in population growth rate. Most observers felt not only that the American colonies had come into demographic balance, but that their inhabitants now were multiplying faster than people back in Europe. Peter Kalm was one European who inquired into this when he visited America. Perhaps because he talked with Franklin, his explanation went directly to the heart of the matter:

It does not seem difficult to find out the reasons why the people multiply faster here than in Europe. As soon as a person is old enough he may marry in these provinces without any fear of poverty. There is such an amount of good land yet uncultivated that a newly married man can, without difficulty, get a spot of

12. Douglass, *Summary, Historical and Political,* I, 156 and 175, II, 346.

ground where he may comfortably subsist with his wife and children.[13]

Kalm also hinted at another reason which may have affected the American increase somewhat. In New York and Pennsylvania particularly, he noticed a growing tendency to marry by license instead of after the normal publication of banns. Although the reason for this was partly a matter of fashion, the result was presumably a quicker road to matrimony and child-bearing.[14]

Colonial governors, of course, had standing instructions to inform the Board of Trade or one of the Ministries of the changes of population which occurred in their colonies. Such census reports, estimates from tax or militia rolls, and other vital data as these men sent to England provided officials in the home government with some idea of the steady rise which went on over the years. By the 1750's the governors were writing of large increases. In 1751 Governor Belcher attributed the increase in the Massachusetts population during the preceding ten years "partly to the healthiness of the Countrey, and partly to the Importation of considerable numbers of people from Ireland." Governor Bernard, however, twelve years later, thought that

13. *Peter Kalm's Travels,* I, 258. Jeremy Belknap expressed this situation somewhat more colorfully a few years later: "A young man who has cleared a piece of land, and built a hut for his present accommodation, soon begins to experience the truth of that old adage, 'It is not good for man to be alone.' Having a prospect of increasing his substance by labour, which he knows himself able to perform, he attaches himself to a female earlier than prudence would dictate if he had not such a prospect. Nor are the young females . . . averse." — Jeremy Belknap, *History of New Hampshire,* 3 vols., 2nd ed. (Boston: Bradford and Read, 1813), III, 178.

14. *Peter Kalm's Travels,* I, 138; and Calhoun, *A Social History,* I, 159.

most of that state's increase over the previous ten years was a natural one, although he acknowledged that the rise in Massachusetts was not comparable to the great population increase of some of the other colonies. The biggest part of the mid-century wave of immigrants, he saw, was passing New England by. Moreover, it seemed to Bernard that Massachusetts was as hard hit by the ending of the French and Indian wars as it had been by their continuation. The deaths of thousands of young men in engagements at Louisburg, Quebec, and other localities had served to restrict the population of the next generation before it got well started. Now the loss was due to migration. The fall of Quebec, it is true, brought great new security to the frontier regions. For just this reason, Bernard reported, in the 1760's large numbers of Massachusetts citizens were migrating to the lands in Maine and New Hampshire that were no longer barred by the enemy.[15]

One colony's population loss thus was often another's gain. Governors of colonies other than those in New England reported similarly that their frontier areas were opening up to the populating processes. In New York, settlers were finally free to move into the devastated areas north and west of Albany. Western Pennsylvania, which at one

15. Benton, *Early Census Making,* pp. 22ff. Bernard observed, moreover, that many more had died from disease than from battle. To decrease deaths from disease in future campaigns, he recommended: 1) providing the troops with good clothing, 2) keeping them from rum, and 3) substituting spruce beer in the diet.

Lieutenant Governor Thomas Hutchinson, who reconstructed these and earlier population trends in his *History of Massachusetts,* first published in 1764, commented: "It is probable there would have been 200,000 souls more than there are at this time in New England, if the French had been driven from Canada an hundred years ago" (II, 150). Hutchinson included in his reckonings not only actual battle deaths but death from disease contracted in the service.

time had gained refugees from frontier New York, Maryland, and Virginia, only to suffer a severe population setback with Braddock's defeat, also began to recover. From that point, as well as from Virginia and the Carolinas, the white population even began trickling out beyond the Alleghenies and into the Ohio, Kentucky, and Tennessee areas.

The English government, alarmed by a trend which seemed likely to provoke further Indian hostilities, tried to seal off the frontiers. Through the Proclamation of 1763 it tried to bar the trans-Allegheny region to settlement and to divert would-be settlers to new colonies of Quebec, East Florida, and West Florida. But the population pressures from the old areas toward the contiguous western areas, along with pressures of land speculation, were so powerful as to leave the Proclamation largely ineffective.[16]

While governors documented in part the population shifts of the mid-eighteenth century and a few other observers called attention to the expanding birth rate, only two persons went into such demographic matters at all deeply. These were Franklin and Stiles. Few if any other colonial Americans were as familiar as they, either with the statistical literature of their day or with the vital data of the American colonies.[17] No others made contributions to demographic ideas which had comparable influence on both sides of the Atlantic. With their studies, along with

16. See Sutherland, *Population Distribution*, pp. 1–60, passim; Hansen, *Atlantic Migration*, pp. 30–70, passim; and Ray A. Billington, *Westward Expansion* (New York: Macmillan, 1949). In its original form the Proclamation of 1763 was drawn up by Lord Shelburne, who was not only head of the Board of Trade but direct descendant of Sir William Petty. Petty, the Political Arithmetician, might well have approved the policy of population restriction in the American West.

17. See discussion in Chapters V and VI.

the statistical analyses of disease by Douglass, Boylston, and Mather, American demography began to become something more than a purely descriptive science and much more than a purely collecting one.

Franklin had more than a little in common with Sir William Petty, whose works and ideas he knew well. True, the two looked at colonial population matters from opposite sides of the ocean. But both considered such things in essentially the same way, that is, from the broad viewpoint of political economy. Both were realistic men of this world who looked inquisitively into vital statistics for what they could show about the strength of society and governments.

The views on marriage which Franklin printed were essentially those he shared in common with his fellows of the colonial middle and upper classes. If he enjoyed spoofing the marital state in some of the doggerel verse he put in his almanacs, he also knew that such spoofs were good for sales. Actually, he consistently opposed the single state and strongly encouraged marriage. In his *Gazette* as early as 1734 he replied somewhat sententiously to a correspondent that, "if common Planting and Gardening be an Honourable Employment . . . I think *Human Planting* must be more Honourable." And to press his point he tossed in a quotation from *Paradise Lost*:

> Our Maker bids increase; who bids abstain,
> But our Destroyer, foe to God and Man?
> Hail wedded Love! [18]

From simple statements such as this which reflected the popular morality, Franklin grew interested in every phase

18. Franklin, "Reply to a Piece of Advice," *The Pennsylvania Gazette,* March 4, 1734/5.

of demography.[19] He collected statistics bearing upon population, and reported upon them in a variety of publications. Much of his attention focused upon the phenomenon of American population increase. Even his concern with the data of smallpox was essentially only a part of his interest in the demographic advancement of the colonies. Human increase, he wrote, "has indeed been more obstructed by that distemper than is usually imagined. For the loss of one in ten therby is not merely the loss of so many persons, but the accumulated loss of all the children and children's children the deceased might have had, multiplied by successive generations." [20]

One of Franklin's most original demographic contributions was his speculation about the natural rate of human increase in America. He posed the problem first in his *Poor Richard* article of 1749: "What the natural Increase of Mankind is, is a curious question." Further on he presented and discussed some suggestive, if preliminary, statistics on the question.

First, he pointed to the classic European figures which had formed the basis of Halley's study of human life expectancy:

19. There is an extensive scholarly literature on Franklin's views on population. Much of this has approached the subject as a component of Franklin's economic and political thought. Other treatments have tended to consider Franklin's demographic ideas chiefly as they anticipated those of Malthus. Among the useful works are the following: Alfred O. Aldridge, "Franklin as Demographer," *Journal of Economic History,* 9 (1949–50), 29–44; Joseph J. Spengler, "Malthusianism in Late Eighteenth Century America," *American Economic Review,* 25 (1935), 691–707; Conway Zirkle, "Benjamin Franklin, Thomas Malthus and the United States Census," *Isis,* 48 (1957), 58–62; W. A. Wetzel, *Benjamin Franklin as an Economist* (Baltimore, Md.: Johns Hopkins Press, 1895); and Lewis J. Carey, *Franklin's Economic Views* (New York: Doubleday, Doran, 1928).

20. Franklin, in Heberden, *Some Account of Inoculation,* in Cohen, *Benjamin Franklin,* p. 198.

In Breslau, the Capitol of Silesia, a healthy inland City, to which many Strangers do not come, the Number of Inhabitants was found to be generally about 34,000. An exact Register is kept there of the Births and Burials, which taken for thirty Years together, amount as follows,

> Births, *per Annum* 1238
> Deaths, *per Annum* 1174
> Yearly Increase but 64

Let the expert Calculator say, how long it will be, before by an Increase of 64 *per Annum,* 34,000 People will double themselves?

The evidence for America indicated something quite different from that for Europe, Franklin thought. To be sure, the evidence which he now brought forward was far from exhaustive, consisting as it did of data for only two colonies. Population estimates which he had obtained for Massachusetts showed an increase of 5573 in the seven years between 1735 and 1742, an increase of about one sixth. Census figures for New Jersey, on the other hand, indicated a seven-year increase of about one third. "*Query,* At this Rate of Increase, in what Number of Years will that Province double its Inhabitants?" A comparison between such European and American data, meager as it was, seemed to warrant some generalization:

I believe People increase faster by Generation in these Colonies, where all can have full Employment, and there is Room and Business for Millions yet unborn. For in old settled Countries, as England for Instance, as soon as the Number of People is as great as can be supplied by all the Tillage, Manufactures, Trade and Offices of the Country, the Overplus must quit the Country, or they will perish by Poverty, Diseases, and want of Necessaries. Marriage too, is discarded, many declining it, 'till they can see how they shall be able to maintain a Family.[21]

Within two years of his *Poor Richard* notes, Franklin was willing to hazard a guess about the actual length of the doubling period of natural increase. This he did in his *Observations Concerning the Increase of Mankind,* as part of a broad sketch of America's demographic situation.[22] As a publication, the *Observations* is insignificant in size — a pamphlet of merely ten pages. And statistically it must be regarded as a most unsatisfactory document; there is not a single table or reference to support the sweeping statements of its argument. Despite this, the work became widely quoted and regarded as authoritative.

Actually, the work was not intended as a scholarly demographic study, but as a protest against the British Iron Act of 1750. That Act prohibited the erection in the colonies of slitting or rolling mills, plating forges, and steel furnaces.[23] Many, not just Americans, argued that the measure

21. From *Poor Richard Improved, for 1750* (pub. 1749).
22. Although Franklin had written his *Observations* by 1751, they were not published until 1755, in the *Gentleman's Magazine.* The work also appeared in pamphlet form that same year in Boston, *Observations Concerning the Increase of Mankind, Peopling of Countries, &c* (Boston: S. Kneeland, 1755). References are to this edition. It was subsequently issued in a number of other places. See Carey, *Franklin's Economic Views,* pp. 54–60.
23. See Labaree, ed., *Papers of Franklin,* vol. IV. Dorfman, on the other hand, argues that the tract was written to offset pressures on Parliament by British sugar colonies for measures to reduce the trade of the northern colonies with foreign sugar islands: *Economic Mind in American Civilization,* I, 181–182.

would harm the British Empire as a whole by hampering colonial growth and strength just at the time it was most needed, that is, the climatic years of the British-French struggle for North America. At the same time, Franklin, among others, professed to see no likelihood that the American colonies could pose a threat to English manufactures for an indefinite future. On the contrary, the colonies constituted a "glorious" market for British goods, and one which was growing in population so fast that it would doubtless soon exceed the capacity of the home country to supply. For these reasons, he felt, *"Britain* should not too much restrain Manufactures in her Colonies. A wise and good mother will not do it. To distress is to weaken, and weakening the children weakens the whole family."

The expected increase in American population which Franklin envisaged was premised upon a past rate of natural increase which seemed to have been statistically demonstrated. The European statistics on this matter, he showed, were obviously not relevant to America. Such data pertained to crowded cities where luxurious living was common, to countries where labor was so plentiful as to keep wages low, and to states where most of the land was taken up — all of these conditions which deterred marriage and child-raising. Various other conditions common in Europe tended to discourage marriage and cause a decline of national populations: foreign exploitation, loss of territory, loss of trade and food supplies, bad government and heavy taxes, and excessive consumption of foreign luxuries.

America, by contrast, had almost no barriers to population growth, but instead had the most fundamental advantages. The principle of such growth, Franklin wrote, was that "people increase in proportion to the number of marriages, and that is greater in proportion to the ease and convenience of supporting a family. When families can be easily supported, more persons marry, and earlier in life." In America, ready availability of land made possible a population dynamism which was no longer possible in Europe. People in the colonies were not afraid of marriage economically.

Hence Marriages in *America* are more general, and more generally early, than in *Europe*. And if it is reckoned there, that there is but one marriage per annum among one hundred persons, perhaps we may here reckon two; and if in *Europe* they have but four Births to a marriage (many of their marriages being late) we may here reckon eight, of which if one half grow up, and our marriages are made, reckoning one with another at twenty years of age our people must at least be doubled every twenty years.

Slavery, Franklin admitted, was an adverse factor for American population growth. American experience had already shown by 1750, he observed, that "the Whites who have slaves, not labouring, are enfeebled, and therefore not so generally prolific; the slaves being work'd too hard, and ill fed, their constitutions are broken, and the deaths among them are more than the births; so that a continual supply is needed from *Africa*." Happily, he pointed out, the Northern colonies, having few slaves, make up for the other colonies with their rapid increase of Whites.

Franklin implied that certain personal characteristics which were prominent among Whites in the Northern and Middle colonies also promoted population increase. Principal among these were some of the essential traits of the

Puritan Ethic: thrift, hard work, and simple living. While he felt that the pursuit of fashion makes people cautious of marriage, Franklin was certain that honest labor on the part of parents encourages the children to early marriage, since the latter learn by example what a good subsistence is obtained through labor. "If there be a sect, therefore, in our nation, that regard Frugality and Industry as religious duties, and educate their children therein, more than others commonly do, such sect must consequently increase more by natural generation, than any other sect in *Britain*."

The strenuous observance of the Puritan Ethic in the garden of America was just an added assurance that human increase in the colonies would continue bountifully and unabated. There was, after all, Franklin saw, "no bound to the prolific nature of plants or animals, but what is made by their crowding and interfering with each others' means of subsistence." With "upwards of One Million English Souls" in the colonies now, what might the future not produce? Were the doubling of American population to continue, even at a slightly slower rate, say every 25 instead of the 20 years he calculated, "the greatest number of *Englishmen* will be on this side of the water. What an accession of Power to the British empire by the Sea as well as Land! What increase of trade and navigation! What numbers of ships and seamen!" [24]

In subsequent years Franklin grasped eagerly at whatever further statistical evidence he could find about America's doubling period. In 1753 he passed on a nugget of this sort to Richard Jackson, London barrister and colonial agent: "Dr. Elliot writes me, that in their Town of Killing-

24. The preceding discussion and quotations are from Franklin's *Observations*.

worth [Ct.] in which few or no Strangers come to settle, the People double every 15 years, as appears by examining the Train band Lists taken annually." [25] But Franklin's most dramatic evidence continued to come from New Jersey. In his almanac for 1754, he published comparative population tables for the counties of West Jersey, an area little affected by immigration. Starting from a 1699 enumeration of 832 freeholders, he estimated a total population that year of 4,992 (assuming an average six souls per freeholder). Along with this he printed the 1745 census totals for the same counties, which amounted to 31,821. "By which it appears," he concluded, "that West Jersey has increased in Forty-six Years, more than six for one; tho' some of its Counties are from their Situation reckoned not very healthy." [26]

Observers other than Franklin, of course, obtained statistical evidence of the rapid rate of colonial population increase. Some of the English themselves were alert to such matters. For instance, a 1759 British compilation of vital statistics literature included a striking chart of Rhode Island census data:

	Whites	Blacks
1730	15,302	2,633
1748	29,755	4,373
1755	35,939	4,697

If one accepted the censuses at their face value, as did the compilers, it was evident that the Rhode Island population had "nearly doubled in eighteen years . . . What then

25. Franklin to Jackson, Dec. 6, 1753, in Labaree, *Papers of Franklin*, V, 148. Franklin referred here to the pastor-physician Jared Eliot.
26. *Poor Richard Improved, 1754*.

are we to think of the inhabitants of Great Britain, who increase so slowly, if they do at all . . . ?"[27]

Apart from his interest in the doubling rate of the colonial population, Franklin's involvement in the affairs of Pennsylvania led him to study a number of demographic problems of that colony.[28] One occasion was during the 1750's, when he was member and chairman of an Assembly committee inquiring into currency, trade, and population. A 1752 report of the committee drew together bills of mortality back to 1722, yearly data on new buildings, and tax records of the various counties, in order to establish business trends in the colony. It concluded that although in 1723 trade had been languishing and population diminishing (as indicated by the many vacant houses), the colony had since increased steadily in every respect. The committee's 1754 report noted that subsequent gains in population and in domestic trade had been proportional.[29]

For some, immigration had become a graver problem

27. [Thomas Birch ?, ed.], *A Collection of the Yearly Bills of Mortality from 1657 to 1758 Inclusive* (London: A. Millar, 1759), p. 14. Although Birch's name has long been associated with this volume, it is often and plausibly attributed to William Heberden, Sr.

28. The long epic poem, "On Publick Spirit," which Franklin printed in *Poor Richard* in 1752, included several penetrating lines on overpopulation:

> And when too populous at length confess'd,
> From confluent Strangers refug'd and redress'd;
> When War so long withdraws his barb'rous train,
> That Peace o'erstocks us with the Sons of Men;
> So long Health breathes thro the pure ambient Air,
> That Want must prey on those Disease would spare;
> Then will be all the gen'rous Goddess seen,
> Then most diffus'd she shines, and most benign.
> *Poor Richard Improved, 1752* (pub. 1751).

29. "Report on the State of the Currency," Aug. 19, 1752, Labaree, *Papers of Franklin*, IV, 344–350. The Committee discovered burial

than trade in mid-eighteenth-century Pennsylvania. If most of the Scotch-Irish went elsewhere, Palatines and other Germans were flooding into Pennsylvania in huge numbers, as the newspaper reports of ship arrivals attested. Ironically, observers on both sides of the Atlantic thought that this particular population movement was entirely needless. In Germany the Cameralist writer Johann von Justi observed that "if we had wise police and economic administration, there would be no need of allowing emigration to America . . . Nevertheless we must bow to the wise providence of God, which perhaps in this way will make the most remote regions of the earth moral, reasonable, and enlightened in religion." [30]

In Pennsylvania most people took a different view. Franklin feared that if the German influx were not checked Pennsylvania might well "in a few years become a German colony," and needlessly so. But, given a different policy, he thought,

> equal Numbers might have been spared from the British Islands without being miss'd there, and on proper Encouragement would have come over: I say without being miss'd, perhaps I might say without lessening the Number of People at Home. I question indeed, whether there be a Man the less in Britain for the Establishment of the Colonies. An Island can support but a certain Number of People.[31]

---

lists or bills of mortality for Philadelphia for 1722, 1729–1732, and 1738–1744. See also, "Report on the State of the Trade," Feb. 6, 1754, *ibid.*

30. Translation from Johann von Justi, *Staatswirtschaft* (1758), in Albion W. Small, *The Cameralists* (Chicago, Ill.: University of Chicago Press, 1909), p. 342.

31. Franklin to James Parker, March 20, 1750/51, Labaree, *Papers of Franklin,* IV, 120.

Franklin developed this theory in his *Observations* and in correspondence with men whose ideas he sought on the problem. Meanwhile, he recognized that the Germans, who had been induced to settle in Pennsylvania, should be treated with "great tenderness" and in good faith. Otherwise, "how shall we be believed another time, when we want to People another Colony?" Some of Peter Collinson's ideas on this problem seemed good, particularly that of establishing free English schools among the Germans. Franklin thought, however, that Collinson's proposal for encouraging intermarriages between the English and Germans, through financial and other inducements, would not only be too expensive but also ineffective upon aesthetic grounds.

> The German Women are generally so disagreeable to an English Eye, that it wou'd require great portions to induce Englishmen to marry them. Nor would the German Ideas of Beauty generally agree with our Women: *dick und starcke,* that is, *thick and strong,* always enters into their Description of a pretty Girl.[32]

Franklin had a clear idea of how he wanted the American garden peopled. To some extent his preference was based not only on "thickness" but on color. He thought it was still not too late, "by excluding all blacks and tawneys, of increasing the lovely white and red." He confessed to prejudice in this matter, "for such a partiality is natural to Mankind." [33]

32. Franklin to Collinson, probably late 1753, Labaree, *Papers of Franklin,* V, 158–159. The idea of free English schools was tried out in Philadelphia by the Reverend William Smith.

33. *Observations,* p. 10. By "tawneys," he included virtually all Europeans except Anglo-Saxons.

Above everything else, however, he considered it all-important for Britain to conquer and exclude the French from the areas north and west of the English colonies. Upon that achievement, in fact, rested the demographic future of the English colonies. In the *Observations*, Franklin pointed out that Britain must always be careful, in negotiating colonial boundaries with the French, "to secure room enough, since on the room depends so much the increase of her people." During the mid-1750's, he advanced his plan to establish two new colonies in the Ohio country, an area whose natural richness made it seem certain to become powerful and populous, "perhaps in less than another century." If the English failed to move in, the French obviously would, with all that meant:

1) Our people, being confined to the country between the sea and the mountains, cannot much more increase in number; people increasing in proportion to their room and means of subsistence . . .
2) The French will increase much more, by that acquired room and plenty of substance, and become a great people behind us.[34]

This argument, by Franklin and others, had much to do, at the end of the Seven Years' War, with Britain's

34. Franklin, "A Plan for Settling Two Western Colonies," probably 1754, Labaree, *Papers of Franklin*, V, 457. Lord Hillsborough, in 1772, was among those who criticized Franklin's proposal. Franklin, however, pointed out further that the colonists had no desire to migrate either to the cold of Canada or the heat of Florida. He also observed that failure to provide the colonists with enough land was forcing them together in cities, where they were beginning to establish manufactures and compete with Britain. See discussion in Spengler, "Malthusianism in Late Eighteenth Century America, *American Economic Review*, 25 (December 1935), 697.

decision to annex Canada.[35] Annexation, however, did not end Great Britain's demographic problem in North America; it only changed it. If, before the war, the French in North America constituted a continuing threat to the empire, after the war the thought of her overly prolific colonists remained almost equally unsettling to the British. As a consequence, just as it seemed like a good idea to tax these numerous subjects to pay for subsequent Crown projects in America and for their continuing defense against the Indians, it seemed equally logical to throttle their capacity to increase by barring their way to the new lands in the West.[36] The colonists obviously did not take kindly to either proposal.

Apart from any political effect they had, Franklin's ideas on population were an important addition to the mid-eighteenth-century discussion of the subject. Fothergill wrote, "I don't find anyone has hit it off so well." [37] While there were those who could not or would not believe that the American population was doubling every twenty years, many thinkers had no doubt that it actually did. In France, Montesquieu, in *L'Esprit des Lóis* (1748), had earlier reached some conclusions quite similar to Franklin's on marriage and human increase, while both Buffon and the Abbé Raynal readily adopted Franklin's population ideas.[38]

35. See further Franklin's 1760 pamphlet, "Interest of Great Britain Considered with Regard to her Colonies and the Acquisitions of Canada and Guadalupe."

36. One proposal of the period to limit American population expansion is discussed in Thomas C. Barrow, "A Project for Imperial Reform: 'Hints Respecting the Settlement for [sic] our American Provinces,' 1763," *William and Mary Quarterly*, 3rd ser., 24 (1967), 108–126.

37. Collinson to Franklin, Sept. 27, 1752, Labaree, *Papers of Franklin*, IV, 358.

38. Montesquieu observed, among other things, that "a rising

During the sixties and early seventies, in England, Franklin knew Adam Smith, who ultimately also accepted the American's views on the rapid doubling of colonial population. Also in Great Britain, Franklin's friend David Hume was interested in these matters, although he contributed most to a somewhat different phase of the discussion in his 1752 essay, "The Populousness of Ancient Nations." [39]

In the summer of 1766 Franklin visited the University of Göttingen, where among others he met Professor Gottfried Achenwall, coiner (in 1749) of the term "Statistik." Achenwall, in the chapter on population of his 1761 volume, *First Principles of Politics,* had referred his readers to three works: Short's *New Observations . . . on Bills of Mortality,* Mirabeau's *L'Ami des hommes, ou Traité de la population,* and "Benedict Franklyn's" *Observations.* Franklin's work was by then available in Germany in the *Hamburgischen Magazin* (Vol. XVII). Achenwall now questioned Franklin closely in order to obtain the kind of information which interested him and other German university "statisticians," that is, a systematic description of the state. Later, from his notes, Achenwall prepared an article, "Some Observations on North America and the

---

people increase and multiply extremely," but he did not attempt to establish the rate of increase. *The Spirit of Laws,* transl. Thomas Nugent, rev. ed., 2 vols. (New York: Colonial Press, 1899), I, 6.

39. See Frank N. Egerton III, "The Longevity of the Patriarchs: A Topic in the History of Demography," *Journal of the History of Ideas,* 27 (1966), 575–584. A review of Hume's and other English writings on fertility is found in Robert R. Kuczynski, "British Demographers' Opinions on Fertility, 1660–1760," *Annals of Eugenics* (1935), reprinted in Lancelot Hogben, ed., *Political Arithmetic* (London: Allen & Unwin, 1938), chap. 7. A review of some of the Europeans who knew and were influenced by Franklin's *Observations* is found in Carey, *Franklin's Economic Views,* pp. 59–60.

British Colonies from Verbal Information of Dr. Franklin." This was published in 1767 in *The Hanoverian Magazine* and was later reprinted in Leipzig and Frankfort periodicals. In the interview Franklin suggested that Germans read Douglass's *Summary* and Kalm's *Travels,* which he considered the best and most detailed sources of information about the colonies. He then gave his own short description of American institutions, cities, trade, occupations, religion, governments, and other matters, including a summary of his views on population.[40]

In the colonies, as in Europe, Franklin's views on population became well known. *Poor Richard* introduced them relatively painlessly into many households. The *Observations* was published in Boston as well as in England and Germany. Colonial officials and intellectual leaders read and discussed it. In New England the number of readers naturally included Ezra Stiles.

Stiles, in contrast to the worldly and politically minded Franklin, speculated upon population just as he carried on his various statistical-gathering activities, within the general framework of his church-oriented life.[41] Like the work of Derham and Süssmilch, his demographic contributions are no less important for that orientation. Indeed, the relationship serves as a reminder that few persons in the mid-eighteenth century had better access than clergy-

---

40. G. G. Rosengarten, ed. and trans., *Achenwall's Observations on North America, 1767* (Philadelphia, 1903), reprinted from *Pennsylvania Magazine of History and Biography,* January 1903. Achenwall himself listed the Douglass and Kalm works in the bibliographies of later editions of his *Staatsverfassung der heutigen vornehmsten Europäischen Reiche und Folker im Grundrisse,* 5th rev. ed. (Göttingen: Vandenhoeck, 1768).

41. Other aspects of Stiles's statistical activity are discussed above, Chapter V.

men to the vital data necessary for population generalizations or greater motivation for using them. The Puritan belief in large families had an enthusiastic advocate in Stiles. He earnestly wanted Congregational Church members to breed plentifully in order to ensure the continued dominance of the Puritan way of life in New England. To make specific his hopeful computations of the future growth of the Congregational churches, he prepared genealogies of his friends by which he computed the issue of a single Congregational couple during a given number of generations.[42] For his own family, he constructed a projection based upon hypothetical progeny for ten generations. More profitably, like a poultryman keeping track of the layers among his chickens, Stiles kept in touch with the midwives of Newport in order to have current breeding information about the city. In 1774 Mrs. Dennis, the principal midwife, told him that there had been 430 births in the city in 1773 and that there would be 440 in 1774. She and her associates, it turned out, had current parturient information upon each of the nearly 900 women of childbearing age in Newport, virtually all of whom had children every one and a half or two years.[43]

It is uncertain precisely to what extent Stiles's more elaborate views on population derived from Franklin. In his principal published work on the subject, the 1761 *Discourse on the Christian Union,* Stiles acknowledged his use of some of the other's concepts on immigration, and he several times quoted Franklin's passages on the doubling of population. It appears that he also adopted as his own Franklin's views of the relationship of population to means of subsistence. Still, having thought through these

42. Morgan, *Gentle Puritan,* p. 140.
43. *Literary Diary of Ezra Stiles,* Nov. 24, 1774, I, 488.

matters for himself, with the aid of the growing European literature, Stiles arrived at independent ideas. In fact, it was the Rhode Island clergyman rather than the Pennsylvania printer who, in 1761, formulated a pioneer statement of scope and purpose for the pursuit of demography as a science:

> I cannot but remark that Population; or the laws of human increase and degeneracy are as properly a subject of systematical Science, as botany, the theory of agriculture, or raising and improving stock — and like all other branches of philosophy is to be founded on experiments. These experiments in all their variety are already made to our hands in the sufficiently authoritative history of the last 3000 years in different parts of the world. There remains the classing and generalizing of experiments or facts, and pursuing their obvious inductions to certain general Laws; with which we may be prepared for useful and interesting applications. These researches will not only [be] very pleasurable, but lead to several Things of great moment, hitherto little attended to by politicians, philosophers, or divines.[44]

Stiles's demographic interests naturally centered upon the people of the area he knew best, New England. The 1760 population of that region, roughly 500,000, was essentially, he felt, the result of a natural increase of the original Puritan stock which had arrived before 1643. This was so, he claimed, because "since that time more have

---

44. Stiles, undated note, probably 1761, intended to be added to the *Discourse on the Christian Union,* but not included in the published form. Quoted in Morgan, *Gentle Puritan,* pp. 139–140.

gone from us to Europe, than have arrived from thence hither." This natural increase, he pointed out, had been accomplished at a doubling rate of about twenty years, "or according to Dr. Franklin 25 years." Stiles viewed this period of rapid increase as part of a more or less standard population cycle. To explain the operation of this cycle, in his *Discourse* he linked the experience of New England with that of ancient Israel but carried on the discussion in the unmistakable terminology of the Enlightenment.

"In new-settled Countries," he explained, "the transplanted Colonies, by an established Law of Nature, in a good Climate, do increase to a certain patrial Maturity; then they begin to decline." The demographic history of the chosen people of Israel illustrated this perfectly many years before; that of New England appeared to demonstrate it again. At the beginning, the period of population doubling is always very short; in early Israel it was unusually so, only 14 years. Then, "in consequence of another Law of Nature," the doubling period becomes much greater, a phenomenon Stiles saw he would have to leave to posterity to explain. New England could expect, he calculated, around another 160 years of rapid increase at the 20-year doubling rate, "by which time, thro' the Blessing of Heaven, we in the Province of New England may become many million." After that, the area's period of patrial maturity might ordinarily be expected to go on for something like a thousand years. But, "as it may have then advanced us into the millennial times," the whole process would possibly have become exceedingly academic.

Moving on in the *Discourse* beyond his speculations about the population cycle, Stiles got back on firmer ground when he addressed himself to the more immediate population trends of eighteenth-century New England. To be sure, he produced little more statistical material for his discussion than did Franklin in his *Observations*. What data he had, however, were about as good as any of that period, either in America or Europe. These consisted mainly of summaries of the Rhode Island census counts of 1730 and 1755. Compared, these gave evidence of the rapid doubling period of New England population. From these and other data, Stiles felt it was clear that the doubling rate of settled coastal areas had already slowed down. There the doubling period was over 25 years, while inland it ranged between 15 and 20 years. It was evident that "Agriculture and the rural life are peculiarly friendly to increase." Assuming the 25-year doubling rate for the entire region during the near future, Stiles compiled a table of projected New England population figures for each year up to 1785 and for the two next doubling years of 1810 and 1835.

The current area of New England, Stiles estimated, would support an increase of up to 7,000,000. There seemed little doubt that this figure would be reached about 1860, even if there was some emigration from the older parts of New England to such newer provinces as Nova Scotia and the interior of New Hampshire. (Quitrents in some neighboring colonies deterred migrations there, he thought.) The 1760 prospect of a future territorial enlargement of British America was another thing. Such an event might well give New England a demographic mission which would occupy her for years to come:

If Providence shall complete the reduction of Canada and an honorable peace annex it to the british crown, we may extend our settlements into new provinces, or to the western part of those provinces which by the charters cross the continent to the pacific ocean. With pleasure we anticipate the rapid settlement of new towns and provinces around us, and filling up with millions of inhabitants.

As Stiles looked out over the wilderness bordering New England, he saw, like Franklin, that the wilderness must be peopled before it could blossom into a garden. The process, however, seemed eminently simple:

Plantations may be made with encouragements but cannot successfully be forced. *Free polity, free religion, free property,* and *matrimony,* will soon populate a fertile country, in a good climate. These have been the basis of our increase.[45]

Stiles's demographic views spread much further than the religious audience which heard and read his *Discourse on the Christian Union.* A critic, in his own colony of Rhode Island, writing in the *Providence Gazette,* gently satirized the concepts, but particularly Stiles's "Spiritual Multiplication Table." [46] There were some who did not appreciate the religious setting within which he presented his views. There were others, however, especially in New England, who thought of demography, when they did at all, only in such a religious frame of reference as Stiles used. Still,

45. Unless otherwise noted the foregoing discussion and quotations are from Stiles's *Discourse on the Christian Union,* pp. 102–123.

46. *The Providence Gazette and Country Journal,* vol. 8, Feb. 3–March 2, 1771.

it was only through the intervention of an Englishman that the scientific portion of Stiles's views reached important audiences in Great Britain and Europe. This boost came from the enthusiastic Thomas Short.

In his *Comparative History of the Increase and Decrease of Mankind*, Short made a new and vigorous case for the use of vital statistics in the pursuit of many kinds of human knowledge. Attention to such data, he felt, along with the promotion of health and population increase, would strengthen Great Britain to "cope with our most envious or perfidious Enemies, and transmit our Laws, Liberties, and Possessions [to posterity]." As a prominent part of the preface to his book, Short presented several pages from Stiles's *Discourse*. He did so, not because he considered the publication an oddity, but because he regarded it as important. He felt that Stiles's work "will throw a greater light on the [subject of population increase], and show more clearly the quick Increase of that colony [Rhode Island], than any Thing I have yet met with upon that Subject, and must highly gratify the Curious, as very few Copies of that Sermon are in England." [47]

During the decades after 1760, other Englishmen, among whom were such thinkers as Richard Price and Thomas Malthus, found the contributions of Stiles and Franklin statistically useful. At the same time, scrutiny of the demographic relationship between the colonies and the mother country continued on both sides of the Atlantic. The process seemed to draw American demographic thinkers into ever closer ties with some of their British counterparts. Quite logically, no one perceived more clearly

47. Thomas Short, *A Comparative History of the Increase and Decrease of Mankind in England, and Several Countries Abroad* (London: W. Nicoll and C. Etherington, 1767), p. ii.

than these men that British policy and the plain facts of American population growth were leading inexorably to confrontation between the mother country and colonies that no longer felt dependent.

Chapter VIII

The Numerical Basis of Revolt

To some observers who had been watching colonial population changes the American Revolution was as much a demographic phenomenon as a political upheaval. Contemporaries on both sides of the Atlantic between 1760 and 1775 saw that American population growth was a powerful if not an irresistible factor. While some ignored the growth or sought to throttle it, others realized that it was already leading to a redefinition of the colonies' position vis-à-vis Great Britain. Demographic thinkers, as often as other Englishmen both at home and in the colonies, sought some compromise which would keep the colonies within the Empire. Few, however, found anything in the population figures which might give comfort to lovers of the status quo. When the Revolution broke out, the protracted hostilities disrupted in considerable measure the mechanisms that had been developed in the colonies for the recording and quantification of human events. At the same time, justification of the colonists' position called forth appeals to the authority of statistical data as well as to that of abstract concepts.

When the Stamp Act passed in 1765, Ezra Stiles did a few quick calculations. Backers of the Act, he noted, had estimated that half of the existing Americans, paying only one shilling each per year, would produce revenue amounting to 60,000 pounds per year. "Hence the subjects in North America are reckoned by the Lords at about two million and a Quarter of souls; this I believe the Truth, inclusive of the Negroes." [1]

Neither Stiles, the Lords, nor anyone else could have calculated in advance the violence of colonial opposition to the Stamp Act. But, once unleashed, it had to be dealt with. In London, the Quaker physician John Fothergill was among those who pleaded for repeal of the Act and for an imperial policy which treated Americans as brothers rather than as subjects. In an appeal for reconciliation, he stressed the colonies' importance both as markets and as sources of troops. Noting the rapid increase of colonial population, he advocated a scholarship plan to send the proliferating American youth to English universities and thereby promote understanding and friendship on both sides. The results, he felt, "will be more lasting benefit to both countries, than all the armies that Britain can send thither." [2]

The correspondent "Publicola," writing during the mid-1760's in *The Publick Ledger* and *General Evening Post* in London, went beyond Fothergill to argue that oppressive acts like the Stamp Act were bound to lead to re-

1. Stiles, *Extracts from the Itineraries,* p. 225.
2. Fothergill, "Considerations Relative to the North American Colonies," *Works,* III, 416.

sistance, "and perhaps, in the End, Revolution." He noted also that colonial communities naturally begin having feelings of insubordination or independence as soon as they achieve a respectable population in relation to the parent countries. Logically, it was imprudent for Great Britain to stimulate the growth of American population, especially since America was already doubling by propagation every 20 or 25 years. "It should therefore be our Policy to let them go on increasing from their own Numbers, without exterior Aids therein, which we ought rather to obstruct than encourage; while by all Means we should endeavour to increase our Stock of People at home." Publicola looked ahead with some apprehension from the few million people then in the colonies to the many millions which would beyond any doubt be there after a century of doubling:

> And what then will become of our Awe and Power over them, tho' we had Stamp and every other Kind of Taxes established there, and, with Herds of Revenue Officers, an Army of an hundred thousand native Britons? Alas! Hundreds of such Instruments will not be able to controul, by Force, Millions of Men, whose Hearts glow with the Flame of Liberty.

Conciliation, then, was essential, and creation of a harmonious relationship between equals. For, "as mere Friends they will be more useful to us than they now are as Dependents, from the immense Extent of their Numbers." In turn, the great land area of America would keep that population scattered, agricultural in their pursuits, and consequently of no danger to English manufactures:

> I say, with a right Attention, this Kingdom may keep the Americans, with their natural Increase of People,

in a scattered State for Ages, and every way highly contributive to its own Power and Prosperity; But it cannot be for our Interest to aid their Population . . . [for this] will be hastening them into the very State of Population which will be most dangerous to ourselves, that of peopling large Towns and Cities, which must introduce all Kinds of Manufacturing.[3]

Such reasoning appealed so much to Thomas Short that he reprinted all twenty of Publicola's letters in an appendix to his own *Comparative History of the Increase and Decrease of Mankind*. Adam Smith, somewhat similarly, a few years later, advocated incorporating the American colonies as equals in a British commonwealth.[4] And, in various ways, other scholars who were political moderates or friends of the colonies used demographic arguments to work for conciliation and for reversal of the British policies of the 1760's and '70's.

In London during those years Franklin was a member of several brilliant groups of men who gathered at St. Paul's Coffeehouse, the London Coffee House, and other meeting places. Most members of these groups were, in varying combinations, religious nonconformists, political liberals, and scientists. Several of them had conspicuous interests in population problems or the statistical approach to human affairs. These included Collinson, Fothergill, Joseph Priestley, and the prison reformer John Howard. But most important of all, from the viewpoint of Amer-

3. Short, *Comparative History*, pp. 162–166.
4. Adam Smith, *An Inquiry into the Nature and Causes of the Wealth of Nations* (Chicago: Encyclopedia Britannica, Inc., 1952), pp. 270–271.

ican demography and vital statistics, was Richard Price.[5] Price was an established moral philosopher of some note who frequently discussed philosophy or religion with friends like Hume and Priestley.[6] He was humanitarian by instinct and infinitely curious. He sometimes did small favors for Franklin; on one occasion he suggested the names of dissenting preachers in London whom the latter might go to hear. In turn, during the 1760's, Franklin was among those who not only fanned Price's deep affection for the colonies but helped turn the Presbyterian clergyman's interests increasingly toward demographic and actuarial matters.

One of Price's earliest demographic writings not only involved Franklin but, so far as it criticized Crown policies toward the colonies, earned for itself peremptory treatment at the hands of the Royal Society. This was his 1769 communication to the Society, broadly entitled "Concerning Observations on the Expectations of Lives; the Increase of Mankind; the Number of Inhabitants in London; and the Influence of great Towns, on Health and Population." As read to the Society, in the form of a letter to Franklin, the paper at one point referred parenthetically but pointedly to the violent colonial reactions to the Stamp Act and the Townshend duties. Price's sympathies were clearly with the colonies, "formerly an increasing number of FRIENDS, but now likely to be converted . . .

5. A delightful account of Franklin's extensive club life and acquaintances in England may be found in Verner W. Crane, "The Club of Honest Whigs: Friends of Science and Liberty," *William and Mary Quarterly*, 3rd ser., 23 (April 1966), 210–233.

6. Among the biographies of Price, see Carl B. Cone, *Torchbearer of Freedom: The Influence of Richard Price on Eighteenth Century Thought* (Lexington: University of Kentucky Press, 1952); and Roland Thomas, *Richard Price, Philosopher and Apostle of Liberty* (London: Oxford University Press, 1924).

into an increasing number of ENEMIES." Not all the members of the Royal Society shared Price's sympathies, and many did not want the Society to mix politics with science. In any case, the passage proved so offensive that it was suppressed when Price's paper was published in the *Philosophical Transactions*.[7]

In 1771 Price published his book, *Observations on Reversionary Payments*. This established him as an authority both upon public finance and life insurance.[8] It proved to be a useful volume for American scholars and statesmen. It provided cautions and techniques for forming insurance societies. It provided summaries of vital data from all over Europe which the Americans could compare with their own figures. And it brought together under one cover the demographic and statistical concepts of European thinkers from Graunt and Halley down to DeMoivre, Süssmilch, and Maitland.

Well before preparing this work, Price had become familiar with the demographic writings of Stiles and Franklin and with some of the sources of colonial vital data. He was much interested in what these showed about the rapid doubling rate of the American population. As he discussed the matter in his *Observations,* Price matched almost any colonial writer in enthusiasm for America's demographic prospect. Comparing Stiles's vital data, however, with those which Thomas Prince had published on Boston, Price made Boston something of an object lesson. He showed

7. Read to the Society in April 1769, the paper appeared in vol. 59 of the *Philosophical Transactions.* Price revealed the Society's censorship and the missing passage some fourteen years after the event, in the fourth edition of his *Observations on Reversionary Payments,* 2 vols. (London: T. Cadell, 1783), I, 284.

8. See Chapter X below for more on the development of life insurance in the United States.

that in the midst of the rapid population increase of New England, Boston, the only sizable city, had an excess of burials over births between 1731 to 1762, and would have decreased but for a constant supply from the country. The demographic moral was clear: the colonies should value and preserve their predominantly rural way of life. Even at the beginning of the Industrial Revolution, in Price's eyes, city crowding was already a condition to shun:

> The greatest part of that black catalogue of diseases which ravage human life, is the offspring of the tenderness, the luxury, and the corruptions introduced by the vice and false refinements of civil society. [And, conversely,] . . . the further we go from the artificial and irregular modes of living in great towns, the fewer of mankind die in the *first* stages of life, and the more in its *last* stages.

America, Price felt, was at the best and happiest of the levels of civilization: it was in a time of abundance, simple and long living, and painless population increase. He accepted Stiles's prediction that New England would have 4,000,000 people within seventy years. By extension, he had no doubt that all of the colonies together would then amount to twice as many people as Great Britain. Meanwhile, he wrote, "What a prodigious difference must there be, between the vigour and the happiness of human life in such situations and in such a place as London?" [9]

The young physician Benjamin Rush, in a 1774 paper before the American Philosophical Society, showed himself to be among those who were not a little influenced by

9. Richard Price, *Observations on Reversionary Payments* (London: T. Cadell, 1771), pp. 197–204 and 274ff.

Price's viewpoint.[10] Rush had little doubt that the rapid increase of American population was a result of the simple rural life in combination with the special conditions of the colonies:

> The population of a country is not to be accomplished by rewards and punishments. And it is happy for America, that the universal prevalence of the protestant religion, the checks lately given to negro slavery, the general unwillingness among us to acknowledge the usurpations of primogeniture, the universal practice of inoculation for the smallpox, and absence of the plague, render the interposition of government for that purpose unnecessary. These advantages can only be secured to our country by AGRICULTURE. This is the true basis of national health, riches, and populousness.

Rush felt that scrutiny of any nation's bills of mortality would give a good idea of its essential vigor. From a look at the bills "of many countries," he asserted that the proportion of the aged was greater in civilization than among savage nations. But, conversely, referring to the London bills, he asserted that more persons die of diseases in civilized nations than among the American Indians. He was not able to back these claims up with vital data of the Indians. He did relate them statistically to the Philadelphia experience:

10. Another was the Roxbury, Massachusetts, preacher William Gordon. See Gordon's booklet, *The Plan of a Society for Making Provision for Widows, by Annuities for the Remainder of Life, and for Granting Annuities to Persons after Certain Ages, with the Proper Tables for Calculating what must be paid by the Several Members, in order to secure the said Advantages* (Boston: J. Edwards and J. Fleeming, 1772), pp. v–vi. See also Chapter X below.

> I am sorry to add . . . that the number of patients in the Hospital, and incurables in the Almshouse of this city, show that we are treading in the enervated steps of our fellow subjects in Britain. Our bills of mortality likewise show the encroachments of British diseases [nervous fever, consumption, hysteric and hypochondriac diseases] upon us . . . All these diseases have been produced by our having deserted the simple diet and manners of our ancestors.[11]

The encroachments of British diseases, revealed by statistical analysis, then, joined the growing list of grievances which hitherto good American subjects increasingly held against the mother country. As the British tightened their control over colonial life, tensions and incidents multiplied. With ever closer controls the British needed ever more and better statistical data from the colonies.[12] Some colonial governors made efforts to supply the needed information. But, as tensions grew, colonists became less and less cooperative in furnishing data. It is no wonder that, when the colonists themselves came to need demographic or other figures, the data were neither very accessible nor very reliable.

In the fall of 1774, as differences came to a head, delegates to the First Continental Congress assembled in Phila-

11. Benjamin Rush, "An Inquiry into the Natural History of Medicine among the Indians of North America: and a Comparative View of their Diseases and Remedies with those of Civilized Nations," *Medical Inquiries and Observations,* 4th ed., 4 vols. in 2 (Philadelphia: M. Carey, 1815), I, 72–89.

12. Although the colonial vital data which British government agents or agencies collected were the most extensive anywhere available on the subject, most were of no value to contemporary demographers since they were not made public until long after Independence.

delphia. Before the group could proceed to its substantive business, it spent several days working out procedures and organizational matters. The allotment of delegates to each colony proved a difficult problem. Some proposed that apportionment be made in accordance with the population and property of the respective colonies; others wanted it on the basis of population alone. Although Congress ultimately fell back on the expedient of giving each colony a single vote, population figures of sorts were obtained from the colonies for the discussions. Both within the Congress and outside, these figures were themselves a subject of considerable discussion and disagreement.

Stiles was annoyed at finding the estimates published in a Rhode Island paper, since he considered them altogether "too large and indefinite." Although he made no public rebuttal, he took up several pages of his diary to analyze and correct the data. Only the figures for three states (Massachusetts, Connecticut, and Rhode Island), he thought, were based upon substantially reliable information. The others, resting upon sketchy data, seemed considerably overestimated. The corrected figures which he jotted down from the various sources were themselves estimates in many cases. However, they undoubtedly gave a closer account than the Congress figures of colonial population on the eve of the Revolution (see table).[13]

At Harvard College, Edward Wigglesworth, Professor of Divinity, found the Congress estimates more useful than Stiles did. He adopted them without change, in fact, in a pamphlet, *Calculations on American Population,* which he wrote for "recreation" late in 1774. There the figures became not only part of an analysis of American manpower strength but part of a last-minute plea for colonial recon-

13. Dexter, *Literary Diary of Ezra Stiles,* I, 486–488.

Continental Congress estimates September 1774			Stiles's estimates November 1774		
			Whites	Negroes	Total
Massachusetts	400,000				
New Hampshire	150,000	New			
Rhode Island	59,678	Eng.	725,000	15,000	740,000
Connecticut	192,000				
New York	250,000		150,000	6,000	156,000
New Jersey	130,000		130,000		130,000
Penna. & Delaware	350,000		300,000		300,000
Maryland	320,000		200,000	50,000	250,000
Virginia	650,000		300,000	100,000	400,000
North Carolina	300,000		200,000	50,000	250,000
South Carolina	225,000		70,000	110,000	180,000
TOTALS	3,026,678		2,075,000	331,000	2,406,000

ciliation with England. Using the Congress figures along with other data (see accompanying table), Wigglesworth compared America's demographic resources for carrying on a conflict with those of Great Britain. He found that Price had estimated a population of five million for England along with one and a half million for Scotland. Of these, an estimated one fourth, or 1,550,000, were fencible men — that is, males between 15 and 56. By the same ratio (and omitting some half-million slaves from consideration), Wigglesworth noted that America had 625,000 white males between those ages. He calculated further that out of the 70,284 person increase in American population in 1774, "17,571 effective men [were] added to the Americans." Was it only a coincidence, Wigglesworth wondered, that Lord Barrington had moved in the House of Commons, "that 17,542 effective men be employed for the land service this year?"

Although Great Britain in 1774 had roughly double the

population of America, Wigglesworth had no more doubt than Stiles that the rapid colonial rate of increase would enable the colonies to exceed the home country within seventy years. "Happy had it been for America," wrote Wigglesworth, "if its present contest with the parent state had been postponed to the middle of the next century! And more happy still had [they both remained] subservient to each others prosperity and happiness; and have formed one of the most populous, potent, wealthy and happy kingdoms that ever existed."

Apart from its consideration of military manpower resources, Wigglesworth's pamphlet included some of the most extensive mathematical calculations yet produced in America upon population matters. Wigglesworth made his calculations from the current "Capital Stock" of about 2,500,000 white British-Americans which the Congress figures suggested, and from the premise of a 25-year doubling period caused by natural increase. He used these to construct a mathematical formula from which, at least in theory, various population unknowns might be calculated. Employing the same principles used to compute compound interest on money, he worked out a ratio of annual population increase in America and constructed a table "to compute the number of inhabitants in any American colony for any given year," past or future.

The examples which Wigglesworth gave for using his formula were carefully worked out and had some plausibility when applied to years which were relatively close to the base year of 1774. His extensions into the distant past or future, however, like Stiles's population cycle, had an air of unreality about them. Even Wigglesworth himself, as he contemplated the hypothetical results of unrestricted doubling continuing throughout the nineteenth and twentieth centuries, found that the figure "overwhelms the mind with astonishment! At that time [the year 2000], should their future population be as rapid as their past, the Americans would amount to ONE THOUSAND TWO-HUNDRED AND EIGHTY MILLIONS! . . . What an amazing source of commerce will be opened to Great Britain," should the rulers of the home country decide to adopt a policy of conciliation!

As he took his pamphlet to the printer early in 1775, Wigglesworth sought an appropriate text to go upon the title page. Wavering, like many other Americans, between pride in the demographic outlook for his country and profound disquiet over the heightening quarrel with the mother country, it was only natural for the Harvard divine to look for his text in the Bible. Given the ambiguity of the situation, the words he chose from Abraham were remarkably apt:

Look now toward Heaven, and tell the STARS, if thou be able to number them. So shall thy Posterity be. [from Genesis 15: 5]

Let there be no STRIFE, I pray thee, BETWEEN US; for we are BRETHREN. Is not the WHOLE COUNTRY before thee? [from Genesis 13: 8–9][14]

The Second Continental Congress met in an atmosphere of greater urgency than had the First, for in the spring of 1775 military engagements had already taken place at Lexington and Concord. Congress's resolve to help Massachusetts resist the British put all of the colonies on a war footing. As one measure, they agreed to apportion costs of war

14. Edward Wigglesworth, *Calculations on American Population* (Boston: John Boyle, 1775).

in accordance with the population. Since it still lacked reliable data, the Congress called upon each colony to determine its own population. Only two colonies carried out census enumerations in response to this request.[15] Undaunted, Congress later sought to formalize the apportionment and census-taking procedure through precise provisions in the Articles of Confederation. These were as follows:

> All charges of war and all other expenses that shall be incurred for the common defence, or general welfare, and allowed by the United States assembled, shall be defrayed out of a common treasury, which shall be supplied by the several colonies in proportion to the number of inhabitants of every age, sex, and quality, except Indians not paying taxes, in each Colony, a true account of which, distinguishing the white inhabitants, shall be triennially taken and transmitted to the Assembly of the United States.[16]

Compliance with such a provision, even for those states that were willing, proved to be out of the question during much of the war.[17] Even in 1781 a resolution to have the census carried out failed to pass the Congress, although several states were able to make enumerations around that time.[18]

15. Discussed in Rossiter, *Population Growth,* pp. 3–5.

16. Original draft of Article XI of the Articles of Confederation, in *The Papers of James Madison* (Washington: Langtree and O'Sullivan, 1840), I, 27–28.

17. Massachusetts conducted an enumeration in 1776. In 1777 an enumeration of Philadelphia was carried out for Lord Howe during the British occupation.

18. "Proceedings of the Hartford Convention," *The Papers of Thomas Jefferson,* ed. Julian P. Boyd (Princeton, N. J.: Princeton University Press, 1950–   ), IV, 141.

It was not particularly remarkable that the first political arrangements of the new United States included some mechanisms for obtaining population data from the individual states. Nor was it strange that the statistical approach was useful to and compatible with prerevolutionary and revolutionary idealism. As a form of intellectual activity, statistical method fitted easily and logically into the inquiring spirit of the Enlightenment. Statistical studies of epidemics and inoculation marked a distinctly rational approach to disease and one which abandoned old metaphysical factors. Part of Stiles's appeal in England and on the continent lay in his having framed his ideas on population dynamics within the context of natural law. The comprehensive view (of men like Fothergill and Rush) that vital statistics could illuminate many of the dark corners of society harmonized with the idea that men and society could be improved by projects devised for the purpose. Traditional authority, finally, that ultimate bugaboo of Enlightenment minds, was as unsatisfactory a basis for population policy in a free land as it was for providing just government.[19]

The Declaration of Independence brought together strands of Enlightenment thought and idealism which had crystallized since John Locke. The shapers of the Declaration well knew that their act was of demographic significance. Their formal list of grievances against the King included, in fact, a protest that he had violated the natural right of Americans to increase:

> He has endeavoured to prevent the population of these States; for that purpose obstructing the Laws for

19. The broad concepts of the Enlightenment are discussed in Carl Becker, *The Heavenly City of the Eighteenth Century Philosophers* (New Haven, Ct.: Yale University Press, 1962), pp. 1–63.

Naturalization of Foreigners, refusing to pass others to encourage their migrations hither, and raising the conditions of new Appropriations of Lands.[20]

Now, under Independence, all of this would be corrected. The restrictions on western settlement would go. Achievement of a free government would finally assure the conditions necessary to populate adequately the great and abundant land. The young Charlestown physician David Ramsay in 1778 expressed what many others felt on the subject:

> Our Independence will naturally tend to fill our country with inhabitants. Where life, liberty, and property are well secured, and where land is easily and cheaply obtained, the natural increase of people will exceed all European calculations . . . The population of this country has been heretofore very rapid; but it is worthy of observation that this has varied more or less, in proportion to the degrees of liberty that were granted to the different provinces by their respective charters. Pennsylvania and New-England, though inferior in soil, being blessed originally with the most free forms of government, have out-stripped others in the relative increase of their inhabitants. Hence I infer that as we are now completely free and independent, we shall populate much faster than we ever have done, or ever would, while we were controuled by the jealous policy of an insignificant island.[21]

20. From the Declaration of Independence.
21. Ramsay, "Oration on American Independence," in Robert L. Brunhouse, ed., *David Ramsay, 1748–1815: Selections from his Writings* (Philadelphia: American Philosophical Society, 1965), pp. 187–188.

In England, meanwhile, throughout much of the war, Price and others argued about the British population. Scholars for years had been debating whether the country's population trend was up or down. Their debates remained inconclusive for lack of a national census and because of poor vital statistics registration. The question took on new interest during the American Revolution, particularly in the light of the spectacular American increase. Price, blaming some of the same British policies which had estranged the Americans, consistently argued that the English population had steadily declined since 1688.[22] Repeated during wartime, the thesis brought down upon him not only statistical but patriotic opposition. The most effective rebuttal came from the English physician John Heysham of Carlisle. Heysham thought that the subject of English population deserved the "attention of every lover of his country, and especially since the commencement of the present war." From his own census and carefully kept vital statistics of the Carlisle parish, he reported large population increases in the region, and coming, significantly, at the "very period, in which *Dr. Price* asserts the depopulation of *Great Britain* to have been rapid and progressive." Heysham went on to accuse Price of virtual disloyalty for deprecating British population resources while magnifying those of the enemy.[23]

22. See, for instance, Price, *An Essay on the Population of England, from the Revolution to the Present Time,* 2nd ed. (London: T. Cadell, 1780). See also Cone, *Torchbearer of Freedom,* passim, and Bonar, *Theories of Population,* passim.

23. John Heysham, *Observations on the Bills of Mortality in Carlisle* (Carlisle, Eng., 1780–1787). See especially the *Observations* for 1779 (publ. 1780), p. 2; and *Observations* for 1780 (1781), p. 1. Others who refuted Price included John Howlett, William Wales, John Wesley, and Arthur Young. Among those who essentially shared Price's views on this subject were Robert Wallace and Montesquieu. Americans, of course, by accepting Price's view of British popula-

There was no doubt that Price gave comfort, if not actual aid, to the colonists. Before Independence he was an outspoken supporter of their rights as Englishmen. Afterward, he continued to speak out in admiration, both of American ideals and of the favorable conditions which existed for American population increase. His *Observations on the Nature of Civil Liberty* brought him far more of a colonial following than his *Observations on Reversionary Payments*. The former prompted Congress in 1778 to offer Price American citizenship. But it was his mathematical talents that the members had in mind when they asked him to organize the finances of the new nation. He was doubtless well advised to decline, considering the unsettled conditions at the time.

The alterations which the Revolution brought about in the lives of the colonists, in the composition of society, in institutions, culture, and governments, were many and complex.[24] It was a convulsive period, many of the effects of which were beyond statistical measurement. In the case of matters that ordinarily might have been counted or recorded, many of the mechanisms were disrupted or shattered. It was hard enough at the national level, now that the corps of British collectors, surveyors, and other officialdom had been packed off, along with their information-gathering systems. Congress had much difficulty forming

---

tion, were led to an excessively rosy idea of the comparative manpower situation at the beginning of the Revolution. There was no definite disproof of Price, however, until the countrywide British census of 1801.

24. William H. Nelson discusses these complex effects in "The Revolutionary Character of the American Revolution," *American Historical Review*, 70 (July 1965), 998–1014. See also Merle Curti, *The Growth of American Thought*, 3rd ed. (New York: Harper & Row, 1964), pp. 120–130.

an idea of what resources it could count on. At the local level, where most statistical activity heretofore had taken place, the situation was even worse. Registration mechanisms, along with various other basic components of an orderly society, were among the early casualties of the war in many places. As the enemy approached, registrars and sextons marched off with their neighbors to join the fight. When the towns and villages became parts of the battle-field, their churches, town offices, and libraries were often burned, and with them, unknown quantities of church and town registers were destroyed.[25] In places where the personnel and buildings remained intact, wartime paper shortage sometimes intervened. As generals sometimes lacked the paper even to send written orders to their subordinates, similarly clerks were hard-put to find enough paper for keeping their registers or preparing bills of mortality.[26]

With vital registers thus emasculated and any general census-taking out of the question, one of the great demographic dramas of the time, the exodus of the Loyalists, remained poorly accounted for. The broad outlines, however, emerged later in the records of courts and property assessors, while the Episcopal parish registers which sometimes survived recorded the exile of Loyalists or the division of their property. Nobody knew then, and we still do not know, exactly how many Tories left America. But almost certainly upwards of 70,000 persons, including a large

25. See, for instance, *Guide to Vital Statistics Records in New Jersey*, II, 2–3.
26. In Boston the brief summaries or bills of mortality which newspapers had been printing since 1704 were casualties of the war. Attempts to revive them in the mid-1780's did not succeed. See John B. Blake, "The Early History of Vital Statistics in Massachusetts," *Bulletin of the History of Medicine*, 29 (1955), 47.

segment of the intellectual, governmental, and civic elite, were lost to the country.[27]

Records of other population movements were perhaps even more inadequately kept. Several of the cities occupied by British forces experienced marked decreases of population. Many residents of Newport and Boston, for instance, dispersed to the countryside, while Philadelphians went in considerable numbers to Baltimore. But no one knew just how many.[28]

Nor were there thorough data on the slaves who left the states during or after the Revolution. Unknown thousands were carried on British ships to East Florida, the Caribbean Islands, and Canada, some with their Loyalist masters and some seeking freedom. Others, who had gone into the possession of British or French officers, were taken back to Europe by their masters. At the time of the British withdrawal from Atlantic ports after Yorktown in 1782 and 1783, British leaders made some attempt to account for the departures of slaves. Lists of refugees or embarkation returns which British officials prepared in Savannah and Charleston included large numbers of Negroes. And, in the spring of 1783, Sir Guy Carleton directed that a special register be kept of all Negroes evacuated from New York. Kept by three British Commissioners, and inspected by

27. See Jones, *O Strange New World*, pp. 313–321; and Samuel E. Morison and Henry S. Commager, *The Growth of the American Republic*, 4th ed., rev. and enl., 2 vols. (New York: Oxford University Press, 1955), I, 198–199. The author of an interesting recent article, while acknowledging the absence of reliable contemporary data, estimates the number of wartime Loyalists at 19.8 percent of the white Americans, or 513,000. He does not discuss figures for the exodus. Paul H. Smith, "The American Loyalists: Notes on their Organization and Numerical Strength," *William and Mary Quarterly*, 3rd ser., 25 (April 1968), 259–277.

28. See Rossiter, *Population Growth*, pp. 6–13.

three American Commissioners, the register eventually included the names, descriptions, former masters, dates, and departure ships of nearly three thousand Negroes.[29]

The record of Revolutionary casualties was poorly documented. True, Ezra Stiles kept a tally on the wartime scalpings of Whites which were reported in upper New York. But it was a matter of guesswork just how many settlers perished in the Indian and Tory attacks along the whole frontier. Vital statistics of the troops themselves were not much better. Although individual military units normally kept some records, such as those of current strength, losses, and recruitments, in practice their data were often sketchy and sometimes nonexistent for crucial periods. The cumulative data on these matters which were sent on to higher echelons suffered badly in transmission.[30]

Military medical statistics, though not far developed anywhere, were not unknown either in Europe or the United States in the late eighteenth century.[31] Daily sick returns

29. Benjamin Quarles, *The Negro in the American Revolution* (Chapel Hill: University of North Carolina Press, 1961), pp. 58, 163–172. Quarles notes that some 10,000 Negro departures were registered, but estimates that over 5000 unregistered slaves were taken away before Yorktown, together with over 14,000 afterward.

30. Stiles, *Literary Diary*. See also Ray A. Billington, *Westward Expansion*, p. 174. Twentieth-century military historians agree as to the poor state of record-keeping in the Revolutionary armies. From the sketchy data that have been preserved, however, they have estimated variously: that some 250,000 individuals saw service; that the average annual strength of the army was 50,000; and that there were over 70,000 deaths, out of which about 7,000 died of battle wounds, 11,000 died on the prison ship *Jersey*, and most of the rest succumbed to diseases. For a summary, see Stanhope Bayne-Jones, *The Evolution of Preventive Medicine in the United States Army, 1607–1939* (Washington, D. C.: Government Printing Office, 1968), pp. 54–55.

31. Walter F. Willcox felt that such statistics were negligible. "The Development of Military Sanitary Statistics," *Publications*, American Statistical Association, 16 (1918), 908.

were kept in some European armies. Indeed, John Pringle had analyzed such data from the British armies in the 1740's to obtain some idea of the incidence of diseases among the troops.[32] The general principle of keeping vital records was also agreed upon for the American revolutionary forces. The most extensive data were the hospital records. John Morgan, placed in charge of army hospitals in 1775, ordered that weekly sickness records be kept in the general hospital at Roxbury, Massachusetts. After Congress made this a general requirement for the Army in 1776, attempts were made in many hospitals to keep some records.[33] There were continuing problems, however, such as the failure of some surgeons to forward sickness returns regularly from regimental to general hospitals. This neglect led to much suffering among patients since, because of the deficiencies of the figures, sufficient medical supplies and personnel were not always obtained. Later in the war, Benjamin

32. John Pringle, *Observations on the Diseases of the Army in Camp and Garrison* (London: Millar, Wilson & Payne, 1752). Following Pringle, Richard Brocklesby also used such data in his book, *Oeconomical and Medical Observations . . . tending to the improvement of medical hospitals . . .* (London: Becket & De Hondt, 1764).

33. The law which the Continental Congress passed on July 17, 1776 was based on suggestions by Morgan. It provided, in the pertinent part: "That the several regimental and hospital surgeons in the several departments make weekly returns of the sick to the respective directors [of hospitals] in their departments." Quoted in Packard, *History of Medicine in the United States*, I, 546; but see also 544–545, 576–577, and 584–587. Somewhat more extensive reports were required after the reorganization of the Army Medical Service under William Shippen in 1777. Congress's reorganization law provided for "daily returns of sick and wounded, to be made to the physician and surgeon general [of each district], and for monthly returns to the Director General." Percy M. Ashburn, *A History of the Medical Department of the United States Army* (Boston: Houghton Mifflin, 1929), pp. 18–19.

Rush, critical of William Shippen's management of the hospitals, kept his own figures of hospital mortality. Asked where he obtained his figures, he replied that it was simply by counting the number of coffins buried each day. "From their weight and smell I am persuaded they contained hospital patients in them, and if they were not dead I hope some steps will be taken for the future to prevent and punish the crime of burying the Continental soldiers alive." [34]

Reports kept by military hospitals in South Carolina consistently showed a large preponderance of patients with diseases over those with battle wounds. We know that "Colonel William Moultrie's Second Regiment of Provincials had a small hospital census in December, 1775: of eleven patients only one had a wound, four had fevers, four had diarrheas, one had dropsy, and one had venereal disease." A Continental General Hospital report early in 1780 indicated only twelve wounded patients out of 302. The May 9–June 9, 1781, report of the Southern Department hospitals, however, indicated 52 men with wounds out of 280 admitted.[35]

Baron von Steuben's Army Regulations, which were drawn up in 1780, made the keeping of vital medical records a permanent requirement in the Army in peace as in war. The appropriate regulation read as follows:

Once every week, and oftener when required, the surgeon will deliver to the commanding officer of the regiment, a return of the sick of the regiment, with

34. Rush to Nathaniel Greene, quoted in Whitfield J. Bell, Jr., *John Morgan, Continental Doctor* (Philadelphia: University of Pennsylvania Press, 1965), p. 225.
35. Waring, *History of Medicine in South Carolina*, p. 98.

their disorders, distinguishing those in the regimental hospital from those out of it.[36]

If military vital statistics generally left much to be desired, that did not mean that no one thought about such matters during the war. As a matter of fact, Alexander Hamilton, with time on his hands in 1777 while he was with the Army in New York, used the opportunity to acquaint himself with statistical studies and demographic ideas. Lacking a special commonplace book, Hamilton appropriated space at the back of the Pay Book of the State Company of Artillery, and in it kept notes on his private reading of the period. There, along with quotations from Plutarch and Demosthenes, he copied long extracts from Postlethwayt's *Universal Dictionary of Trade and Commerce*.[37] In Postlethwayt, Hamilton discovered Petty, Davenant, and other political arithmeticians. He noted Postlethwayt's figures on the English population, as well as the latter's claim for England, "that 100,000 people augment annually one year to another to 100,175." He was interested that "Mr. Kerseboom [sic] agreeing with Dr. Halley makes the number of people thirty five times the number of births in a year." He went on to copy some of Edmund Halley's original data, particularly the "Table of Observations Exhibiting the Probabilities of Life," summaries of the average of Breslau births and deaths, and various demographic generalizations on infant mortality and longevity.[38] Most of this material was of little immedi-

36. Quoted in Ashburn, *Medical Department of the U. S. Army*, p. 22.

37. Malachy Postlethwayt, *The Universal Dictionary of Trade and Commerce* (London, 1751ff.).

38. *The Papers of Alexander Hamilton*, ed. Harold C. Syrett (New York: Columbia University Press, 1961–   ), I, 387–410, passim.

ate value to Washington's aide-de-camp, but it proved useful fourteen years later when Hamilton became Secretary of the Treasury.

As the revolution dragged on, it became increasingly important for the young nation to obtain recognition, commercial exchanges, and loans from Europe. Such a possibility sometimes depended, at least in part, upon offsetting adverse British propaganda about American strength, resources, and stability. Former Governor Pownall of Massachusetts, for instance, circulated through Europe his propagandistic pamphlet of 1777, "A Memorial Humbly Addressed to the Sovereigns of Europe on the Present State of Affairs Between the Old and New World." John Adams had to face the effects of this document when America in 1780 sought aid from Holland. In the course of negotiations that year, Adams replied at some length to the questions of the Dutch lawyer, Calkoen. In his seventeenth inquiry, the latter asked whether there were any reliable population data for America. Adams provided Calkoen with the estimates, totaling 3,026,678, which had been made in 1774 for the Continental Congress, though he candidly agreed that the figures were quite imperfect. At the same time, he made it clear that he considered them much more accurate than the figure of 2,141,307 for the same year which Pownall was circulating.

Calkoen also asked whether the American population had increased since the outbreak of the war. Here Adams could reply with assurance: "It is an undoubted fact that America daily increases in strength and force." The experience of previous ages, he maintained, had always been that countries increase their populations nearly as much during wartime as in peace. Although America had had no wartime census which would bear this out, Adams pointed to the extensive wartime migration of Americans to frontier areas as equally strong proof that increase was going on. Still, it was his version of America's population doubling figures that must have carried the most weight in his exposition:

> It has been found by calculations, that America has doubled her numbers, even by natural generation alone . . . about once in eighteen years . . . There are near twenty thousand fighting men added to the numbers in America every year. Is this the case of our enemy, Great Britain? Which then can maintain the war the longest? [39]

Thus, in a variety of ways demographic statistics were useful in justifying the American Revolution and in helping advance it to a successful conclusion. With independence and military victory achieved, the reconstruction of society, government, and institutions in the new American image could go on. Some people seemed to act as though patriotic rhetoric alone would be enough to accomplish this. But other Americans realized that a firm base of vital and other data, as well as the scientific capacity to reason from that base, was essential in an increasingly complex and competitive post-Revolutionary world.

39. *The Works of John Adams,* ed. Charles Francis Adams, 10 vols. (Boston: Little, Brown), VII (1852), 265–273.

Chapter IX

The Statistical Mind in the New Nation

The United States that emerged from the Revolution needed the best demographic data they could bring together. This was true both in carrying on the nation's internal business and in making a place for itself in the world of nations. Recognizing this, American political leaders did what they could at the very beginning to pass statistical legislation and organize the registration mechanisms which they felt were necessary. Intellectuals, in an outpouring of surveys, histories, geographies, and other studies, produced an extensive quantitative inventory of the human and physical resources of the young nation. The total statistical effort made within the federal and state governments, as well as in the scientific and scholarly community, was an impressive one for that period of history. That the effort was not completely successful should not obscure the fact that it was made and certain results achieved.

Among the postwar demographic trends, one of the most obvious was the continuing pattern of rapid population growth. Patriots were happy with this situation. George Washington himself was certainly partly in earnest when, at the end of the Revolution, in an uncharacteristically jocular letter to Lafayette, he touched on the subject of population:

> I wish to see the sons and daughters of the world in peace and busily employed in the . . . agreeable amusement of fulfilling the first and great command-ment — Increase and Multiply: as an encouragement to which we have opened the fertile plains of the Ohio to the poor, the needy and the oppressed of the Earth.[1]

Not that very much encouragement was needed. Benjamin Rush felt that the increase of patriotic fervor during the Revolution had already contributed to an increase in the birth rate. It appeared to him that "marriages were more fruitful than in former years, and . . . a considerable number of unfruitful marriages became fruitful during the war." [2] Others did not think this at all farfetched, particu-larly in Pennsylvania. The French traveler Brissot de Warville concluded in 1788 that that state's population had "more than doubled in twenty-five years, notwithstanding the horrible depopulation of a war of eight years." [3] To most Americans it was a thoroughly desirable objective

1. Quoted in Henry Nash Smith, *Virgin Land*, p. 203.
2. Rush, quoted in George Rosen, "Political Order and Human Health in Jeffersonian Thought," *Bulletin of the History of Medicine*, 26 (1952), 40.
3. J. P. Brissot de Warville, *New Travels in the United States of America, Performed in MDCCLXXXVIII*, 2nd ed., corr., 2 vols. (London: J. S. Jordan, 1794), I, 279.

that this rapid doubling be continued and encouraged.

Meanwhile, the population situation in the post-Revolutionary United States was much more than one great patriotic orgy of mating and increasing. War deaths, huge for a country with such a small population, left great gaps in families and in every kind of local institution. It took time, moreover, for communities to recover from the human dislocations caused by the British occupation and the Loyalist exodus. And it was not until the French troops departed that America was relieved of the "eternal sexual problems associated with armies." [4] Many Americans had turned westward and were settling in the back country and on land across the Alleghenies. As the Whites began to form new states, the Indians were forced out. In the old pattern, many of the latter went to war or just as often succumbed to smallpox. By 1790, less than ten thousand Indians remained east of the Alleghenies. Only in New York and Pennsylvania were enough left to maintain any tribal organization on the reservations where they were placed.[5] Meanwhile, immigration from Europe had resumed, though for several decades the volume remained less than before the Revolution.[6] Along the Eastern seaboard, refugees from the French Revolution, Santo Domingo, and various European wars began appearing at American ports during the 1790's, along with liberals, such as Priestley, who were forced out of England.

Once in a while data might be found which illuminated some of these demographic movements, but not often. It was hard enough just to get a record of the stationary population and of the basic vital events of birth, marriage, and

4. Jones, *O Strange New World*, p. 322.
5. Rossiter, *Population Growth*.
6. See Maldwyn Allen Jones, *American Immigration* (Chicago, Ill.: University of Chicago Press, 1961), pp. 64–91.

death which occurred to these citizens. The new states met these needs in various ways.

From a legislative point of view, independence gave the new states the opportunity of forming governments based at least partly on the principles for which they had fought. It was an occasion to reexamine the whole body of law which had accumulated during the colonial period. In the case of vital statistics laws, as with other civil legislation, the results were mixed. Massachusetts, like several other states, updated its basic colonial registration provisions (those of the 1692 law), but did not change them in any important respect. The state's 1796 law in turn provided the basis for the registration system until the 1840's.[7] Few if any basic changes in marriage laws or registration were made by any state. Some states, however, acted upon the fact that their provisions for registering births and deaths had been anything but successful. Framers of the North Carolina Constitution of 1776, recognizing that county registers had been unable to keep adequate vital statistics, eliminated that duty from the office in their reorganization of county government. The fee bill of 1778 in that state, moreover, terminated the payment of fees for registration of births and deaths.[8] New Jersey, by giving its Court of Chancery sole jurisdiction over divorces in 1795, became the first state to have central files and data on divorce. At about the same time, however, that state, like several others subsequently, made the reporting of births and deaths a strictly voluntary matter which individuals could attend to within three years of the event.[9]

7. Gutman, *Birth and Death Registration in Massachusetts,* pp. 21–23.

8. *Guide to Vital Statistics Records in North Carolina,* I, 1–3.

9. *Guide to Vital Statistics Records in New Jersey,* p. 2. See also Jacobson, *American Marriage and Divorce,* pp. 12ff.

In some states, enactment of new vital statistics legislation was hampered by the pressures for separation of church and state. Fervently secular states could not very well continue old arrangements which made church registers in effect the official sources of vital data. Thus, when religions were disestablished, some states were left without adequate registration provisions and failed to build new systems. New York, Maryland, and most of the southern states neglected to develop systematic vital statistics registration arrangements in the early national period. In some cases the omission persisted for over a hundred years.[10] Virginia failed to adopt such new provisions despite the best intentions of her early state leaders. During the revision of laws which went on between 1776 and 1786, Jefferson was a member of the committee which approved a birth and death registration bill designed to replace the Registration Act of 1713. Madison presented the bill to the Virginia legislature in October 1785, and the House passed it in December. The Senate, however, pigeonholed the measure. A bill providing for civil marriage and civil registration of marriage data similarly failed to pass.[11]

Whatever provisions they made for the gathering and recording of vital data, the states remained individually autonomous in this respect. As a result, the new nation presented a far from united front so far as the vital statistics of its people were concerned. The state registration systems and collections of vital data developed as totally independent entities, with no more relevance to or connection with

10. See, for example, discussion in *Guide to Public Vital Statistics Records in New York State,* I, viiff. See also Cordell, *Medical Annals of Maryland,* p. 12; and James H. Cassedy, "The Registration Area and American Vital Statistics," *Bulletin of the History of Medicine,* 39 (1965), 221–231.

11. Boyd, *Papers of Thomas Jefferson,* II, 491–492, 556–558.

those of neighboring states than with those of European nations. This potpourri of registration legislation, systems, and incompatible data presented large obstacles to scientific studies of demographic events or trends in the nation as a whole. Still the situation did not become serious so long as would-be scholars in this subject area were few and European vital statistics provisions generally remained little better than American. Only as European nations created efficient mechanisms in the course of the nineteenth century did the uncoordinated condition of American state registration begin to reveal the extent of its shortcomings.

In the late eighteenth century, few people envisaged anything more than the most modest of formal statistical roles for the new federal government. When Congress legislated in 1787 for the organization of the Northwest Territory, it provided population formulas for establishment of the territorial legislature and for subsequent creation of new states. It did not see fit, however, to prescribe the registration of vital events in such places. The Territorial government itself by 1788 provided for marriages to be reported to county registers and recorded within three months, but it did not require births or deaths to be registered.[12] Governments of later continental territories generally made similar minimal registration provisions.

Only with the national population census did many leaders agree that there was a need to have some statistical mechanisms and data in the national government. Even this required much resolution of differences. Fundamen-

12. See *Guide to Public Vital Statistics Records in Indiana* (Indianapolis: Indiana Historical Records Survey, 1941), and similar volumes for other Central states. Although no census was taken at the time, in 1790 Governor St. Clair estimated that there were about 4000 Whites, surrounded by hostile Indians, in the Territory's scattered settlements. Rossiter, *Population Growth,* p. 48.

tally, the states had to work out an equitable formula for determining state apportionment of national expenses. The wartime debate over a proposed triennial census under the Articles of Confederation continued just as fruitlessly after the peace, despite some concessions, such as elimination of a provision calling for the enumeration of slaves. Nevertheless, in 1783 the Congressional Committee on Revenue reported that only the small states of New Hampshire, Rhode Island, Connecticut, and Maryland "had produced authentic documents of their numbers." [13] The large states continued by and large reluctant to assume equitable proportions of the national debt.

When the Constitutional Convention met at Philadelphia in 1787, the apportionment dilemma quickly came up again. The debates on the subject followed lines very similar to the earlier ones in Congress. Again, as in 1774, each of the delegations submitted to the Convention population estimates for their respective states. In marked contrast to the 1774 estimates, however, it turned out that for every state except Georgia the population was now considerably underestimated. The figure for North Carolina was "less than two-thirds what it should have been," while the total of the states' estimates was short by over half a million.[14] The states admittedly were taking no chances on excessive taxation.

The clause on apportionment which the Convention finally adopted as part of the Constitution was a masterly arrangement, even if, demographically, it left each slave with only three fifths of an existence.

Representatives and direct taxes shall be apportioned among the several States which may be in-

13. *Papers of James Madison,* I, 431.
14. Rossiter, *Population Growth,* pp. 46–49.

cluded within this Union, according to their respective numbers, which shall be determined by adding to the whole number of free persons, including those bound to service for a term of years, and excluding Indians not taxed, three-fifths of all other persons. The actual enumeration shall be made within three years after the first meeting of the Congress of the United States, and within every subsequent term of ten years, in such manner as they shall by law direct.[15]

The delegates took no public notice, even if they realized the fact, that their solution provided for the first regular population census of any modern nation. They took satisfaction instead that the demands of conflicting interests and sections had been reconciled through workable compromises. Madison explained some of them a few months later in *The Federalist*. One of the most important was the ingenious use of the population base not only to determine the proportion of the states' tax contribution, but also to determine the states' representation in the House of Representatives:

As the accuracy of the census to be obtained by the Congress, will necessarily depend in a considerable

15. Article 3, Section 2, of the Constitution. Actually, in the context of another phase of the Convention's debate, the three-fifths rating of the Negro slave's life was made to appear not entirely illogical demographically. Oliver Ellsworth of Connecticut, in fact, was convinced that the pressures of general population growth would lead quickly to the complete disappearance of slaves from the United States: "As population increases, poor labourers will be so plenty [sic] as to render slaves useless. Slavery in time will not be a speck in our country." Quoted in J. J. Spengler, "Malthusianism in Eighteenth-Century America," *American Economic Review*, 25 (1935), 704–705. See also William G. Brown, *The Life of Oliver Ellsworth* (New York: Macmillan, 1905), pp. 147–157.

degree on the disposition, if not the cooperation of the States, it is of great importance that the States should feel as little bias as possible to swell or reduce the amount of their numbers. Were their share of representation alone to be governed by this rule they would have an interest in exaggerating their inhabitants. Were the rule to decide their share of taxation alone, a contrary temptation would prevail. By extending the rule to both objectives, the States will have opposing interests, which will controul and ballance each other; and produce the requisite impartiality.[16]

Some people, Madison noted, criticized the Convention's decision to have only 65 representatives (or 1 for about 45,000 people) chosen for the House of Representative's first session. Compared with the ratio of 1 for 4000 in the Pennsylvania legislature, 1 in 1000 in Rhode Island, and 1 in 10 in Georgia, the proposed ratio in the House, on the face of it, seemed too small to guard the liberties of the people adequately. In answer, Madison pointed out that such a variety of formulas demonstrated the breadth of possible choices which were open in organizing a representative government. "Nothing can be more fallacious than to found our political calculations on arithmetical principles" or hard-and-fast formulas, he warned. Besides, following the census which was to be held in three years, the number of representatives would immediately rise substantially. Using the convention-approved formula of ulti-

16. "The Federalist, no. 54" (Feb. 12, 1788), in *The Federalist*, ed. Jacob E. Cooke (Middletown, Ct.: Wesleyan University Press, 1961), pp. 371–372.

mately having one representative for each 30,000 population, he showed that the 65 representatives would go up almost at once to at least 100, assuming a base population of around three million. Moreover, "at the expiration of twenty and five years, according to the computed rate of increase, the number of representatives will amount to two hundred; and of fifty years to four hundred. This is a number which I presume will put an end to all fears arising from the smallness of the body." [17] Large states and expected new states would have a self-interest in frequent reapportionment, the latter particularly so, as they would doubtless increase rapidly in population in their early years.[18]

In early 1790, with the Constitution adopted and a new government formed, Congress considered a bill to provide for conduct of the first national census. In its original form, the bill provided only for the barest enumeration of individuals. Madison, however, was instrumental in expanding it to include a schedule of six items of inquiry: heads of family, free white males over 16, free white males under 16, free white females, other free persons, and slaves. Madison had hoped that the census could also be used to obtain information on occupations. This, he thought, would be the "kind of information extraordinarily requisite to the Legislator, and much wanted for the science of Political Economy. A repetition of it every ten years would hereafter afford a most curious and instructive assemblage of facts." Much to his regret, as he informed Jefferson, that

17. "The Federalist, no. 55" (Feb. 13, 1788), Cooke ed., pp. 374–375.
18. "The Federalist, no. 58" (Feb. 20, 1788), Cooke ed., pp. 391–397.

provision "was thrown out by the Senate as a waste of trouble and supplying materials for idle people to make a book." [19]

The carrying-out of the first census was no small task for the new government. That it took eighteen months to account for the 3,929,214 inhabitants was a measure of its magnitude. Jefferson, as Secretary of State, transmitted the necessary instructions to the governors or the seventeen marshals.[20] He also took it upon himself to obtain a census of the Southwest Territory. Hamilton guided through Congress the money bills to pay the enumerators: one dollar for every three hundred persons counted in cities of over 5000; one dollar for every 150 in country areas; and one dollar for every 50 in very dispersed areas. Remuneration was by no means liberal, especially since there were no standard forms and many enumerators had to supply their own paper sheets for the returns. Actual conduct of the census involved most of the same problems which had hampered the colonial censuses: transportation difficulties, uncertain geographic boundaries, recurring fears of the "Sin of David," and a citizenry out of principle always suspicious of authority, especially when its members fancied new taxes might result. Once the district returns were completed, the federal marshals compiled and posted the results in two or more prominent places, sometimes gave them to the local newspapers, and forwarded summaries to the Secretary of State. The latter passed them on to

19. Madison to Jefferson, Feb. 14, 1790, *Letters and Other Writings of James Madison*, 4 vols. (Philadelphia: Lippincott, 1865), I, 507.

20. It is not known certainly whether Jefferson corresponded directly with the marshals or whether the marshals received their instructions through the governors. Merriam believes the latter to be probable. W. R. Merriam, "The Evolution of American Census-Taking," *Century Magazine*, April 1903, pp. 832–833.

Congress just as he received them and had them published.[21]

Washington and his advisers were more than perfunctorily interested in learning the results of the census; they particularly counted on the data to help project the image of an ever-stronger America to the rest of the world. American diplomats sent abroad during the mid-1780's were armed with only the vaguest of population figures. Although they used what data they had forcefully enough, they frequently felt the need for more in their crucial efforts to get recognition and trade arrangements for the new country and in their attempts to dissuade European powers from undertaking new adventures at America's expense. For instance, John Adams in 1786 had only the most general of demographic facts to warn England against underestimating America:

> The Americans are, at this day, a great people, and are not to be trifled with. Their numbers have increased fifty per cent since 1774. A people that can multiply at this rate, amidst all the calamities of such a war of eight years, will in twenty years more, be too respectable to want friends.[22]

Jefferson, who was trying at the same time to convince the French that American markets were worth their while, fell

21. This summary of the 1790 census relies heavily upon standard secondary accounts. See especially Merriam, "Evolution of American Census-Taking," *Century Magazine*, April 1903, pp. 831–838; Rossiter, *Population Growth*, pp. 15–50, passim; and Carroll D. Wright and William C. Hunt, *The History and Growth of the United States Census*, Senate Document no. 194, 56th Cong., 1st sess. (Washington, D. C.: Government Printing Office, 1900), pp. 7–20.

22. Adams to Matthew Robinson, March 2, 1786, *Works of John Adams*, VIII, 385.

back, for lack of anything better, on population arguments that were little different from those that Franklin had used thirty-five years earlier.

A century's experience has shown, that we double our numbers every twenty or twenty-five years. No circumstances can be foreseen, at this moment, which will lessen our rate of multiplication for centuries to come. For every article of the productions and manufactures of this country [France] then, which can be introduced into the habit there [the United States], the demand will double every twenty or twenty-five years.[23]

The need of American officials for better demographic information had become a matter of some urgency by the time of the organization of the federal government under the Constitution. In October 1790, while the census was being taken, Hamilton met with the British agent, George Beckwith, in order to impress upon him that the new nation was not as impotent as many Englishmen seemed to think.

. . . our government acquires daily strength and consistence in the public mind . . . I am persuaded when our Census is completed we shall have at least three Millions and a half of people; at this time we are capable of making considerable exertions, even Maritime ones, if from circumstances it became a measure of government to encourage them, and I must beg leave to repeat its being my opinion, that looking forward particularly to what may be the expected

23. Jefferson to the Count de Montmorin, June 23, 1787, *Writings of Jefferson*, ed. A. E. Bergh, 20 vols. (Washington, D. C.: Jefferson Memorial Association, 1903), VI, 186.

condition of this country in a few years, it would be an Act of Wisdom in the Minister of Great Britain to attach and consider the States upon political as well as commercial considerations.[24]

For similar reasons that same year, Hamilton urged Washington to stress, in his address to Congress, the "symptoms of greater population than was supposed, a further proof of progressive strength and resource." [25]

As the census returns came trickling in from the various states, there was some surprise that the figures were not higher than they were. Washington confided to Gouverneur Morris that he had been misled by estimates supplied by members of Congress, each of whom appeared to have been "looking through a magnifier." At the end of July 1791 it was apparent that, contrary to some hopes and estimates, the total would not come to four million. But, Washington thought, there were certain adjustments to be made that would eventually raise the figure:

. . . the real number will greatly exceed the official return, because, from religious scruples, some would not give in their lists; from an apprehension that it was intended as the foundation of a Tax, others concealed or diminished theirs; and from the indolence of the mass and want of activity in many of the deputy enumerators, numbers are omitted. The authenticated number will, however, be far greater, I believe, than has ever been allowed in Europe, and will have no

24. Hamilton, "Conversation with George Beckwith," Oct. 15-20, 1790, *Papers of Alexander Hamilton,* VII, 114.
25. Quoted in J. J. Spengler, "Malthusianism in Late Eighteenth-Century America," *American Economic Review,* 25 (1935), 701, n. 32.

small influence in enabling them to form a more just opinion of our present growing importance than have yet been entertained there.[26]

After the final returns were in, other leaders were similarly skeptical of, if not somewhat disappointed with, the announced figures. When Jefferson forwarded copies of the census report to diplomatic officials abroad, he was careful to emphasize that the report did not reflect what he considered to be the full population. He indicated in red ink his own estimates for returns which he thought were incomplete.[27]

Despite its deficiencies, the census provided the factual base about the American people which officials and scholars needed. In no way was it put to better use than to refute the views of the Englishman, Lord Sheffield. In 1783 Sheffield had published his *Observations on the Commerce of the American States,* which went through six editions by 1791 and had great influence in shaping European ideas about post-Revolutionary America.[28] Striking harshly at sensitive points, he belittled America generally, its products and its capacity for trade or manufacture, and predicted it would long be dependent upon Great Britain. He supported parts of his polemic by references to American population trends. Obviously unimpressed by Franklin, Stiles, or Price, Sheffield argued that it was most unlikely that American population would continue to increase as

26. Washington to Gouverneur Morris, July 28, 1791, quoted in Rossiter, *Population Growth,* p. 48.

27. Carroll D. Wright, *History and Growth of U. S. Census,* pp. 16–17.

28. John Baker Holroyd, First Earl of Sheffield, *Observations on the Commerce of the American States,* 1st ed. (London: J. Debritt, 1783).

it had previously. In fact, numbers had already fallen off in 1784, according to his information. Increasingly chaotic conditions under the newly independent nation would doubtless even bring about a considerable emigration.

American officials were much disturbed by the adverse effects of Sheffield's book. Among the replies, one of the most detailed was that made in 1791 by Tench Coxe, then Assistant Secretary of the Treasury, in a series of articles in *The American Museum*. Coxe attempted, with his own figures, to refute the fabric of prejudice and error which he found in Sheffield's sections on manufactures, agriculture, resources, and commerce. In particular, with the results of the national census before him, he picked apart Sheffield's population data. Where Sheffield had denigrated 1783 estimates of 35,000 people for Delaware, Coxe triumphantly pointed to the state's official 1791 census total of 59,094. Where Sheffield had questioned the 1783 estimate of 150,000 for New Jersey, the census showed that only eight years later the figure had soared to 184,139. Connecticut had increased between 1783 and 1791 from an estimated 206,000 to a demonstrated 237,942, despite the fact "that it has been incessantly sending emigrations" to Maine, New Hampshire, Vermont, Pennsylvania, Maryland, Virginia, and the Western territories. Even Rhode Island had increased, despite "the unhappy condition of that government, and the consequent interruption of its trade, fisheries, and manufactures, from 1786 to the beginning of 1790, [which] occasioned great emigrations thence into other states." Where its 1783 population was put at 51,896, in 1791 it had increased to 68,825. With similar examinations of the other states, Coxe maintained that, on population grounds at least, Sheffield's argument had little validity. He showed that throughout the nation the great increases had continued during the 1780's, even though most of those years "were extremely disordered and discouraging." The reasons that Coxe found for the increase were much like those ascribed by previous observers: "the simplicity of living amongst *the great body* of the American people; the extraordinary facility of obtaining the means of subsistence; migration to our country; and the non-existence of emigrations." [29]

Coxe republished his replies to Lord Sheffield in 1794, together with other papers, in his book, *A View of the United States of America.* He showed himself to be thoroughly imbued with the concept of political arithmetic as an essential ingredient in the methodology of good government. His fiscal ideas, particularly the concept of a national bank, had been favorably received by Richard Price and by British bankers and economists.[30] His collected papers provided an impressive early demonstration of statistical method in the service of the commercial interests of the new nation. Since talk about commerce and trade ultimately involved people in their roles as consumers, various of the papers went into population matters and their statistics. Coxe noted that the end of the slave trade, gradual emancipation, and the increase of the white population, had already reduced the proportion of slaves in the total population, and he gave rough figures on the numbers of Negroes in each region. In presenting data for the benefit of prospective immigrants, he noted that

29. Tench Coxe, "Statements Relative to the Agriculture, Manufactures, Commerce, Population, and Public Happiness, of the United States; in Reply to the Assertions and Predictions of Lord Sheffield," in Coxe, *A View of the United States of America* (London: J. Johnson, 1795), pp. 197–200.

30. Coxe to Hamilton, March 5–9, 1790, *Papers of Alexander Hamilton,* VI, 290.

American taxes were low and that no state had the hearth taxes or window taxes so frequently found in Europe and so often used there as bases for population estimates. It was apparent to him that "the population of no [other] country can increase so rapidly: because living is no where so cheap, and we are constantly gaining people from the nations of the old world."

Several of Coxe's papers were designed to boost his own state of Pennsylvania. In pursuing this aim, he presented comparative population tables of each county for 1760, 1770, and 1793, together with broader tabular information which included population for 1790. He stressed the rapid settling of new land west of Philadelphia, a phenomenon which had increased the state's numbers from an estimated 360,000 in 1783 to 434,000 in 1791. All in all, Coxe maintained, the extraordinarily favorable demographic trends, along with other factors, suggested the brightest of futures for the state:

> The population of Pennsylvania appears to have increased, in 23 years [1770–1793], nearly in the proportion of from 39 to 91; though the whole term of a revolutionary and invasive war of seven years was included. This considerably exceeds Dr. Franklin's estimate of doubling in twenty years. Now that all New-England is full, except Main and Vermont, the contiguous states of New-Jersey and Delaware are overstocked, and Maryland nearly so; and above all, now that Europe is full and much disturbed, a curious rapidity of population is to be expected in a state with so much unimproved land, disposition and capacity for manufactures, wealth, foreign intercourse, energy, and enterprise, as Pennsylvania.[31]

31. Coxe, *View of the United States,* pp. v, 97–101, 481–505.

Benjamin Rush had a less numerical outlook than Coxe on the population of Pennsylvania, but a more imaginative and selective one. He thought of Pennsylvania as a sieve, screening and keeping the industrious newcomers and passing on the remainder to the southern states and western territories. The back-country of the state was filled, he reported, with people at varying stages of civilized life. Of these, the restless ones who were close to the Indians in nature tended to migrate every April. This "passion for migration," Rush thought,

> is wisely calculated for the extension of population in America; and this it does, not only by promoting the increase of the human species in new settlements, but in the old settlements likewise . . . [Removal] of the idle and extravagant . . . by increasing the facility of subsistence to the frugal and industrious who remain behind, naturally increases the number of people, just as the cutting off the suckers of an apple-tree increases the size of the tree, and the quantity of fruit.[32]

Like Coxe and Franklin, Rush offered his advice to would-be post-Revolutionary migrants from Europe. He advised artists, literary men, and the idle rich to stay home as there was no place for them in a busy America. Oh behalf of the new country, however, he extended a warm welcome to schoolteachers, professional men, servants, and especially to farmers, mechanics, and laborers. Ever the

32. Benjamin Rush, "An Account of the Progress of Population, Agriculture, Manners, and Government in Pennsylvania, in a letter to a Friend in England," *Essays, Literary, Moral and Philosophical,* 2nd ed. (Philadelphia: Thomas & William Bradford, 1806), pp. 213–225.

enthusiastic patriot, Rush noted that revolutionary movements were beginning in Europe as a result of the American example. Where free governments were established
due to these, he thought, there seemed no doubt that
populations would increase. But, since European countries
had no available land, the free United States would be
the only logical place for the excess population to go.
Such emigration, Rush assured his readers, would in turn
promote the prosperity of the original country.[33]

Just as Coxe and Rush brought together demographic
data to support the aspirations of Pennsylvania, other
scholars drew upon similar sources to advance, describe,
defend, or glorify their states or the nation as a whole.
In doing so, they unearthed and published considerable
amounts of the surviving colonial data which might otherwise have remained obscure or lost.

Perhaps no writer of the period accomplished this so
thoroughly for a given state as Jefferson, in his *Notes on
Virginia*. This was no matter of chance; probably no one in
America was more imbued with the statistical spirit than
was Jefferson. If his mind was concerned with the most
elevated political and philosophical issues of the day, it
was also concerned with building a firm base of quantitative information upon which such concepts could rest.
While he appreciated poetry, architecture, and nature with
the most exquisite aesthetic perception, he could quickly
and willingly turn to the process of writing columns of
impersonal figures in his notebooks. If, as a scientist, he
sought knowledge through experiment, he looked for it
equally through observation and measurement of quantita-

33. Benjamin Rush, "Information to Europeans who are Disposed
to Migrate to the United States of America," *Essays, Literary, Moral
and Philosophical,* pp. 189–212.

tive information. In virtually every area of his interests, he exercised an almost compulsive instinct to keep records of data.[34]

Jefferson's knowledge of and interest in population matters came naturally with the amassing of his large library and his reading in the standard demographic works. Before 1776 he was familiar with Franklin's *Observations,* and in his Commonplace Book had copied passages on population from Montesquieu's *L'esprit des lois.* Within a few years he was well acquainted with works of such classical authors in the field as Petty, Halley, Derham, and DeMoivre, together with those of later writers like Buffon, Price, and Douglass.[35] His circle of American scientific colleagues, both within the American Philosophical Society and elsewhere, included many with demographic interests.

The *Notes on Virginia* came into existence essentially in response to a diplomatic need; it went on to serve a broader information role. Much as the English Board of Trade had done earlier, the French government, during the Revolution, made various attempts to obtain reliable information about America. Since Douglass's history (one of the most extensive published compendia) was by then over twenty-five years old, the French in 1780–81 sought up-to-date information from questionnaires which they sent to leading men in each state. Jefferson's reply for Virginia

34. See Edwin T. Martin, *Thomas Jefferson: Scientist* (New York: Henry Schuman, 1952), pp. 3–18.

35. See Joseph J. Spengler, "The Political Economy of Jefferson, Madison, and Adams," in David K. Jackson, ed., *American Studies in Honor of William Kenneth Boyd* (Durham, N. C.: Duke University Press, 1940), pp. 5 and 10; and E. Millicent Sowerby, *Catalogue of the Library of Thomas Jefferson,* 5 vols. (Washington, D. C.: Library of Congress, 1952–1959). See also Gilbert Chinard, ed., *The Commonplace Book of Thomas Jefferson* (Baltimore, Md.: Johns Hopkins Press, 1926), pp. 286–290.

incorporated data he had been keeping for years. As published, it became one of the best and most influential state studies of the day.[36] Few extensive surveys of Virginia had been published since Beverley's volume of 1705. Jefferson's *Notes*, like Beverley's work, included almost every sort of information: geographical, sociological, governmental. Whenever feasible and available, the information was given by number, size, amount, or other form of measurement or quantification. This included charts of such statistical information as river distances, comparative weights of the animals of Europe and America, amounts of government expenses and income, values and sizes of crops and exports, and temperatures for various seasons.

Jefferson marshaled an impressive amount of population data from a search both of earlier historical accounts and of public records. These included charts of colonial immigration, summaries of eight general censuses of the State of Virginia made between 1607 and 1628, and tables of nine censuses of tythes (free males and slaves over 16) taken between 1632 and 1772. He noted that before 1654 there had been sharp fluctuations in the state's population growth due to wars, periodic immigration waves, and epidemic disease mortality. After that time, he thought, growth rates were no longer affected by such sporadic events. From figures for the period between 1654 and 1772, Jefferson calculated that Virginia population had

36. See Brooke Hindle, *Pursuit of Science in Revolutionary America* (Chapel Hill: University of North Carolina Press, 1956), pp. 320–321. Jefferson also used the work to refute adverse European views about the American environment. For an extensive discussion of this intellectual dispute, see Gilbert Chinard, "Eighteenth Century Theories of America as a Human Habitat," American Philosophical Society, *Proceedings*, 91 (1947), 27–57.

doubled once every 27¼ years. Using this rate, he projected the population into the future for three doubling periods; he gave separate projections, one based on natural increase and the other on the basis of possible extra increase through immigration. If the rate continued, natural increase alone would bring Virginia from its half-million people of 1782 to about seven million in 95 years. This would be a density the same as Great Britain, 100 per square mile, and presumably more than the land could provide for, he thought.

It was a complex matter for Jefferson to obtain figures which approximated the Virginia population at the time he wrote his *Notes*. The state had been totally unable to manage a full census for the Continental Congress, and in an attempted count of 1782 eight counties failed to send in any returns at all. From a miscellany of incomplete tax returns, together with militia muster rolls and other data from previous years, Jefferson had to extrapolate to produce the estimated 567,614, separated by sex, age group, and color. He drew special attention to the 270,762 slaves who, he noted, were then in a ratio of 10 for every 11 free whites. However, "under the mild treatment our slaves experience, and their wholesome, though coarse, food, this blot in our country increases as fast, or faster, than the whites." He hoped that the recently passed laws prohibiting the slave trade would, at least in some measure, "stop the increase of this great political and moral evil, while the minds of our citizens may be ripening for a complete emancipation of human nature."

Unlike some of his contemporaries, Jefferson questioned the advisability of increasing the state's population by stimulating importation from abroad. Since most immigrants, he noted in 1782, came from absolute monarchies, they would adversely affect the newly free government and its legislation. "They will infuse into it their spirit, warp and bias its direction, and render it a heterogeneous, incoherent, distracted mass." He felt that the government and the country generally would be more homogeneous, more stable, and more durable with but few immigrants. "If they come of themselves, they are entitled to all the rights of citizenship; but I doubt the expediency of inviting them by extraordinary encouragements." [37]

Apart from the *Notes*, which dealt mainly with Virginia, Jefferson occasionally generalized during the period before his presidency upon the population of the United States as a whole. He was particularly interested in the westward migration. In 1786 he wrote:

We have lately seen a single person go and decide on a settlement in Kentucky, many hundred miles from any white inhabitant, remove thither with his family and a few neighbors; and though perpetually harassed by the Indians, that settlement in the course of ten years has acquired thirty thousand inhabitants.

Jefferson had as little doubt as Franklin, Stiles, or Rush, that these population pressures were virtually irresistible. He outlined their mechanisms in a well-known passage:

The present population of the inhabited parts of the United States is of about ten to the square mile; and experience has shown us, that wherever we reach that, the inhabitants become uneasy, as too much compressed, and so go off in great numbers to search for

37. Thomas Jefferson, *Notes on the State of Virginia* (Paris, 1784–85). See pp. 14, 62–69, 84–86, 136, 141, 151–163, 168–190, 305, and 315.

vacant country. Within forty years their whole territory will be peopled at that rate. We may fix that, then, as the term beyond which the people of those [Western] States will not be restricted within their present limits.[38]

As he contemplated these pressures during the 1780's, Jefferson was formulating his proposals for the social and political organization of the Northwest Territory, a vital step in the orderly accommodation of the large numbers of people going to that region. Given his keen realization of the statistics of American population increase, in 1803, when he was President, he welcomed the opportunity to acquire Louisiana at least partly in order to provide the extra room that would be needed.

Jefferson, Rush, and Coxe used demographic ideas and data for both political and patriotic as well as scientific purposes. Scholars in other states were no less motivated. New England, as usual, had several interested writers. Ezra Stiles, for instance, in a 1783 election sermon, resumed briefly some of the line of population speculation he had pursued earlier in his *Discourse on the Christian Union*. He now predicted great "secular glory" for the United States, with its favorable combination of free government, the true religion, industry, and rapidly increasing population. This nation might well within two or three hundred years, he thought, absorb the entire western hemisphere and reach a population of 300 million. And within a thousand years, the country seemed likely even to exceed China in population.[39]

38. Jefferson to M. de Meunier (1786) in Paul Leicester Ford, ed., *The Writings of Thomas Jefferson* (New York: Putnam's, 1892–1899), IV, 180, 181.

39. Ezra Stiles, *The United States Elevated to Glory and Honor*, pp. 8–10, 14–15, and 35–36.

Perhaps more important demographically in this period was Stiles's publication in 1787 of the vital statistics of New Haven for some thirty years. The vital records kept by the Reverend Chauncey Whittelsey at the First Church in New Haven between 1758 and 1787 had the good fortune of falling into Stiles's hands upon Whittelsey's death. Stiles analyzed these records, tabulated them, and included them, along with vital data of other New Haven churches, as a three-page appendix to his published funeral sermon for Whittelsey. The figures provided a statistical profile of the membership, baptisms, marriages, and deaths in the New Haven church community, separated as to sex and with deaths classified in five-year age groups as well as by causes.[40]

Still more extensive statistically was the Reverend Jeremy Belknap's *History of New Hampshire,* published between 1784 and 1791. Belknap's chapters were liberally illustrated with tables and other statistics of such matters as imports and exports, shipping, wildlife and trees, educational institutions, churches and clergy, taxes and government. He presented current population figures for all the towns of the state and resurrected the results of various colonial attempts to determine population, particularly the estimates of 1767, 1774, and 1775. On the basis of these estimates and others up to the census of 1790, he worked out the average increase and constructed a state population table for the years from 1767 to 1790. He found, much as Coxe had for other states, that, despite seven years of war and an estimated 1400 war deaths, the state's population had doubled in less than 19 years — to 142,018 in 1790.

Belknap also brought together an unusual collection of

40. Ezra Stiles, *A Funeral Sermon, Delivered Thursday, July 26, 1787* (New Haven, Ct.: T. & S. Green, 1787), pp. 35–37.

vital statistics. In his account of the presence of the "throat distemper" in New Hampshire, he reproduced considerable data from such sources as Fitch, Douglass, and the 1786 observations of Dr. Hall Jackson. In addition, following the example of Stiles, and with the aid of the New Hampshire clergy, he ferreted out what he could of the surviving vital records of the state's Congregational churches. The principal series of data which he found, and most of which covered several decades of baptisms and deaths, came from the churches of Dover, Hampton, Newmarket, East Kingston, Wilton, Conway, and Exeter. After tabulating and summarizing the records, he included them in his book essentially in the form of bills of mortality.[41]

Another New England writer of the time, cut out of much the same religious, cultural, and intellectual cloth as Belknap and Stiles, was Jedidiah Morse. Morse's famous work on American Geography has not a little in common with Belknap's history. What Belknap did to describe New Hampshire in words and figures, Morse attempted to do for all of the states. Although there were but two maps, Morse's work was indeed a geography which dealt extensively with such subjects as rivers, mountains, and other physical features, as well as raw materials, natural history, agriculture, and commerce. At the same time, it contained far more than we expect of a geography at the present day. Much like Belknap's work, it was also a compendium of all kinds of facts, current and historical, about the United States: government, churches, educational institutions, economy, and miscellaneous curiosities.

41. The records included those kept by the following preachers: Ward Cotton and Ebenezer Thayer (Hampton), John Moody (Newmarket), Belknap (Dover), Peter Coffin (East Kingston), Abel Fiske (Wilton), and Isaac Mansfield (Exeter). Belknap, *History of New Hampshire,* II and III, passim, but esp. II, 171–190.

Morse's demographic data were extensive in quantity, but they did not match Belknap's in depth. He drew from several good secondary works of the day. He included, for instance, long passages from Jefferson's *Notes on Virginia*, but he failed to find more than sketchy data for most other states. He included few vital statistics or bills of mortality. Morse included summaries of some of the past population estimates and censuses of the various states, though in some cases these were only the rough estimates given to the Continental Congress or the Constitutional Convention of 1787. While he had various current population figures, most of them quickly proved inadequate, since the national census occurred within two years after the book's appearance in 1789. (Later editions included a summary of the census as an Appendix.)

Morse nevertheless did not hesitate to venture some generalization about the population trends of the period. He aptly described New England as a "nursery of men," which annually was furnishing thousands to other areas. Much of New York's increase in the 1780's, he noted, was due to this migration. Despite the constant drain, New England, with a total population of around 823,000, remained the most populous part of the country; of its total, a fifth were fencible men. "Few countries on earth, of equal extent and population," Morse thought, "can furnish a more formidable army than this part of the union." Connecticut, he concluded, had been increasing despite war and emigration. On the other hand, he erroneously thought that fractious Rhode Island was declining in population in the wake of emigration following its widespread civil disturbances.

Like Coxe and Rush, Morse concluded that Pennsylvania was in an extremely favorable position due to its rapid population doubling, extensive immigration, available land, and good government. At the same time, he noted that Pennsylvania, as well as New Jersey and Maryland, was furnishing many emigrants to the western territories. Kentucky, which was receiving large numbers of these persons, though virtually uninhabited in 1780, by 1790 had accumulated more people than several older states. Such rapid growth "can scarcely be produced from the page of history." Morse considered such speed wholly desirable. Otherwise, he thought, people who were left widely dispersed in frontier areas tended to become unsocial, slovenly in dress, and generally indolent and lacking in spirit. Moreover, such growth hastened the fulfillment of America's natural destiny as a nation. To be sure, the estimate of Thomas Hutchins, Geographer of the United States, showed only a few thousand Whites at the time in the Northwest Territory. But Morse had little doubt that the territory would soon follow the pattern of Kentucky. And already American migrants were beginning to move on to New Madrid, in the Spanish territory opposite the mouth of the Ohio. Along with Stiles, Morse looked ahead to that "not far distant" period when all the great trans-Mississippi West would be part of the "American Empire." When this mighty territory was once peopled, then America would come into its own. For, "here the sciences, and the arts of civilized life are to receive their highest improvement." [42]

While Morse and other writers of the day mined the statistical, descriptive, and factual materials of the country, scholars in several places recognized the need to organize,

42. Jedidiah Morse, *The American Geography*, pp. 63, 144, 164, 171–173, 201, 218, 248–250, 284–285, 311–314, 346–352, 374–378, 406–408, 460, 468, and 536.

preserve, and take care of these accumulating records. Such concern, along with patriotic sentiment generally and increased interest in genealogy in particular, led in the post-Revolutionary period to the formation of state historical societies and related organizations.[43] Some historical writers, meanwhile, acknowledged the value of a systematic approach to the treatment of the large masses of materials. One, the Charleston physician and protégé of Rush, David Ramsay, even adopted a formal statistical methodology for his historical work. This, he asserted, was adapted from a contemporary English model: "I have followed Dr. John SinClair's [sic] Statistic account of Scotland in a great measure or rather I have grafted Statistics on history. I endeavored to make both subservient to the cause of virtue and human happiness." [44]

The increasingly systematic activity of the scholars, and the organization of the historical societies, were parts of a general post-Revolutionary intellectual quickening. Writers like Coxe could send their articles to an increasing

43. In Boston, for instance, since part of Thomas Prince's great collection of books, manuscripts, and notes had been destroyed in a fire at the Old South Church, Belknap became increasingly concerned for the preservation of his own valuable materials. His concern was a prominent factor in the founding of the Massachusetts Historical Society in 1792.

44. Ramsay to John Coakley Lettsom, in Brunhouse, ed., *David Ramsay*, p. 163. Sinclair's work, *The Statistical Account of Scotland . . .* , which was published in 21 volumes at Edinburgh between 1791 and 1799, is usually credited with introducing the word "statistics" into English usage. Among Ramsay's writings was a life of Washington, together with histories of the Revolution, of South Carolina, and of the United States. In the population chapter in his *History of South Carolina* (1809), Ramsay discussed the contributions to South Carolina which had been made by the Scots, Irish, Swiss, Germans, Dutch, and New Englanders, but made no reference at all to the Negro slaves in the state. This was not unusual with writers of the day. See Jordan, *White Over Black*, p. 340.

number of journals or papers. In Philadelphia, for instance, Mathew Carey's *American Museum* during the 1790's published a number of articles dealing with population matters.[45] Scientific societies also emerged or found new life. Several of the important ones devoted considerable attention to the vital statistics and population trends of the country. The American Philosophical Society, it is true, in 1774 had agreed that questions from the Abbé Raynal of France with respect to colonial commerce, wealth, and population "were not proper objects of the Society's enquiries."[46] But, in the postwar period, demographic matters were of concern to a sizable group of the members, from Franklin, Rush, and Morgan, to Jefferson, John Foulke, and William Barton. Barton was only one of several in the group who not only hoped but expected that independence would bring improvement in the vital statistics of the country:

> It is greatly to be wished that the several religious denominations of Christians, throughout the United States, at least in our considerable towns and well-settled parts of the country — would be at the pains of obtaining and publishing, every year, lists of the births and deaths in their respective parishes or congregations; together with the proportion of the sexes in each list, the ages of the deceased, their diseases, and the numbers dying in each month. The number of marriages should also be added: and it would, moreover, be useful to notice in what instances those

45. See discussion in J. J. Spengler, "Malthusianism in Late Eighteenth-Century America," *American Economic Review*, 25 (1935), pp. 699–701.
46. American Philosophical Society, *Proceedings*, 22, pt. 3 (1885), Condensed Minutes of Dec. 30, 1774, p. 93.

dying after eighty years of age were foreigners. But a laudable spirit of inquiry is gaining ground among us, so fast, that there is reason to expect the introduction of great regularity and precision in such arrangements, in the several departments of our public economy, as may lead to further attainments in useful knowledge, and particularly to improvements in this branch of science.[47]

In New Haven, the new County Medical Society itself undertook for several years the task of drawing together the records of births, marriages, and deaths in the community. It was soon apparent that the physicians required the cooperation of the clergy in this task. In 1788, therefore, the Society asked the county ministers "to give us a quarterly list of deaths in their several societies, with the disease." [48] No substantial data resulted from this relationship.

The American Academy of Arts and Sciences had a far more elaborate program than any of the other societies, to reform the vital statistics of the entire state of Massachusetts. The Academy was statistically minded from the very first. The invited European membership included some of the leading contributors of the day to vital statistics theory and practice — men like Price of England,

47. William Barton, *Observations on the Progress of Population and the Probabilities of the Duration of Human Life, in the United States of America* (Philadelphia: R. Aitken & Son, 1791), p. 3.

48. Quoted in Ira V. Hiscock, "The Background of Public Health in Connecticut," Thoms, *Heritage of Connecticut Medicine,* p. 141. Among other medical societies which interested themselves at this time in vital statistics registration was the Medical Society of South Carolina. (See below, Chapter XI.) For discussion of the growth of scientific and medical societies during this period, see Hindle, *Pursuit of Science,* pp. 111–113 and 290–295.

Buffon and D'Alembert of France, and Wargentin of Sweden. The American membership included professors, clergy, and physicians who were proven enthusiasts of the statistical approach, men like Wigglesworth, Stiles, Belknap, and Benjamin Gale.

Among the Americans, the one who best saw what was needed to be done for vital statistics in Massachusetts was Dr. Edward Holyoke of Salem. Although some of the clerks and churchmen of the state were still gathering various kinds of vital data, Holyoke knew that what they had was of little value for scientific and medical purposes so long as it remained dispersed, unrelated, and undigested. It was apparent that physicians and scientists had to interest themselves more actively in the registration process if they were to obtain worthwhile data. Holyoke thus published, in the first volume of the Academy's *Memoirs,* his own vital statistics report for Salem, to illustrate what could be done in one community. It was not, he showed, an easy or clear-cut procedure. To estimate the town's population, he obtained the number of "rateable polls" — males over 16 — from the Town Assessor's list. He obtained lists of marriages by canvassing the local clergy and justices of the peace. The total mortality of Salem was complete, he thought, since he had kept that record himself. But the lists of births and causes of death, he acknowledged, were uncertain:

> . . . the best account I could procure of the disease is sometimes taken from the sextons, the reports of nurses or persons about the sick . . . As to the *births,* I believe the account is as compleat as can be expected, considering from whom we are obliged to collect the greatest part of it; and, I suppose, approaches much

nearer to the number of persons actually born, than accounts of christenings ever can, in any country where there is a general religious toleration; indeed, in a town where there are various religious sects, some of which never administer baptism at all, and others, which never administer it but to adults, which is our case, births can never be tolerably guessed at from an account of christenings.[49]

Impressed by Holyoke's demonstration for Salem, the members of the Academy wondered if similar data could not be drawn together regularly from all the towns of Massachusetts. A committee, including Wigglesworth, the Reverend Manasseh Cutler of Ipswich, and three others, was appointed to find out. Taking the direct approach, the committee in November 1785 sent a circular request to all Massachusetts physicians and ministers. The broadside explained the aims and purposes as follows:

The American Academy of Arts and Sciences, apprehending that useful and important information may be obtained, by collecting regular and uniform Bills of Mortality from the several Towns within this Commonwealth, have directed that a form for such Bills be transmitted to the towns and parishes within the same; and that the several Ministers and Physicians be solicited to attend to this subject, and favour the Academy with annual returns. For by a regular return of such Bills for the course of a few years, the rate of our population may be determined; the present value

49. Edward Augustus Holyoke, "A Bill of Mortality for the Town of Salem, for the Year 1782," *Memoirs of the American Academy of Arts and Sciences*, I (1785), 546–550.

of estates, holden for life, or in reversion, ascertained; and a natural history of the diseases incidental to our climate, compiled.

Going on, the broadside spelled out the specific information that the committee desired: population totals by sex and different age groups, as well as the numbers of families and houses, were to be furnished every five years; births, marriages, deaths, and numbers of immigrants and emigrants, should be returned each year. Data on deaths were to be given by age groups, sexes, months of the year, and in accordance with a list of nearly seventy well-defined diseases or other causes. Correspondents were also asked to furnish topographical descriptions of their towns and parishes.[50]

This ambitious scheme did about as well as could have been expected, considering that it depended upon voluntary returns from a heterogeneous, loosely organized body of contributors. Actually, a substantial number of persons submitted some kind of material during the several years following the appeal, though few were able to comply with all of the desires of the Academy. Some of the fuller reports were published individually in the *Memoirs* of the Academy; others appeared in *The Massachusetts Centinel* and other Boston periodicals. Those obtained in any one year, however, never covered the whole state.[51]

50. "Sir, The American Academy of Arts and Sciences . . .", broadside of the American Academy of Arts and Sciences (Boston: S. Hall, Nov. 10, 1785).

51. Wigglesworth subsequently used 62 of the reports, for Massachusetts and New Hampshire communities, in his analysis of life expectancies (see next chapter). For further discussion of this aspect of the Academy's work, see John B. Blake, "The Early History of Vital Statistics in Massachusetts," *Bulletin of the History of Medicine*, 29 (1955), 46–68.

Within a few years the Academy's project had been given up. This left the vital statistics of Massachusetts just about where they had been before. For the City of Boston, in fact, the reform effort hardly seemed to have made any difference. A wistful observer in 1795 wrote the following plea to his neighbors in the hope that the city could at least get back to its earlier statistical practices:

It is to be sincerely regretted that no regular account is kept of births and burials; nor has been, since the revolution. Every child born, ought to have its name entered in the office of the town clerk: And as we have a census of the inhabitants, it would be an easy matter for a person of leisure to observe how many burials there are. The keepers of the several burial places might give an account, once a week, to the printers, as they did formerly. Would it not be worth while for some young printer to engage to publish accordingly? There are a number of the inhabitants would engage to encourage the paper of this very account.[52]

Obviously, more than abstract scientific interest or civic responsibility was needed to bring about any marked measure of change or improvement in the quality of vital statistics, either in Massachusetts or elsewhere. In America at the end of the eighteenth century too many people still shared the doubt that vital statistics had any immediate utility for the community. This doubt began to dissipate

52. "Account of Burials and Baptisms in Boston, from the Year 1701 to 1774," Massachusetts Historical Society, *Collections*, ser. 1, 4 (1795), p. 216.

only when communities had to mobilize to fight repeated onslaughts of new epidemic diseases.[53]

Meanwhile, although none of the scientific societies got far at that time with their hoped-for reforms of vital statistics registration, their efforts were not wasted. The attempts served admirably to focus the postwar attention of a variety of scholars increasingly upon some of the scientific aspects of vital statistics and population data. Of these, none provided a more fertile ground, both for practical application and for speculation, than those relating to the length and probabilities of human life.

53. See below, Chapter XI.

Chapter X

Length of Human Life in the Garden

Few scientific questions were pursued so intently or success-fully in America during the last quarter of the eighteenth century as those having to do with the probable duration of life. Even earlier humanitarian concerns for this matter, along with the steady accrual of scientific knowledge in Europe and the increasing accumulation of domestic mortality data, made it possible for actuarial science gradually to take root in simple American life insurance ventures which at first were practically untainted by commercial motivations. This same combination of circumstances encouraged investigations into the expectancies of life and the facts about longevity in the American environment.[1]

1. Professor Gilbert Chinard used some of the sources for this chapter and the next in his long discussion of eighteenth-century ideas about America as a human habitat. His article should be read in its entirety to appreciate the extent to which demographic data were utilized in that extended philosophical argument, both by Europeans and by Americans. Chinard, "Eighteenth Century Theories of America as a Human Habitat," *American Philosophical Society, Proceedings,* 91 (1947), 27–57.

As these expectancies became known, political leaders and patriots as well as scientists found uses for them in the service of the newly independent nation. Mathematical analyses of mortality data by Halley, De Moivre, and a few others made scientifically based life insurance and annuities possible in England early in the eighteenth century. Actual establishment was quite another thing. Speculators with an eye to quick profits were not the ones to introduce scientific principles into their companies. Humanitarians floundered in ignorance or mistakes before their many mutual benefit societies and annuities schemes began to hold out more promise of good than of bad. Although there were some who realized at least part of what was involved in sound insurance, little progress toward this occurred until after the laborious scientific work and exposés of Price in the 1770's. Meanwhile, the concept of life insurance and annuities passed to the American colonies, though it took root there somewhat more slowly than in the mother country.

The young Franklin, stimulated in part by reading Cotton Mather's *Bonifacius: An Essay Upon the Good,* and partly by other Enlightenment authors, developed an early interest in mutual benefit societies.[2] In 1722, writing in his brother's newspaper, *The New England Courant,* he attempted to bring one such humanitarian proposal to the attention of Americans. There, as part of his "Silence Do-Good" series, he reprinted a long passage from Daniel Defoe's 1697 *Essay on Projects,* in which the latter proposed a "Pension Office" for the poor. Franklin was impressed with its provisions of "Ensurance for Widows," because, like Mather, he knew well their "lamentable condition" in New England. In 1722 it appeared that America was

2. *Bonifacius* was published in Boston in 1710.

already "ripe for many such *Friendly Societies*" as Defoe had described. Franklin thought that the clergy in particular had an urgent need for such an arrangement.[3] The clergy clearly agreed with Franklin. Charitable organizations of various kinds had already appeared in some of the American colonies when Franklin wrote, and others followed soon. Some of these were designed for the clergy. The Presbyterian Synod of Philadelphia in 1717 established its Fund for Pious Uses, which served not only to aid missionaries and new churches, but to help ministers in distressed circumstances. The Convention of the Congregational Ministers in Massachusetts was extending similar help by the 1740's. Other American groups which existed by the 1760's included the Society for the Relief of Poor and Distressed Masters of Ships, Their Widows, and Children (1765), and the Deutsche Gesellschaft von Pennsylvanien, established in 1764 for needy, newly-arrived Palatines.[4]

Insurance enterprises also began appearing in the colon-

3. Quoted by Benjamin Franklin, in "Silence Do-Good, No. 10," *The New England Courant*, Aug. 13, 1722, *Papers of Benjamin Franklin*, ed. Labaree, I, 32–36. Franklin observed that soldiers and sailors would not be covered in Defoe's plan, "because the Contingencies of their Lives are not equal to others." Franklin's interest in insurance was long-lasting. During the 1770's he was reading life insurance proposals of such writers as Francis Maseres, the English mathematician and historian, and suggesting to Price an annuities plan for "old-age housing for the industrious poor, like that he had admired in the Netherlands." Crane, "Club of Honest Whigs," *William and Mary Quarterly*, 3rd ser., 23 (1966), p. 224. He was also involved in a Philadelphia fire insurance company. Carey, *Franklin's Economic Views*, pp. 100–105.

4. Alexander Mackie, *Facile Princeps: The Story of the Beginning of Life Insurance in America* (Lancaster, Pa.: Lancaster Press Inc., 1956), pp. 66 and 120; and Carl Bridenbaugh, *Cities in Revolt* (New York: Knopf, 1955), passim.

ies by the 1720's. During that decade, general insurance brokerage offices were established in Philadelphia, Boston, and New York. Most of the colonial business of such firms was in marine insurance, although some fire insurance was underwritten. The public life insurance that was sold in the eighteenth century was small in amount, although marine policies sometimes covered sea captains or individual passengers for given trips.[5] Lives of slaves, each one a valuable property, were sometimes insured. Some medical practitioners, moreover, found it expedient to insure the slaves whom they inoculated.[6]

The substantial beginnings of life insurance in America, however, were not made by profit-seekers or brokers in the coffeehouses of New York, Philadelphia, or Boston. They resulted from the hard-nosed but humane works of church leaders — ministers and elders — seeking to make some minimal arrangements for their own people in a

5. For further details on the development of life insurance, see John Gudmundsen, *The Great Provider, The Dramatic Story of Life Insurance in America* (South Norwalk, Ct.: Industrial Publications Co., 1959); Charles Kelley Knight, *The History of Life Insurance in the United States to 1870* (Philadelphia: University of Pennsylvania, 1920); John A. Fowler, *History of Insurance in Philadelphia for Two Centuries, 1683–1882* (Philadelphia: Review Publishing and Printing Co., 1888); and J. Owen Stalson, *Marketing Life Insurance, Its History in America* (Cambridge, Mass.: Harvard University Press, 1942).

6. Inoculators in Annapolis and Charlestown, S. C., for instance, during the 1760's and 1770's were insuring at a rate of five percent of the value of the slave. See Guerra, *American Medical Bibliography*, pp. 522, 613, 663, and 679, for citations from various local newspapers. Franklin cited insurance among the more or less standard expenses of slave labor: "Reckon then the interest of the first purchase of a slave, the Insurance or risque on his life, his cloathing and diet, expenses in his sickness and loss of time, loss by his neglect of business." Franklin, *Observations Concerning the Increase of Mankind,* p. 5.

cold world. Like most similar British associations of the day, the enterprises they founded could not claim to have a fully reliable scientific grounding. They did try, however, to achieve soundness by judiciously empirical practices.

The first of these church-related insurance societies came into being in 1759 as an outgrowth of the Presbyterian Fund for Pious Uses. This was the Presbyterian Ministers Fund (its full name, the Corporation for the Relief of Poor and Distressed Widows and Children of Presbyterian Ministers). The Fund followed closely what was the only reliable model in Great Britain, the Widows Fund of the Church of Scotland. The latter had been established in 1744 using Halley's table of life expectancies as its essential base of calculations. Its founding and subsequent record of stability and success, in an era of excesses and failures, was due to the scientific and businesslike guidance of the Edinburgh minister, Alexander Webster.[7]

The Philadelphia Presbyterians who initiated and administered the new American fund managed — by good sense, care, and luck — to achieve a success comparable to that of their Scottish colleagues. Of the initiators, the principal organizer and first president as well as de facto actuary, was the Reverend Francis Alison. Alison was not a mathematician, but he was well read in the sciences and carefully studied various of the mathematical and demographic works upon which life insurance depended. The pastor John Ewing, on the other hand, who helped and then succeeded Alison in doing the actuarial work, was

7. Despite earlier skepticism, Richard Price, in the third edition of his *Observations on Reversionary Payments,* changed his mind and singled out the Scottish plan as virtually the only British annuities or life insurance scheme that was worthy of praise.

well known for his competence in mathematics, surveying, and astronomy. During the years of their leadership, the Fund continued to operate upon a base of Scottish mortality experience. This probably did not represent any special lack of faith in American mortality data; rather, it constituted a conservative reliance upon data which had been well tested and which turned out to be reasonably relevant to Presbyterian clergymen who happened to be in the environment of colonial America.[8]

Ten years after the Presbyterian Ministers' Fund began, Anglicans of Pennsylvania, New York, and New Jersey established their own similar organization. The Reverend William Smith, provost of the College of Philadelphia, was the prime mover of the Anglican fund, mainly due to his close relations with Alison, who was Vice-Provost of the College. Alison shared with Smith his books on actuarial matters as well as the records of the Presbyterian Fund's experience. In England, Franklin sought out Price's evaluation of the new fund. Price advised that the scheme and its rates would be adequate "if the experience of the Corporation should happen to conform to that of the ministers in Scotland, and if interest be taken at six per cent." [9] Like the Presbyterians, the Anglicans took some chances in using a Scottish rather than American base of mortality data, but the fund appeared to work out satisfactorily until it was disrupted by the Revolution and by the exile of many of its participants.[10]

The Congregational ministers of New England, in contrast to the Philadelphia Presbyterians and Anglicans, were

8. For details about the history of the Fund, see Mackie, *Facile Princeps.*
9. Quoted in Knight, *History of Life Insurance*, p. 63.
10. See Mackie, *Facile Princeps*, pp. 127–130.

unable to establish an annuities plan. This was not for lack of interest, effort, or scientific knowledge. True, when Price in 1772 sent a copy of his *Observations on Reversionary Payments* to the Reverend Charles Chauncy of Boston, the book fell into unprepared hands. Chauncy admitted that he was not a good judge of the work, since he had not previously given any thought to such subjects. He passed the book on, however, to Harvard Mathematics Professor John Winthrop, "who red [sic] it with pleasure" and expressed great admiration for the author.[11]

The life insurance interests of William Gordon, pastor at the Third Church, Roxbury, were of a more active sort. In 1772 Gordon published the earliest substantial treatise on life insurance to be issued in America, only a year after Price's *Observations* and based directly upon that work. This was his *Plan of a Society for Making Provision for Widows, by Annuities for the remainder of Life; and for granting Annuities to Persons after certain Ages.*[12] In the hope of "contributing my mite towards the happiness of the Colonists," Gordon proposed establishment of a general annuities society open to persons from several colonies, so far as their life expectancies were compatible. He was confident that if Price's rules were carefully followed, such a society could be established without the help of an

11. Chauncy to Price, Oct. 5, 1772, *Letters to and From Richard Price, D.D., F.R.S.* (Cambridge, Mass.: John Wilson & Son, Harvard University, 1903), p. 6.

12. Boston: Joseph Edwards and John Fleeming, 1772. Gordon acknowledged three sources for his pamphlet: 1) Price's *Observations*; 2) The Constitution of the London Annuity Society, established in 1765; and 3) an abstract of the Deed of Settlement of the Laudable Society for the Benefit of Widows, established in 1761 in England. He used the latter two as models for the details of operating and governing his Society; Price was his scientific authority.

able mathematician.[13] His own tabular material followed Price's use both of Halley's data and of De Moivre's hypothesis for calculating life probabilities. Although he did not attempt to draw up a table of life probabilities for the colonies themselves, he commented on some of the factors which would affect such a table. With the aid of Massachusetts census data of 1764, he asserted that differences between colonial males and females in natural life expectancy were not real but only apparent, since neither the thousands of men lost in the French wars nor those absent on merchant ships at sea were accounted for. He also pointed out the scientific inadequacies of baptism figures.[14]

Although Gordon's proposed society of from 40 to 2000 persons was not necessarily to be church-run, it might well have formed the basis for a Congregational ministers' fund. As it happened, the Revolution intervened and the Boston Congregational community did not adopt any scheme for several years. Nor was it ready to entrust leadership of any such enterprise to Gordon, who was considered somewhat unstable and disputatious.[15]

A man who did enjoy the necessary community confidence was Edward Wigglesworth, orthodox scion of a well-known and orthodox Massachusetts family. Probably as well qualified as Gordon, Wigglesworth had attained, through his prewar *Calculations on American Population,*

13. Price himself was ambiguous on this point. At one place in his book Price stressed the necessity of having a good mathematician, while a few pages later he made the point which Gordon grasped. Gordon, *Plan of a Society,* p. iii.

14. *Ibid.,* especially Preface, pp. i–vi and 27–35.

15. Mackie, *Facile Princeps,* pp. 124–126; and Fowler, *History of Insurance in Philadelphia,* p. 612n. There is a fairly substantial biography of Gordon in Clifton K. Shipton, *Sibley's Harvard Graduates* (Boston: Massachusetts Historical Society, 1965), XIII, 60–85. See also *Dictionary of National Biography,* XXII, 235.

at least a local reputation for his knowledge of demography and vital statistics.[16] There is no doubt that his continuing interests in these matters played a leading part in bringing the American Academy of Arts and Sciences to turn a good share of its early attention to vital statistics. It is a question, however, whether the Academy would have pursued its vital statistics campaign so vigorously, or indeed at all, had it not been for the simultaneous post-Revolutionary development of an annuities plan among the members of the Congregational clergy. Not surprisingly, since Wigglesworth played a key role in this latter plan as well as in the Academy's campaign, the two projects were closely connected. The AAAS questionnaire was undoubtedly designed as much to obtain vital data for the proposed annuities fund as for any other purpose.

Proposals for a Congregational annuities plan to benefit the Massachusetts clergy, the Harvard faculty, and the widows of each, took concrete form in 1785 at the time the Massachusetts Congregational Charitable Society finally secured a charter of incorporation. The committee which the Society chose to look into such a plan was composed of Joseph Willard, President of Harvard, Judge James Sullivan, and Wigglesworth, who carried the whole matter along, at least in its scientific aspects.

Wigglesworth was convinced that Americans could not rely upon European tables of life probabilities to form the basis of domestic life insurance, and that they must

16. The Reverend James Freeman of Boston, for instance, in 1792 drew extensively from Wigglesworth's *Calculations* in criticizing Belknap's tabular projection of New Hampshire population, though Freeman himself thought that American population was doubling closer to every 21 years than to Wigglesworth's figure of 25. See Freeman to Belknap, in Belknap, *History of New Hampshire*, III, App. 33, pp. 344–354.

construct their own tables from the records of American experience. Stiles, to be sure, had written to Gordon that any such effort "would require more complete records of births and deaths than New England had been accustomed to keep." [17] But Wigglesworth thought there was a possibility that such records existed if they could but be located. By way of illustrating his argument, in the first volume of *Memoirs* of the AAAS, he described two excellent collections of such records kept by Massachusetts clergymen. One included the records of births and deaths kept in the parish of Ipswich between September 1771 and September 1781 by its preacher, Manasseh Cutler. The other bill was constructed from the records of baptisms, marriages, and burials kept in Hingham between 1726 and 1779 by the Reverend Ebenezer Gay. Wigglesworth thought that Gay's extraordinary registers would be useful in constructing a life expectancy table for New England. Cutler's data, though covering a shorter period, served to illustrate the inappropriateness of relying upon the European data in American actuarial or demographic calculations. According to the Breslau data which Halley had used, 5 out of 12 children died before the age of five, while 1 out of 30 persons lived to the age of eighty. In Ipswich, by contrast, only 6 out of 33 were found to die before five, while 1 out of every 8 lived to be eighty.

Interesting as these comparisons were, Wigglesworth realized that the isolated experience of only two parishes was by no means broad enough to construct a reliable American life table. "This can only be done by keeping regular bills of mortality, and comparing them together, and making proper deductions from their joint result." Hence, Wigglesworth's personal appeal to readers of the

17. Cited in Kraus, *The Atlantic Civilization*, p. 139.

Memoirs to send in copies of their registers or bills of mortality. And hence his great interest in the results of the AAAS questionnaire.[18]

Meanwhile, until data for an American life table could be accumulated, it was necessary for Wigglesworth (like Alison twenty-five years earlier) to settle upon the most nearly comparable European experience as a foundation for the Congregational Fund. Price's *Observations* served as Wigglesworth's guide to most of the technical questions on this. When that volume failed to reveal the full answer, the New Englander worked out tentative solutions and then wrote Price for an opinion.

To determine a basis of comparability of the New England clergy's life experience with that of Europe, it seemed natural in 1785 to fall back upon the talent and record of Harvard itself. Wigglesworth suspected that the mortality and life expectancy of ministers and college professors might differ appreciably from that of the general populace, but he found no tabular data in Price's book to verify this. Since data on local ministers themselves were equally unavailable, he turned, for an alternative, to the published catalog of Harvard graduates of the period 1711 through 1784, and to the register of University admissions from 1775 to 1781. From these sources he determined mathematically the mean ages and then the life expectancies of the graduates at various ages. Comparing his figures with general life expectancy calculations in Price, Wigglesworth concluded that Harvard graduates — and by extension, Congregational ministers and the Harvard faculty — did

18. Edward Wigglesworth, "Observations on the Longevity of the Inhabitants of Ipswich and Hingham, and Proposals for Ascertaining the Value of Estates held for Life and the Reversion of Them," *Memoirs of the American Academy of Arts and Sciences*, I (Boston: Adams & Nourse, 1785), 565–568.

have markedly greater expectation of life than ordinary mortals. Accordingly, the most nearly comparable European life experience to that of the Harvard graduates, he thought, was that of Sweden.[19]

Price responded quickly and sympathetically to questions which Wigglesworth and Willard wrote him upon these matters. He confirmed Wigglesworth's assumption as to the higher life expectancy of the clergy. He likewise agreed as to the wisdom of using the Swedish life tables at the beginning, and he went on to suggest various other elements which might be incorporated into the annuities plan, including an interest rate of 6 percent in place of the 4 percent common in England.

The committee adopted virtually all of Price's recommendations in the annuities plan which it recommended to the trustees of the Massachusetts Congregational Charitable Society. The latter, in turn, voted to adopt the plan as soon as fifty subscribers were obtained. This turned out, in the unsettled economic conditions of the mid-1780's, to be a more difficult matter than it had been before the Revolution for the Presbyterian and Episcopal funds. Recruiting of subscribers was further complicated by disagreements over certain procedural details. In consequence, despite the careful scientific preparations, the activation of the fund was delayed and finally the plan was given up entirely.[20]

19. Edward Wigglesworth to Joseph Willard, Oct. 6, 1785, in *Letters to and from Richard Price*, pp. 71–75.

20. Wigglesworth to Price, July 27, 1786, and Willard to Price, July 29, 1786, both in *Letters to and from Richard Price*, pp. 86–89. See also Cone, *Torchbearer of Freedom*, passim; and Mackie, *Facile Princeps*, pp. 120–124. This failure, along with Wigglesworth's death in 1794, eliminated one of the chief motivations for continued collection of vital data from New England ministers and physicians.

In the meantime, by 1789 a sizable number of replies to the AAAS vital statistics questionnaire had arrived from Massachusetts and New Hampshire communities. Wigglesworth in that year began to collate and study the varied data. Although relatively few of the sixty-two bills covered long or strictly compatible periods of time, the total collection proved fairly representative of the area of the two states. Wigglesworth was confident that the data provided an accurate view of the rate of population doubling, that is, every 25.3 years, and virtually all of it by natural increase.

With this substantial cross section of the New England mortality experience, Wigglesworth went on to prepare a native life probability table, the first in America for a general population. Published subsequently in the AAAS *Memoirs* of 1793, the table served various uses — legal, actuarial, and eventually, sanitary — in Massachusetts for many years.[21] Soon after its preparation, however, Wigglesworth himself suffered a disabling stroke (1791) and died in 1794. What hopes still lingered of launching the Con-

21. Edward Wigglesworth, "A Table showing the Probability of the Duration, the Decrement, and the Expectation of Life, in the States of Massachusetts and New-Hampshire, formed from sixty-two Bills of Mortality on the files of the American Academy of Arts and Sciences, in the year 1789," AAAS, *Memoirs,* II, pts. 1 and 2 (Boston, 1793), pp. 131–135. See also Knight, *History of Life Insurance,* passim.

Despite Wigglesworth's care, certain shortcomings were discovered by the mid-nineteenth century. Among these, "Allowance was not made for the fact that the population had been rapidly increasing, and the table was framed on the assumption that it had been stationary." E. B. Elliot, "On the Law of Human Mortality that Appears to Obtain in Massachusetts, with Tables of Practical Value Deduced Therefrom," *Proceedings,* American Association for the Advancement of Science, 11 (1858), 53n.

gregational Widows fund seem to have died with him.[22] In the brief remarks which accompanied his Life Table, Wigglesworth expressed the hope that bills of mortality comparable in accuracy to those of Massachusetts towns and parishes could be kept in other states. They obviously would be useful to investigators in preparing life expectancy tables for other sections of the country. They would, moreover, "afford entertainment to persons of a philosophical disposition, both in Europe and America." [23]

During the post-Revolutionary decades, Philadelphia was about the only other American community in a position to provide either the vital data or the talent for constructing native life tables.[24] None of its insurance enterprises, however, attempted to do this until the early nineteenth century.[25] To be sure, Mathematics Professor Robert Patterson of the University of Pennsylvania helped the Presbyterian Ministers' Fund overhaul its procedures in the 1790's by working out a revised premium schedule in keeping with Price's principles. Nevertheless, outside the ministers' funds, there was still little American interest in life insurance and few Americans purchased commercial policies. Out of 24 insurance companies chartered in the

22. Wigglesworth merits further scholarly attention. For brief biographical details, see article in *Dictionary of American Biography,* XX (New York: Scribner's, 1936), pp. 192–193.

23. Wigglesworth, "A Table Showing the Probability," AAAS, *Memoirs,* II (1793), p. 135.

24. In New Haven, Stiles might have done so had he found enough adequate registers and had he not by then had the responsibility of running Yale College.

25. The Pennsylvania Company for Insurances on Lives and Granting Annuities prepared a life table, after its founding in 1809, in which the data of the Christ-Church Parish bills of mortality were used in conjunction with those of Wigglesworth's table and Price's standard Northampton Table. Fowler, *History of Insurance in Philadelphia,* pp. 627ff.

United States between 1790 and 1800, only one wrote any life insurance. And that one, the Insurance Company of North America in Philadelphia (established 1792), issued only a few policies. As a rule, most life insurance was still purchased from English firms, and then only on special occasions and after special negotiation.[26] The trip of Houdon to the United States provides an example.

In Paris in mid-1785, Jefferson, acting for the State of Virginia, had engaged the famous sculptor to make a statue of Washington. Because of the substantial funds which had been committed, Jefferson decided to insure Houdon's life when the latter went to America that same summer. Adams, whom Jefferson asked to inquire in London about insurance, in turn brought in Price. In early August, Adams wrote that the insurance would run about five percent, "two for the Life and three for the Voyage," but that Price would try to get it for less. Jefferson told Adams to go ahead and obtain a six-month policy to cover Houdon during the round trip. In late September, Jefferson, by then quite uneasy since Houdon already was on the high seas, wrote for news about the policy. A leisurely two weeks later, Adams replied that Price had forgotten all about the matter. Now, wrote Adams, "I am afraid that Certificates of Heudon's [sic] State of Health will be required, and the Noise of Algerine Captures may startle the Insurers. The Doctor However will get it done if he can." About October 19 Price finally persuaded the Equitable Society, which he himself had built into England's most reliable firm, into underwriting the insurance, and Adams paid the premium. Adams finally sent the policy on

26. For further details on insurance developments of this period, see Gudmundsen, *The Great Provider,* pp. 1–30, passim; and Mackie, *Facile Princeps,* passim.

to Jefferson on October 24, over three weeks after Houdon's arrival at Mount Vernon.[27]

Price's favor to Adams was only one of the continuing services, direct and indirect, that the former performed for America and Americans. Few Englishmen were spoken about so often and in such complimentary terms in America during the 1780's as was Price. In New Haven, Yale College awarded Price and Washington honorary degrees at the same ceremony in 1783. In the Continental Congress, Price's work and authority were cited in the debates over the claims for overdue pay and bonuses of Revolutionary officers. Hamilton, Madison, and James Rutledge, who composed the subcommittee to deal with the officers' petition, were in full agreement that a formula should be worked out "in conformity to tables of Dr. Price, estimating the officers on the average of good lives." [28]

Again, Price's influence was strong in the congressional debates of 1790 and 1791 over the questions of the public credit and federal assumption of state debts. Hamilton's notable "Report on Public Credit" owed much to various writers or precedents; but to none did it owe more than to the British sinking fund which William Pitt established in 1786 upon Price's suggestion. The mechanics of the annuities plans which Hamilton proposed as means of paying off the assumed debts, moreover, almost certainly came more or less directly from Price. Hamilton put his technical discussion of the debt refunding and assumption upon a standard actuarial basis. He argued, from the one side, that "the capital of the debt of the United States,

27. This episode is described in Jefferson's correspondence with John and Abigail Adams, August to October 1785. See Boyd, *Papers of Thomas Jefferson*, VIII, xxiii, 340, 577, 653, and 663–664.

28. "Report on Army Memorial, Continental Congress," Jan. 22, 1783, Syrett, *Papers of Hamilton*, III, 245 n. 6.

may be considered in the light of an annuity at the rate of six percent. per annum, redeemable at the pleasure of the government, by payment of the principal." On the other side, he spelled out the advantages which the various deferred annuities in his plan would offer "for securing a comfortable provision for the evening of life, or for wives who survive their husbands." The strength of his plan, and the carefully drawn-up statistical tables that Hamilton presented in support of his concepts showed that he had by no means halted his study of demography and life probabilities with the few extracts he had found in Postlethwayt. His tables included his

Schedule F. Table Shewing the Annuity which a person of a given age would be entitled to during life, from the time he should arrive at a given age, upon the present payment of a hundred dollars, computing interest at four percent;

and his

Schedule G. Table Shewing what Annuity would be enjoyed by the survivor of any two persons of certain ages, for the remainder of life, after the determination of the life in expectation, upon the present payment of one hundred dollars, computing interest at four percent. per annum, and the duration of life according to Doctor Halley's Tables.[29]

When the bill was finally passed, the federal government acquired a direct financial involvement in the longevity of its citizens. The doctrine of probabilities applied to

29. Hamilton, "Report on Public Credit," *Papers of Hamilton*, VI, 84–127.

annuities thus was well established in the United States before 1800, both in private and public ventures.

While Hamilton was preparing life probability figures for service in the cause of national fiscal stability, Jefferson was using them to assert an essentially contrary point of democratic principle. Jefferson might well have inquired into the probabilities involved in decisions of representative governments. But Condorcet had already produced, in 1785, his exhaustive mathematical examination of this matter, his *Essai sur l'application de l'analyse à la Probabilité des décisions rendues à la pluralité des voix*.[30] Instead, Jefferson had a concern of a different order. In a letter from Paris in September 1789, Jefferson outlined to Madison his idea that the earth belongs to the living, that any one generation cannot bind the next by legislation, debts, or other forms of contract. Drawing from the well-known table of life expectancies in Buffon's *Histoire naturelle*, Jefferson noted that of all persons living at a given moment, half would be dead in twenty-four years.[31] Leaving out minors, he went on to calculate that half of the voting population alive at any moment would be dead within 18 years and 8 months. Hence no constitution, law, or debt should be valid for over 19 years.

Madison politely conceded to Jefferson that in theory "the idea . . . is a great one." From his 1790 vantage point in the thick of the early legislative struggles, however, he had no illusions as to the practical possibilities of establishing such a principle in law, particularly when he could hardly persuade Congress to provide for a broadened

30. Paris, l'Imprimerie Royale, 1785.
31. Georges Louis Leclerc, Comte de Buffon, *Histoire naturelle, générale et particulière*, 2nd ed., 44 vols., II (Paris: L'Imprimerie Royale, 1750), pp. 588–603.

census. Jefferson did not press for legislative enactment of his principle. But throughout his lifetime he retained his fundamental conviction that a precise demographic limitation should operate on the jurisdiction of the present government and society over those of the future.[32] Thomas Paine, maintaining a position similar to that of Jefferson, felt that governments had an obligation to compensate all citizens who had been deprived of their rightful share of landed property by the action of previous generations. Such compensation should principally take the form of payments (from a national fund) of ten pounds per year for life to all persons reaching the age of 50. Writing in 1797 in *Agrarian Justice,* Paine suggested only the vaguest outline of the actuarial problems which would be involved in paying for such a scheme. "My state of health prevents my making sufficient inquiries with respect to the doctrine of probabilities, whereon to found calculations with such degrees of certitude as they are capable of." He pointed out, nevertheless, that it would be "necessary to know, as a datum of calculation, the average of years which persons above that age [21] will live. I take this average to be about thirty years." [33]

The widespread post-Revolutionary familiarity, on the part of statesmen, clergy, educators, and others, with the calculus of life probabilities, is not particularly surprising. Americans had long been interested in the phenomenon and data of longevity. Owing to some improvement in

32. Madison to Jefferson, Feb. 4 and Feb 14, 1790, *Letters and Other Writings of James Madison,* I, 503–507; also, Jefferson to John W. Epps, June 24, 1813, *Writings of Jefferson,* ed. Bergh, XIII, 269–273 and 356–361.

33. Thomas Paine, *Agrarian Justice,* in *The Writings of Thomas Paine,* ed. Moncure D. Conway, 4 vols. (New York: Putnam's, 1895), III, 331–333.

American teaching of mathematics after the middle decades of the eighteenth century, more intellectuals were acquiring the ability to use figures in population or life expectancy calculations. As the colonial period moved on, inquiries into human longevity became less and less apt to be largely devoted to the lives of Old Testament patriarchs, though those remained popular subjects. Scientifically inclined men, like Mather and Stiles, took notes to document the long-lived persons who resided in the community. Belknap, who noted that many New Hampshire persons died of the diseases of old age, printed two pages of instances of unusual longevity in that state. In South Carolina, "at the request of a worthy citizen," Captain Jacob Milligan in 1790 took a census of the aged inhabitants of Charleston. When David Ramsay compared the results with data for New England, he had to confess that "there are as many of their inhabitants reach 85 as of ours who attain to 70." [34] Stiles, Dr. Thomas Bond of Philadelphia, and Rush were among those who were curious about long-lived Indians. Not a few persons, in an age which had high hopes for social progress and human perfectibility, shared Franklin's view that the human life-span was bound to lengthen, perhaps indefinitely, under the impact of knowledge. Franklin summarized this view in a well-known letter to Priestley: "It is impossible to imagine the Height to which may be carried, in a thousand years, the Power of Man over Matter . . . ; all Diseases may by sure means be prevented if not cured, not excepting Old Age, and our Lives lengthened at pleasure even beyond the antediluvian Standard." [35]

34. David Ramsay, *A Sketch of the Soil, Climate, Weather, and Diseases of South Carolina* (Charleston: W. P. Young, 1796), p. 29.

35. Franklin, *Works,* ed. John Bigelow (New York, 1904), VIII, 174–175. For an extensive review of the literature on this general

With the development of the calculus of life probabilities came the means of figuring the rate of man's progress toward some of these goals. Brissot de Warville, in the late 1780's, expressed the widespread appreciation of this fact: "Tables of longevity may be every where considered as the touchstone of governments; the scale on which may be measured their excellencies and their defects, the perfection or degredation of the human species." As Brissot toured the United States, he made note both of how the Americans rated on such a scale, and also to what extent they were attempting to make their own measurements. The American vital statistics that he obtained enabled him to challenge earlier travelers who had reported that America was a place of excessive disease and short life expectancy. Quite the contrary, his data showed that the garden was a place not only of rapid increase but of long life.

Brissot's friend Myers Fisher told him that, in Pennsylvania, one could measure the longevity of people by their religion. There seemed to be something to this. Denominations having strict precepts of simple personal living clearly had the best records of longevity, Brissot thought. He rated the Quakers, Moravians, and Presbyterians in the top three positions, with other denominations trailing behind. In New England the minister at Andover, echoing Wigglesworth, told Brissot "that men of letters enjoy the greatest longevity. He told me that the oldest men were generally found among the ministers. This fact will explain some of the causes of longevity; such as regularity of morals, information, independence of spirit, and easy circumstances."

---

subject, see Gerald J. Gruman, *A History of Ideas about the Prolongation of Life* (Philadelphia: American Philosophical Society, 1966).

Beyond these considerations, Brissot, who had been well indoctrinated by American patriots, thought that the really important factors in longevity were political and economic. Shortness of life, he said, accompanied arbitrary government, tyranny, and the concentration of wealth in a small class. The character of American principles practically assured the opposite: "there can be no country where the life of man is of longer duration; for, to all the advantages of nature, they unite that of liberty, which has no equal on the Old Continent; and this liberty . . . is the principle of health."

Brissot's search for the data which would back up such assertions was by no means easy. Like Peter Kalm two generations earlier, he soon found that although it was not hard to locate persons interested in longevity, it was often difficult to lay hands on well-kept vital registers or bills of mortality. The reasons for this eventually became clear: "There are some sects who do not baptize their children, and whose registers are not carefully kept . . . Some of the sick have no physicians or surgeons, and their attendants who give the information are not exact. The constant fluctuation occasioned by emigrations and immigrations still increase the difficulty."

These and other complications made it obviously impossible to make the clear demonstration which Brissot would have liked. Still, in the data he found, there were enough examples of long community longevity to leave him feeling that they "approach near the truth." Registers which he obtained in Woodstock, Connecticut, showed that more than 1 out of 9 persons were over 80. This contrasted strikingly with a French community which had only 1 person of such an age out of 42. Edward Holyoke's excellent tables of vital statistics of Salem, Massachusetts, which Brissot reproduced from the AAAS *Memoirs,* showed the situation in another light. Although Salem was popularly regarded as being one of the most unhealthful towns in America, the tables seemed to show that the town still enjoyed greater longevity than most of Europe. While only 1 out of 50 persons in Salem died in 1781, 1 out of 30 died in Paris and 1 out of 23 in London, along with 1 out of 40 in rural England and 1 out of 24 in rural France. From the same number of the *Memoirs,* Brissot reprinted Wigglesworth's and Cutler's tables for Ipswich which showed that town in such a favorable light over Breslau. Along the same line was an original and important "Comparative Table of the Probabilities of Life in New England and in Europe," which Wigglesworth furnished to Brissot. Here, Wigglesworth set the longevity statistics of Hingham, Dover (N. H.), and the Harvard graduates against those of the whole array of European communities which he had found in Price: London and half-a-dozen smaller English towns, Sweden, France, Holland, and the German cities of Breslau and Brandenburg. The result was altogether favorable for the United States.[36]

Brissot's collected evidence was dramatic and, he felt, conclusive. "From all the facts and all the tables which I have given you, it must be concluded that the life of man is much longer in the United States of America, than in

36. If Brissot had read Gordon's 1772 pamphlet, he would have found the following striking example: An anonymous correspondent in March 1772 had sent to the *Boston Evening Post* an account of longevity in Rowley, Massachusetts. Culling the records of the First Congregational Church in that town, the correspondent had reported that of 246 persons baptized between 1682 and 1691, 24 were still alive in 1771, about 1 out of 10. He also concluded that 4 out of less than 1000 persons lived to be over 100 years old in Rowley, while in England only about 1 in 1000 were thought to live that long. Gordon, *Plan of a Society,* pp. 33–35.

the most salubrious countries of Europe." And the results had a practical as well as a philosophical side, Brissot thought. "If any government should wish to revive the speculation of life annuities on selected heads, I should advise to select them in the north of the United States." [37]

About the time of Brissot's visit, a number of Philadelphia scientists, some of them using the American Philosophical Society as their forum, joined the discussion of life expectancies and population in America. Rush, of course, had long been interested in the longevity of Pennsylvanians, and his writings on the subject were widely known. Rush was among those before 1800 (and before Malthus) who thought that the ideal of universal longevity was not necessarily desirable and that the high infant mortality of the time might be a blessing in disguise: "Did all the people who are born live to be seventy or eighty years of age, the population of the globe would soon so far surpass its present cultivation, that millions would perish yearly from the want of food." [38] Nicholas Collin also spoke occasionally to Philadelphia scientists and with no little scientific understanding, upon such subjects as "The Importance of a Correct Table of Population." Other inquiries were made by Dr. John Foulke and William Barton.

In February 1789 Foulke delivered the American Philosophical Society's annual oration, "On the State, Stages and Chances of the human constitution and life, and particularly supporting the chances of Longevity in North America." With the thought that the past might furnish

37. Brissot de Warville, *New Travels in the U. S.,* I, 295 and 302–316, and II, App. I and II.

38. Benjamin Rush, "An Inquiry into the Causes of Premature Deaths," *Essays, Literary, Moral, and Philosophical,* p. 310. For further discussion of Rush, see below, Chapter XI.

hints for such an analysis of the American scene, Foulke drew examples of longevity in Europe and Asia from the classical literature. But he counseled that people should not investigate too closely the cases of great longevity reported in the Old Testament; "It might endanger . . . both philosophy and religion." Moving on to the scientific literature, he reviewed the longevity data and observations of such demographic writers as "Mr. Grant" (John Graunt), Halley, Price, and Buffon. Among other things, he was impressed that Graunt's "old and usefull Book" considered the different proportions of deaths among men and women and that it emphasized that 7 out of every 100 persons in England in Graunt's time died of old age ("natural decay"). Foulke thought that Buffon's mortality table was formed on "a more extensive basis" than that of either Halley or Price, while Halley's was the most "discouraging" of the three so far as longevity expectation was concerned.

Foulke emphasized that all of these studies had their weaknesses. Demography was still far from an exact science.

The difficulty and consequent uncertainty of all political arithmetic weakens our confidence in calculations of this nature; but if the most ingenious in Europe are heard on these Subjects with diffidence, what confidence can we inspire unpossess'd of tables or data calculated to invest the true situation of America, and its inhabitants.

Nevertheless, with "such documents as we do possess," Foulke went on to give what idea he could of life expectancy in America. He produced examples of unusual longevity in Virginia and other states. He cited the views of Ramsay and others on the longevity of slaves. He quoted newspaper items on the longevity of New Haven residents, and gave data which had been furnished by Dr. Samuel Stanhope Smith of Princeton on the longevity of New Jersey families. He also cited the mortality and longevity data from Philadelphia church registers.

In the absence of more extensive data, Foulke could only generalize, with Brissot, that if equal distribution of wealth was conductive to long life, then no country had greater longevity than America. Further, he thought "that paucity of Inhabitants, Salubrity of Climate, and a moderate degree of temperance must insure length of life everywhere." Such sentiments doubtless struck a responsive chord in the Philadelphia audience, but they did not add much to the store of scientific knowledge. Perhaps for this reason Foulke never put his paper into shape for publication. It was manifest that the work did no more than scrape the surface of the subject. It did not utilize some of the best American vital data sources and showed little awareness of American demographic contributions of the previous forty years. In these respects the inquiries and papers of William Barton proved to be of more substance.[39]

Barton, a nephew of the astronomer David Rittenhouse, provided several communications on demographic matters to the American Philosophical Society. In February 1789 his letter to Rittenhouse on population and life expectancy in America was read. In April of the next year, he sent to the Society "Additional observations on the proportion between Births and Deaths in Philadelphia: and a Table of

39. John Foulke, "Oration Pronounced by Doctor Foulke before the American Philosophical Society, February 7 [1789]," microfilm no. 540 at American Philosophical Society of unpaged manuscript at The New York Historical Society.

the number of births and deaths in the German Lutheran Congregation . . . from 1774 'till 1790." These and other findings were combined in a major paper read to the Society in March 1791 and published later that same year in the Society's *Transactions.* This was his "Observations on the Progress of Population and the Probabilities of the Duration of Human Life, in the United States of America." Barton's work was of much interest as a review of the scientific literature, European and American, on demography and life probabilities. It was also one of the most elaborate (and extravagant) late eighteenth-century attempts to enlist these sciences in the American quest for national virtue and respectability. While Barton quoted standard European authorities such as Petty, Price, and Laplace as authorities when he restated the old view that population was one of the main measures of a nation's relative strength, he drew upon Franklin, Stiles, and Jefferson for proof that the American rate of population increase was unparalleled anywhere in the world. While he quoted statistics from Graunt, Süssmilch, Buffon, and others on the contrasting mortality of large and small communities, he showed triumphantly, from the data of Wigglesworth, Holyoke, and others, that the record of the small, democratically governed, and simple-living American communities was better than the European record. Admitting the imperfections of his data, he nonetheless accepted at face value the vital statistics of a handful of scattered American communities as a basis of comparison with a heterogeneous group of European communities on the great questions of longevity and life probabilities. As part of this, he set the vital records of Salem for four years and those of two Philadelphia churches (Christ-Church and St. Peter's) for the period between 1754 and 1790, beside those of Breslau,

London, Paris, Northampton, and other English and continental communities, in the form of tables of life probabilities by various age periods. Similarly, in other instances where the data furnished some basis for comparison, he drew up tables contrasting American towns with the reported European experience. In at least four instances, the American vital statistics seemed to show a distinct general advantage over those of Europe so far as life expectancies and longevity were concerned:

1. The number of deaths under the age of 3 for every 1000 persons:

Ipswich (from Wigglesworth)	181
Hingham (from Wigglesworth)	363
Berlin (from Süssmilch)	598

(Barton also gave similar figures for deaths under age 5.)

2. Numbers out of 1000 dying after age of 80:

Ipswich	128	Berlin	27
Hingham	91	Salem	26
Connecticut	74	Philadelphia	25
Breslau	34	Vienna	15
Paris	32		

3. Proportions which annual deaths bear to the total living:
Lowest proportions (1 out of 50 to 1 out of 43), included:

Isle of Madeira
Ipswich
Philadelphia
German country parishes

Highest proportions (1 out of 33 to 1 out of 22), included all of the large European and English cities.

4. Proportions of annual deaths to 100 annual births:

America (Salem, Hingham, and Philadelphia): averaged about 50 deaths to 100 births.
Europe: ranged from 70 deaths for 100 births to 172 deaths for every 100 births.

Actually, neither Barton nor most of his fellow Americans who wrote on these matters at that period had a very substantial scientific preparation. Accordingly, they often lacked awareness of the variables bearing upon a given situation and failed to realize the degree of compatibility necessary to give their studies validity. But they went on anyway. Barton unabashedly followed an a priori approach throughout his paper. He had no doubt that his relatively meager data sources were sufficient to make broad generalizations. "What has been premised, concerning the longevity of the inhabitants will, I presume, be an ample refutation of those writers who, influenced by European prejudices, or considering the subject in a superficial manner, have asserted that the Americans are not so long-lived as the Europeans." Further, he had no hesitation in concluding that "the probabilities of life, *in all its stages,* from its commencement to the utmost possible verge of its duration, are higher in the United States, than in such European countries as are esteemed the most favorable." With no little irony, he remarked that Buffon's life tables stopped at the age of ninety probably because few centenarians were to be found in Europe.

The motivation behind Barton's work, as well as that of Foulke and some of the American historian-compilers of that period, was as much based in patriotism as it was in science. It was not incongruous, therefore, for Barton's paper to conclude on a high-flown note:

Must not the mind of every American citizen be impressed with gratitude, and glow with emotions of a virtuous pride, when he reflects on the blessings his country enjoys? Let him contemplate the present condition of the United States, — enjoying every advantage which nature can bestow — inhabited by more than three million of the freest people on earth — and possessing an extent of territory amply sufficient to maintain, for ages to come, many additional millions of freemen, which the progression of its population is supplying, with wonderful celerity; — let him, also, contrast this situation of his country, with the condition in which it was found by our ancestors, scarcely two centuries ago; and it will be impossible for him not to experience, in an exalted degree, those sensations, which patriotism and benevolence ever inspire.[40]

In varying degrees of comprehension and sophistication, the statistics of life expectancy were developed or used by laymen, physicians, clergymen, statesmen, and general scientists in late eighteenth-century America. Many of these same investigators sought also, again both on scientific and patriotic grounds, to demonstrate statistically the effects of the American environment upon health and dis-

40. William Barton, *Observations*, pp. 3, 26, 29, 31–38.

ease. Here the pursuit of better vital statistics was joined to the pursuit of accurate meteorological data and to the considerable scientific task of identifying and classifying the diseases which afflicted man in the garden.

Chapter XI

The Statistical Approach to Disease

While the national expectancy of life was a legitimate source of pride during the early days of the Republic, Americans still had to reckon with the certainties of disease and death. As the eighteenth century progressed, the study of these certainties, like that of life probabilities, became increasingly systematic. This was partly due to a growing understanding and use of vital and medical statistics. Many investigators, already influenced by the environmental concept of disease causation of the English physician Thomas Sydenham, were strongly affected by his consciously Baconian approach to disease studies. This approach implied an emphasis upon direct observation and careful description of disease in clinical practice, as well as rational and orderly methods of procedure generally. In its original form, the approach also included the arrangement and classification of diseases in species and genera, but this element remained, during the eighteenth century, more controversial than useful. The concept that weather and climatic conditions were somehow causally connected with disease, on the other hand, was not controversial; the quantitative approach demanded that these conditions be carefully observed and recorded. The analysis of vital statistics, not an original part of Sydenham's approach, nevertheless rounded out the method. It constituted virtually the only means of testing the hoped-for correlation of disease with weather and climate.[1]

The American environment was as much of a mystery and challenge to colonial physicians as it was to others. Both medical people and the world at large were interested in knowing about any new diseases which might flourish in the New World. Fortunately, but prosaically, few exotic or potentially dangerous diseases turned up. By the eighteenth century the more important question was: how does the New World climate and weather affect Old World diseases? Answers to such a question demanded the quantitative approach.

American physicians began early to observe and describe in detail both the diseases and the climate of America. As soon as instruments became available, they were busy measuring weather variations and comparing them with

1. Although Sydenham did not himself specifically point out the possible medical uses of vital data, like-minded friends and contemporaries of his, men like Christopher Wren and John Locke, did. Sydenham's quantitative program was spelled out in his *Medical Observations Concerning the History and Cure of Acute Diseases*, in *The Works of Thomas Sydenham, M.D.*, translated from the Latin by R. G. Latham, 2 vols. (London: The Sydenham Society, 1848 and 1850), I, 12–14. For a summary of the views of Wren and Locke on this matter, see Kenneth Dewhurst, *John Locke*, pp. 6–18; idem, *Dr. Thomas Sydenham (1624–1689); His Life and Original Writings* (Berkeley: University of California Press, 1966).

disease variations. Cadwallader Colden and William Douglass began before 1720 to keep careful registers of weather and climate in order to study the relation of such factors with disease. Several others were doing the same by the 1740's and '50's. John Lining of Charleston went so far as to correlate his meteorological readings with a noteworthy series of quantitative measurements of bodily secretions and excretions.[2]

These early investigators, seemingly less enterprising than colonial journalists in digging out church registers, generally had few vital data with which to verify their attempted correlations. But they went ahead anyway. Even Lionel Chalmers' two-volume *Account of the Weather and Diseases of South Carolina* (1776), doubtless the most ambitious of such works to date in the colonies, was badly lacking in this respect. Although Chalmers had abundant meteorological data and tables, he could obtain only the most meager bills of mortality for the state. Rush's postwar "Account of the Climate of Pennsylvania and Its Influence upon the Human Body" shows the same deficiency. While Rush used various meteorological data to relate

2. "A Letter from Dr. John Lining at Charles-Town in South Carolina, to James Jurin, M.D., . . . Statical Experiments Made on Himself for One Whole Year Accompanied with Meteorological Observations, and Six General Tables," Royal Society, *Philosophical Transactions*, 42 (1743), 491–498; and "A Letter From Dr. John Lining, Physician at Charles-Town in South Carolina, to James Jurin, M.D., F.R.S., serving to Accompany Some Additions to His Statical Experiments," Royal Society, *ibid.*, 43 (1744–45), 318.

Beginning with Cadwallader Colden, who by at least 1718 had both a thermometer and a barometer, some of the investigators in America of the disease-environment relationship were able to bring precision to their meteorological observations through the use of instruments. See James H. Cassedy, "Meteorology and Medicine in Colonial America," *Journal of the History of Medicine*, 24 (1969).

climate generally to disease, he produced no supporting mortality figures.[3]

American physicians, like their colleagues in other countries, by the 1780's generally realized that use of vital data could greatly increase the scientific credibility of such studies. The trouble was that these data themselves were often defective and unreliable. In England, members of the medical profession had worked on this problem for some time. The English had tried periodically since the days of John Graunt to reform the London Bills of Mortality. But the bills firmly resisted change. During the last half of the eighteenth century, a new and energetic group of physician-reformers tackled the problem. Thomas Short, who brought together large collections of British vital and meteorological data, deplored the lack of medical uses to which such data had been put in the past. John Fothergill, however, preparing a monthly series of observations which he entitled "Essays on the Weather and Diseases of London" for the *Gentleman's Magazine* during the early 1750's, found that the bills of mortality were nearly useless for such purposes. His 1754 proposal to improve the bills by bettering parish registration throughout the nation failed to pass Parliament. Subsequent efforts by Thomas Percival, John Haygarth, William Black, and William Heberden, Jr. were equally unavailing on a national scale. They did move some local physicians, however, such as John Heysham in Carlisle, to work for improved registration in their own communities.[4]

3. Rush, *Medical Inquiries and Observations,* II, 23–24. Chalmers's work was published in London in 1776.

4. See Short, *New Observations,* p. xii, and *Increase and Decrease of Mankind,* p. i; Fothergill, *Works,* I, 165–167, and II, 107–113; Thomas Percival, *Essays Medical and Experimental,* 2nd ed., rev.

These British reform attempts probably exerted little direct influence upon American vital statistics. Fothergill, to be sure, wrote some of his American friends in an effort to interest them in better registration.[5] And many colonials were acquainted with the writings of Short, Fothergill, Percival, and others. But American physicians in general for years seemed content to leave the preparation of vital registers and bills of mortality alike to the clerks and churchmen.

Because they were usually prepared by laymen, American bills of mortality suffered from many of the same defects as the British bills. The most glaring of the defects arose out of the original assignment of names of diseases or other causes for each death recorded. In England, as both Graunt and Fothergill had noted, this job was done by "Antient Matrons," who were "as poor and ignorant persons as the parish affords."[6] In America, the church sextons who most often did this work could hardly have been quite such miserable creatures; yet they had no more qualifications for assigning medical names to diseases than did their English counterparts.[7] Actually, throughout the eighteenth century, neither the sextons nor the clerks

(London: Joseph Johnson, 1773), II, 239–252; William Heberden, Jr., *Observations on the Increase and Decrease of Different Diseases, and Particularly of the Plague* (London: T. Payne, 1801); Fox, *Fothergill and his Friends,* p. 229; Heysham, *Bills of Mortality in Carlisle, for the Year 1779*; and William Black, *Observations on the Smallpox.*

5. He wrote specifically on this subject to James Pemberton of Pennsylvania. See Fox, *Fothergill and his Friends,* p. 229 n. 1.

6. Graunt, *Observations,* p. 26; and Fothergill, *Works,* I, 167.

7. Edward A. Holyoke was among the Americans who were well aware of the inadequacies of the sextons for this task. See Holyoke, "A Bill of Mortality for the Town of Salem, for the Year 1782," AAAS *Memoirs,* I, 547.

made sophisticated breakdowns of causes of death, but rather contented themselves with simple lists which generally averaged little more than twenty-five names.[8] Disease nomenclature used both in these lists and in medical writing in the colonies was a hodgepodge. To a mélange of classical words was constantly added terms from newer English-language medical works or the London Bills of Mortality. In a setting considerably removed in time and space from the home country, moreover, colonial medical practice gradually acquired a residue of archaic expressions which lingered on in coexistence with newer ones and rarely seemed to be discarded. As the new immigrant populations pushed back the frontier, the many free, uneducated, and frequently doctor-less spirits among them welcomed the simple remedies and simple medical terms of such popular writers as John Wesley and John Tennent.[9]

Clergymen and clerks in all parts of the colonies were often about as familiar with the names of disease as the physicians. None, however, were guided by standard no-

8. A Pennsylvania gubernatorial report of 1730 included a bill with 27 different causes, but over half were different kinds of accidents. The Christ-Church bills in Philadelphia from the 1750's to the 1790's averaged around 27, but with only 1 or 2 accident categories. One of the New Hampshire bills published by Belknap in the 1780's had 36 different causes. Numbers of causes listed on the London Bills through the eighteenth century varied little. The Bills averaged between 55 and 65 categories of diseases plus 1 to 20 categories of casualties. I have found no American bill before 1800 which included this many categories, though the form sent out by the American Academy of Arts and Sciences in 1785 provided a guide list of nearly 70 causes of death.

9. John Wesley, *Primative Physic*, 16th ed. (Trenton, N. J.: Quequelle and Wilson, 1788; the original edition was published in 1747); and John Tennent, *Every man his own Doctor* (Williamsburg and Annapolis: William Parks, 1734).

menclatures or precise definitions when they recorded deaths in their registers or diaries. If one had looked over the shoulders of these men as they made their entries, one might have gained a vivid sense of the hazards of colonial life. Here were accounts of men "slaine by a bow of a tree in ye cutting downe of the tree," "hang'd at Boston for frequent and notorious theft," "killed with Lightning," "caught in harpoon ropes," or "blown up in privateer." A stillborn infant was "borne before its time." Names of diseases were particular or general almost in turn: "of a consumption," "of a feaver," "by a cansor," "with fitts," or, ever so starkly, "suddenly in the night." Men were murdered, scalded, drowned, or simply "found dead." Others died of drunkenness or any of a variety of "dangerous Fluxes and Surfeits." Where nothing else seemed to fit, the dead were lumped together in one of several general terms, "teething" for infants, and "old age" or "decay of nature" for the elderly.[10] Many of these were the same terms which found their way into the bills of mortality.

The British reformers considered the matter of nomenclature to be of central concern. Fothergill saw that the lists of causes of death used on the bills must be kept up to date and tried to enlist the London medical community in the task. Percival similarly urged regular revision of obsolete and ambiguous terms. He also suggested that the reports of causes of death on the bills be prepared from

10. See, for example, Beverley, *History and Present State of Virginia,* pp. 305–307; Lane, "Deaths in Hampton, N. H., 1727–1755," *New England Historical and Genealogical Register,* 58 (1904), 29–36; Otis, "Scituate and Barnstable Church Records," *ibid.,* 9 (1855), 37–43; "Bradstreet's Journal, 1664–83," *ibid.,* 9 (1855), 43–51; Stiles, "Deaths in Newport, R. I., 1760–1764," *ibid.,* 62 (1908), 283–291 and 352–363; and *The Pennsylvania Gazette,* 79 (May 14–21, 1730).

physicians' death certificates. Heysham, in Carlisle, went one step further in 1779 by classifying the various causes of death on his bills according to the nosology of William Cullen.[11] Some of the British attempts at vital statistics reform had little relevance to America so long as the New World bills of mortality were so few and far between. It might have been expected, however, that late-eighteenth century Americans would have found the classification of disease a compatible enterprise. Like Enlightenment minds everywhere, Americans were indeed frequently caught up in the quest for scientific order through arrangement and classification of species. Many in this age considered the graduated scale of perfection of the Great Chain of Being as the supreme evidence of divine order and arrangement of life in the universe. Others felt that systematic man-made classifications which made no rankings or judgments were more promising. Still others embraced both of these popular ordering concepts. At any rate, in the cases of botany and zoology, American collectors made many contributions to the systematic classifications of Linnaeus, Gronovius, and Buffon. But nosologies seemed to have a less than universal appeal in early America. Unlike the case in botany, there were few chances to have a New World disease named after the discoverer. The potential values of nosologies, moreover, at least as means of revealing God's orderly design for nature and the universe, were largely lost in the noisy claims of competing medical systematists and theorists.[12]

11. For references see note 1 of this chapter.
12. For a review of those theories, see Lester S. King, *The Medical World of the Eighteenth Century* (Chicago, Ill.: University of Chicago Press, 1958).

From the 1770's on, of course, American physicians knew Cullen's disease classification well, both from their personal contacts as students with the master and from Cullen's *Synopsis of Methodical Nosology.* And, through Cullen, if not directly, they knew of other nosologies.[13] Although a good many favored the idea of classifying disease, almost none went so far as to produce their own nosologies during the eighteenth century.[14] In fact, the most substantial American reaction to nosology during this time seems to have been the negative one of Benjamin Rush.

Despite his early training under Cullen, Rush moved around, in his mature view of medicine, to oppose Cullen's ontological approach to diseases as specific entities. By the 1790's he had rejected that part of the Sydenham ideal which advocated the division of diseases into genera and species. He later summarized his view as follows:

Much mischief has been done by nosological arrangements of diseases. They erect imaginary boundaries between things which are of a homogeneous nature. They degrade the human understanding, by substi-

13. Foulke, in his 1789 oration, for instance, contrasted the numbers of diseases included in the nosologies of Cullen, Linnaeus, and Sauvages.

14. Several translations of Cullen's work were published in the United States during the 1790's. In addition, the preacher-physician Matthew Wilson of Chester, Pennsylvania, and Lewes, Delaware, started something along this line for his own use and that of his students during the 1780's. Thacher reported that Wilson had written but not published a compendium of medicine which he called his "Therapeutic Alphabet." "Commencing with the classification of Sauvages, it contained the diseases in alphabetical order, with definition, symptoms, and method of cure." See James Thacher, *American Medical Biography,* 2 vols., reprint (New York: Milford House, 1967), II, 198. Parts of Wilson's compendium are reproduced in Stanton A. Friedberg, "Laryngology and Otology in Colonial Times," *Annals of Medical History,* old ser., 1 (Spring 1917) 86–101.

tuting simple perceptions to its more dignified operations in judgment and reasoning. They gratify indolence in a physician, by fixing his attention upon the name of a disease, and thereby leading him to neglect the varying state of the system. They moreover lay a foundation for disputes among physicians . . . The whole materia medica is infected with the baneful consequences of the nomenclature of diseases, for every article in it is pointed only against their names.[15]

Rush's opposition to nosologies was subsequently passed on to many persons in the next generation of American physicians. This attitude greatly hampered later professional efforts at improving disease nomenclatures, not only those used in medical practice but those for bills of mortality.

This is not to say that Rush opposed the statistical or quantitative approach to disease in toto. On the contrary, he expressed admiration for much of the systematic program for medical progress that Sydenham had outlined. For himself, he wrote, "in the year 1779 I opened a book and recorded in it an account of the diseases of every season, and frequently of every month in the year, together with a history of the weather and the state of vegetation. I have continued this register every year since." [16] Rush's subsequent recommendations to physicians, made in 1789, might almost have been taken directly from the English Hippocrates:

Preserve a register of the weather, and of its influence upon the vegetable productions of the year . . . Re-

15. Rush, *Medical Inquiries and Observations,* III, 19–20.
16. *The Autobiography of Benjamin Rush,* ed. George W. Corner (Princeton, N. J.: Princeton University Press, 1948), pp. 86–87.

cord the epidemics of every season . . . Preserve, likewise, an account of chronic cases. Record the name, age, and occupation of your patient; describe his disease accurately, and the changes produced in it by your remedies; mention the doses of every medicine you administer to him . . . The records will supply [any] deficiency of memory, especially in that advanced stage of life, when the advice of physicians is supposed to be most valuable.[17]

The record-keeping activities which Rush prescribed for American physicians did not include any responsibility for vital statistics (as distinguished from medical statistics). Here he followed the older example of Sydenham rather than that of Percival and Heysham. But, personally, he always looked closely into available bills of mortality and considered that their data were scientifically invaluable.[18]

17. Rush, *Medical Inquiries and Observations,* I, 260.

18. In 1789 Rush entered in his Commonplace Book an unusually detailed twenty-year summary of the vital statistics of the Presbyterian congregation at West Conecocheague (Mercersburg), Pennsylvania. These data for 1769–1789 came from his friend, the Reverend John King:

Baptized	596
Admitted to church communion	292
Married, pairs	106
Died, aged persons 47, middle aged 47, children 60	154
Killed in battle	5
Killed by accidents	5
Died at Camp	2
Died by oppression in New York	3
Emigrated, of the original members and their families	240
Remain, distinct families, the same as in 1769	140 families

(Quoted in *Autobiography of Benjamin Rush,* p. 179.)

He hoped that someone in every community would undertake to assure the supply of such data. He recommended, particularly, that every newspaper editor should "once a month publish a list of all the deaths in the city — and if possible the names of the diseases which occasioned them." [19] American physicians contemporary with Rush were by no means all devoted to quantitative methods in medical practice or inquiry. However, certain of the most patriotic and most inquisitive minds were. Some, like Thomas Bond in 1782, argued from both vital statistics and weather data to show that the success of the Revolution had owed much to the favorable climate of America:

. . . we shall have Reason to conclude with *Hippocrates,* that climates have great Influence in tempering the Bodies and Minds of Men, and that frequent and great Changes in the Atmosphere, are favourable to the Happiness and Dignity of human Nature . . . Had the Councils of Britain been aware of these Circumstances, they would probably have deliberated longer on the Propriety and Means of enslaving, chaining and bringing under their Feet, a People thus destined by the God of Nature to be great, wise, and free . . . [This opinion is] not only confirmed by meteorological and morbid Registers, and the general Laws of

19. See Rush to Andrew Brown, Oct. 1, 1788, in L. H. Butterfield, ed., *Letters of Benjamin Rush,* 2 vols. (Princeton, N. J.: Princeton University Press, 1951), I, 488. See also Rush to Lyman Spaulding, Feb. 9, 1802, *ibid.,* II, 843. Here Rush recommended that Spaulding read a work on the subject by the French physician Guillaume Daignan, *Tableau des variétés de la vie humaine* (Paris, 1786), which Jefferson in turn had sent Rush some years earlier.

Creation, but will further stand the Test of historical Inquiry.[20]

Other physicians of this period joined in the search for still larger amounts of meteorological and vital data with which to refute European critics of the salubrity of the New World.[21]

Serious investigators profited from this postwar interest in quantitative data to further the study of the disease–environment relationship. For almost the first time, some Americans were able to satisfy the criteria for such studies which Christopher Wren and John Locke had laid down over a century earlier.[22] For now they began to demand and find at least some bills of mortality or other vital data with which to bolster their correlations of weather and disease.

Edward Holyoke of Salem was one of those who not only made regular meteorological observations himself but also kept his own mortality records of the community. He was so convinced of their medical value that he too, like Rush, advocated having monthly bills of mortality.[23] In 1787 he

20. Thomas Bond, *Anniversary Oration, Delivered May 21st, before the American Philosophical Society Held in Philadelphia for the Promotion of Useful Knowledge, For the Year 1782* (Philadelphia: John Dunlop, 1782), pp. 27–28.

21. See Gilbert Chinard, "Eighteenth Century Theories . . . ," APS *Proceedings,* 91 (1947), 27–57.

22. These men believed that the greatest promise for studies of disease lay not only in careful clinical observations but in comprehensive parallel observation and recording of meteorological phenomena along with study of bills of mortality. See Dewhurst, *John Locke,* pp. 6–18; and James H. Cassedy, "Meteorology and Medicine," *Journal of the History of Medicine,* 24 (1969).

23. Holyoke to Wigglesworth, Feb. 22, 1790, AAAS, *Memoirs,* II, pt. 2 (1804), 58–61. See also Edward A. Holyoke, "An Account of the Weather and of the Epidemics, at Salem, in the County of Essex,

published his detailed account of the weather and diseases of Salem for the previous year. This not only contained careful meteorological statistics but a bill of mortality which included a chart of thirty-five different causes of death plus accidents. Dr. William Currie of Philadelphia was able, in 1792, to produce a study of climate and diseases which also incorporated substantial vital statistics. In large part a compendium of published accounts, the work drew from such material as Jefferson's meteorological observations for Virginia, Wigglesworth's and Holyoke's mortality and weather data for New England, and various weather data and vital statistics for other states.[24]

In South Carolina, David Ramsay continued the line of outstanding Charleston physicians who employed quantitative methods to study the disease–weather relationship. Owing at least partly to his efforts, the new Medical Society of South Carolina in 1791 purchased meteorological instruments and began sponsorship of observations in Charleston. The Society also prevailed upon sextons of local churches to furnish it with lists of burials during the summer months. Later, the City Marshal was assigned the task of obtaining these lists from the sextons daily from July through October. Ramsay himself, owing the example of Rush, in 1796 published his short *Sketch of the Soil, Climate, Weather, and Diseases of South-Carolina*. He made no attempt therein to achieve the literary scope of Chalmers' earlier study. Instead, Ramsay made a largely tabular and in many ways more effective presentation of

for the Year 1786. To which is added, a Bill of Mortality, for the same Year," Massachusetts Medical Society, *Medical Communications*, I (1787), 17–40.

24. William Currie, *An Historical Account of the Climates and Diseases of the United States of America* (Philadelphia: T. Dobson, 1792).

meteorological data as well as of diseases, mainly of Charleston. A few years later he attempted to launch, as a private venture, an annual narrative and statistical report of the city's health. He hoped, as one result, to stimulate similar local reports elsewhere in the United States in order to gain a broad idea of American health, longevity, and the effects of climate on diseases. But Ramsay could not even keep his own publication going after the first year. Although he had an abundance of pluviometrical and other meteorological data for it, he was unable to obtain the regular and complete bills of mortality which such a report required. He had to confess that, except for the summer months, "no register of the dead is kept" in Charleston.[25]

Many eighteenth-century laymen were as interested in disease as the physicians, both generally and in the possible connection between disease and weather or climate. The number included Mather, Beverley, Franklin, Stiles, and Jefferson. Most of them kept extensive meteorological records along with the population and vital data which they accumulated; and most, on occasion, made more or less perceptive observations of diseases as well. Since few, however, were in a position to carry out systematically sustained observations and descriptions of diseases, they generally left the attempts to correlate the incidence of disease with the weather to the physicians. Epidemic onslaughts, since they were short-lasting community crises,

25. David Ramsay, *The Charleston Medical Register for the Year MDCCCII* (Charleston: W. P. Young, 1803), p. 21. See also Waring, *History of Medicine in South Carolina*, pp. 291–293; David Ramsay, *A Sketch of the Soil; Charleston Gazette and Daily Advertiser*, no. 4034, July 23, 1800; and Robert Croom Aldredge, "Weather Observers and Observations at Charleston, South Carolina, 1670–1871," Historical Appendix, *The Year Book of the City of Charleston for the Year 1940* [Charleston, 1940], pp. 226–230.

were another matter. These sometimes found about as many laymen as physicians involved in the process of observing the progress of the disease and measuring its impact quantitatively. This had been notably true during the Boston smallpox epidemic of 1721 and the New England throat distemper of the 1730's. It was equally true when yellow fever struck coastal cities during the 1790's.

The yellow fever attack upon Philadelphia between August and November 1793 has been frequently described. It was a major disaster which had a frightful mortality and disrupted much of the city's normal activity. Jefferson, who watched the progress of the fever, commented in his letters to Madison on the variations in mortality in proportion to the progressive numbers of sick. Like everybody else's data, his figures of new cases and daily deaths were only guesses.[26] As might have been expected, the calamity caused at least a partial breakdown in the mechanisms of vital statistics registration and other quantitative procedures involving human data just when they were most needed. Enough remained intact so that the extent of the epidemic could at least be reconstructed after the fact. To be sure, there did not seem to be any statistics which could settle the burning question among Philadelphians, of whether the epidemic originated in local unsanitary conditions or whether it was imported. And what data there were did not yield a single, agreed-upon answer to the lesser question of whether the epidemic was affected somehow by the weather.

Among the reports made after the epidemic, one of the most extensive and authoritative was by a layman, the

26. One of the best accounts of the epidemic is that of John H. Powell, *Bring Out Your Dead* (Philadelphia: University of Pennsylvania Press, 1949). Powell summarizes Jefferson's correspondence on these matters on pages 64–65.

journalist and bookseller Mathew Carey. The narrative account which he published immediately after the event was a sensation, partly because it listed the names of all those who had been buried. On the basis of "books kept by Clergymen, Sextons, etc.," Carey reported a total of 4041 deaths, which was about one tenth the estimated population. He also furnished charts of the daily burials in each of the twenty-odd graveyards of the city. Going on, he discussed the mortality of the various periods of the epidemic in relation to the weather and climate. As part of this, he published meteorological observations which had been kept during the epidemic by the astronomer David Rittenhouse. These included daily readings of thermometer, barometer, wind, and weather. Carey concluded that the data showed no special connection between temperature, weather, and the end of the epidemic.[27]

Rush, using essentially the same mortality sources as Carey, as well as Rittenhouse's observations, reached the opposite conclusion. He positively attributed the checking of the epidemic to the light showers and increased coolness which occurred during the week of October 15. His account also drew upon weather data of previous years and on older mortality records from the Friends burial ground. From them he attempted to show that epidemics of 1699 and 1762 had abated under meteorological circumstances similar to those of 1793.[28]

27. Mathew Carey, *A Short Account of the Malignant Fever Lately Prevalent in Philadelphia, with a Statement of the Proceedings that took Place on the Subject in Different Parts of the United States,* 3rd ed., improved (Philadelphia: M. Carey, 1793). Carey's book was widely read both in the United States and abroad. His data were quoted by British medical writers such as William Heberden, Jr.

28. Rush, "An Account of the Bilious Remitting Yellow Fever, as it Appeared in Philadelphia in the Year 1793," *Medical Inquiries and Observations,* vol. III.

Both Rush and Carey used corrected mortality totals, since the burial returns from some of the graveyards were recognized to be considerably deficient. The Lutheran pastor of Philadelphia, J. Henry C. Helmuth, did similarly, though he felt that the figures for his own graveyard were accurate. Helmuth, something like Jabez Fitch a half-century earlier, prepared a partially statistical account of the epidemic "for the Reflecting Christian." Whatever the exact total for the city, Helmuth was certain that "this mortality has proved a harvest for heaven." And few people were inclined to deny his view that the total included the saved as well as sinners.[29]

At the end of the year, the compilers of the Christ-Church bill of mortality, similarly awed by God's terrible will, arranged for embellishment of the 1793 printed bill quite beyond the usual matter-of-fact format. At the top, above the ordinary prosaic heading, appeared a lugubrious cut of Time with his scythe, in the best style of the grave-stone art of the day. At the end, there was a long mortuary poem, of which the first two stanzas give sufficient idea:

> How many precious souls are fled
> To the vast regions of the dead!
> Since to this day the changing sun
> Through his last yearly period run.

29. J. Henry C. Helmuth, *A Short Account of the Yellow Fever in Philadelphia for the Reflecting Christian,* translated from the German by Charles Erdmann (Philadelphia: Jones, Hoff, and Derrick, 1794), p. 50. In New York, the clergyman Samuel Miller preached along these same lines after the epidemic of 1798: "O Death! how large the catalogue of thy trophies!" When Miller published his sermon he specified the size of the catalog (2082) by listing the interments of the city's 19 burial grounds. Samuel Miller, *A Sermon, Delivered February 5, 1799* (New York: Forman, 1799), pp. 11, 35-36.

We yet survive; but who can say?
That through this year, or month, or day,
"I shall retain this vital breath,
"Thus far, at least, in league with death." [30]

People were still talking about the 1793 epidemic four years later. Not everyone, by any means, thought that the huge mortality totals were entirely the work of God. The controversial journalist William Cobbett, in fact, laid a good many of the deaths directly to the doings of Benjamin Rush and his followers. Cobbett specifically attacked the system of "depletion" — bleeding and purging — which Rush considered to be the proper remedy for yellow fever (or for any fever).[31] When Rush resumed use of the remedy during the 1797 yellow fever epidemic, Cobbett began publication of his vitriolic serial, *Porcupine's Gazette,* at least partly to challenge the practice. Rush thereupon sued, ultimately won damages of $5000, and continued bloodletting. Although Cobbett's exposé did little to stop the practice in the United States, it remains one of the pioneer statistical analyses of a form of medical therapy.

Cobbett, to begin with, was angered by Rush's reported claim that 99 out of 100 of his yellow fever patients in 1793 had been cured due to the generous use of the depletion system. Such claims issued during the early, less severe parts of the epidemic, Cobbett said, influenced many Philadelphians who might have fled to safety to remain in the city, where they subsequently succumbed to the fever. Re-

30. Matthew Whitehead, John Ormrod, and Joseph Dolby, *An Account of the Baptisms and Burials in the United Churches of Christ-Church and St. Peters . . . from December 25, 1792, to December 25, 1793* (Philadelphia: William W. Woodward [1794]).

31. Some of the other Philadelphia physicians also strongly opposed the practice of bleeding, at least when done to excess.

constructing the chain of events, Cobbett published extracts from the daily bills of mortality to show that bleeding not only had been of no help whatsoever, but actually had a harmful effect:

Though the lancet was continuously unsheathed; though Rush and his subalterns were ready at every call, the deaths did actually increase; and, incredible as it may seem, this increase grew with that of the very practice which saved more than ninety-nine patients out of a hundred!

When challenged, Rush had to admit that he had merely been guessing about the numbers and cures of his patients. Under the stresses of the epidemic he was unable to keep the careful records which he agreed in principle were desirable. In a few instances he did manage to keep notes of the quantities of blood taken from patients and the times of the bleeding, but this proved impossible for most cases. Accordingly, Cobbett could attack him for a lack of method as well as for falsification of claims:

When the Doctor was called on . . . for a *list* of his patients, he pretended he had kept none; when the dreadful increase of the bill was shown to have begun with the use of his remedies, he replied, that this increase was occasioned by the want of *timely* application, by that timidity which prevented patients from losing blood, or swallowing mercury, enough, and by a want of proper nurses.

Lacking more precise numerical evidence of the adverse effects of bleeding among the total number of Rush's patients, Cobbett was forced to make an inference from the limited record of mortality in Rush's own household. There, four out of six persons who fell ill from the yellow fever died despite the most extensive application of depletion, and in the very presence of the "great Philadelphia Hippocrates." From this sad fact Cobbett concluded his indictment:

> As this is the only authentick record, from which a judgment can be formed of the Doctor's success, we . . . conclude, accordingly, that, instead of *saving* more than ninety-nine, he lost at least sixty-six, out of every hundred of his patients.[32]

Quite apart from the controversial aspects of the epidemics, the incidence of yellow fever in the various communities led boards of health during the 1790's to undertake various official steps to obtain and disseminate relevant statistics. In New York, several public lists of victims were prepared and issued between 1795 and 1800. Individuals like Matthew L. Davis and James Hardie included such lists in their accounts of the New York epidemics. Some observers obtained tabular data of burials in the various graveyards as well as of meteorological observations.[33] The

32. This and the immediately preceding quotations are from Peter Porcupine (William Cobbett), *The Rush-Light* (New York: William Cobbett, 1800), 68–73. This work is the collected essays of *Porcupine's Gazette* put in book form. It must be pointed out that Cobbett also made vicious attacks about the same time not only on Noah Webster, who agreed with Rush on many things, but on Mathew Carey, who did not. See Mathew Carey, *A Plumb Pudding for the Humane, Chaste, Valiant, Enlightened Peter Porcupine* (Philadelphia: M. Carey, 1799).

33. Board of Health, *Names of Persons who have Died in New-York of the Yellow Fever, from the 29th of July, to the Beginning of*

Philadelphia Board of Health, during the 1798 epidemic, employed a man to collect daily information from the sextons as to the numbers of burials. Another man, John Jervis, called on the city's physicians every morning to obtain written returns of the number of new cases of sickness during the preceding 24 hours. Both sets of returns were published daily in the *Philadelphia Gazette*. Somewhat similar official reports were made by the Board in 1799 and 1802. The 1802 data included daily listings not only of the names of newly reported sick people, but also the street locations of their houses. Some observers thought that this measure had "a very great effect in preventing inadvertent exposure to the contagion." [34] Similarly, the Baltimore Board of Health collected death figures beginning around 1797, while in Boston the Selectmen published total numbers of yellow fever cases and deaths during the epidemic of 1798. [35]

Statistical notices of these kinds mark an approach to the regular publication of official reports on health matters in American cities. Effective launching of such official re-

---

November, 1795 [New York, 1795]; Committee of Health, *Record of Death* ([New York], J. Hill & Co. [1799]); M. L. Davis, *A Brief Account of the Epidemical Fever which Lately Prevailed in the City of New York . . .* (New York: Matthew L. Davis, 1795); and James Hardie, *An Account of the Malignant Fever, Lately Prevalent in the City of New York* (New York: Hurtin & M'Farlane, 1799).

34. William Currie and Isaac Cathrall, *Facts and Observations, Relative to the Origin, Progress and Nature of the Fever . . .* (Philadelphia: William W. Woodward, 1802), p. 11.

35. See William T. Howard, Jr., *Public Health Administration and the Natural History of Disease in Baltimore, Maryland, 1797–1920* (Washington, D. C.: Carnegie Institution of Washington, 1924), p. 194; John B. Blake, "Early History of Vital Statistics in Massachusetts," *Bulletin of the History of Medicine*, 29 (1955), 51–52; and John B. Blake, *Public Health in the Town of Boston* (Cambridge, Mass.: Harvard University Press, 1959), pp. 212–216.

porting, however, had to wait until the nineteenth century. And even in that century, many years went by before such reports achieved substantial public health usefulness, except during epidemic periods.

The increased availability of mortality and morbidity data in the late eighteenth century, however, made it possible, among other things, to assess the value of hospital care for yellow fever patients. When Stephen Girard and Peter Helm took over management of Philadelphia's emergency hospital during the 1793 epidemic, they made immediate provisions to keep methodical records of admissions, cures, dismissals, and deaths. The managers subsequently issued several reports to the newspapers to stress that stricken persons had a better chance of survival in the hospital than at home.[36] Similarly, during the 1798 epidemic, the board of managers published a comparison between the mortality at the hospital and that in the city as a whole between August 9 and September 19. The following chart summarizes their data:

Number of cases reported by physicians	2472
Total deaths	1700
Cases treated in the City (outside the hospital)	1937
Deaths in the City (outside the hospital)	1424
Cases sent to the hospital	535
Deaths at the hospital	276

"What is the obvious deduction from the preceding facts?" William Currie asked. "Remove the sick immediately to

36. Powell, *Bring Out Your Dead*, pp. 167–169.

the Hospital, and the well to the encampments, and the excessive mortality will of course subside." [37]

Among the accounts of the various yellow fever epidemics, few relied more fully upon statistics, public and private, than those which Currie published at the time. Currie's detailed presentation of every sort of available morbidity, mortality, and meteorological data was directed at least in part to supporting the view that yellow fever was of imported origin and was contagious. He and his supporters got no further in proving this than did Rush and the miasmatists in their efforts to find the origins in unsanitary local conditions. [38] Both sides in the controversy, however, displayed an awareness that the science of epidemiology, as it existed in their day, depended in increasing measure upon statistical fact and analysis. But the grand eighteenth-century demonstration of this truth came neither from Currie nor from Rush, but from their contemporary, Noah Webster.

In 1799 Webster published his large work, *A Brief History of Epidemic and Pestilential Diseases*. For Webster,

37. William Currie, *Memoirs of the Yellow Fever* . . . (Philadelphia: Thomas Dobson, 1798), p. 85. While the general mortality rate in Philadelphia was thus about 74 percent among those who were treated for the disease outside the hospital, in the hospital a patient had almost an even chance of survival. During the 1798 epidemic, huge encampments were hurriedly erected on the outskirts of the city. Many poor people of the crowded central areas who could not flee to the country were removed to these sites.

38. In addition to Currie's *Memoirs of the Yellow Fever* and his *Facts and Observations* . . . *of the Fever*, previously cited, see also his *A Sketch of the Rise and Progress of the Yellow Fever and of the Proceedings of the Board of Health, in Philadelphia, In the Year 1799* (Philadelphia: Budd & Bartram, 1800); and his *Observations on the Causes and Cure of Remitting or Bilious Fevers* (Philadelphia: William T. Palmer, 1798).

Enlightenment man that he was, this work was at least in part the result of a yearning for social and intellectual order in the new Republic. While statesmen and politicians organized state and federal governments, Webster promoted uniformity and American ideas in the education of school children. While scientists energetically classified the plants, animals, and minerals of the country, Webster put his mind to work at standardizing its grammar and language. Similarly, if he made occasional excursions into such fields as law, politics, and journalism, he did so as a good citizen trying to improve the ordering processes of his community.[39]

Webster had shown his statistical-mindedness in many ways well before 1799. During his lecture tour of several states during the mid-1780's Webster, like Stiles before him, counted houses in the towns he visited.[40] When he prepared his famous spellers and readers he included population data and was careful to bring them up to date in successive editions. He followed fairly closely the population trends in the United States. Like the good Federalist he was, he deplored the continuing drain of all classes of population from New England, but agreed that such a phenomenon could not help but benefit the rest of the country.[41] When he examined the results of the 1790 national census, he was particularly interested in the rough data it provided on longevity. From the respective proportions of free white males over and under 16 in the regions, he concluded that life was generally longer in the northern states, partly, he thought, because much of the southern

39. A good general biography is Harry R. Warfel, *Noah Webster, Schoolmaster to America* (New York: Macmillan, 1936).
40. *Ibid.*, p. 258.
41. Webster, "Remarks on the Population of the United States," *The Spectator* (N. Y.), Oct. 7, 1801.

population lived in low, marshy areas. Later, in 1800, he helped organize the census of New Haven.[42] In 1798 Webster projected a comprehensive statistical account of the State of Connecticut, which was to include data on health, longevity, and population among other items. He went so far as to send a circular request for data to the clergy and other learned men in the state. When insufficient replies came in, he took a similar project to the new Connecticut Academy of Arts and Science. Although the Academy distributed his new questionnaire, this inquiry had no better immediate results than its predecessor.[43]

Webster's interest in epidemic diseases arose in considerable measure out of the disorderly squabbling between miasmatists and contagionists over the causes of yellow fever.[44] He was ultimately convinced both that the continuing squabble was bad for the prosperity of the new country and that the contagionists could be refuted once and for all by a rational and methodical approach. He thus set about to bring the weight of collected facts to bear upon this discussion. At first he tried to do this by publishing the consensus of the experiences of American physicians.[45] Once started in the subject, though he was no

42. Webster, *Letters on Yellow Fever Addressed to Dr. William Currie*, ed. Benjamin Spector (Baltimore: Johns Hopkins Press, 1947), pp. 105–106.

43. See Emily E. F. Skeel, compiler, *A Bibliography of the Writings of Noah Webster* (New York: New York Public Library, 1958), p. 343; and Warfel, *Noah Webster*, pp. 252–258.

44. Among the fuller discussions of Webster's epidemiology, see George Rosen, "Noah Webster — Historical Epidemiologist," *Journal of the History of Medicine*, 20 (April 1965), 97–114; and C.-E. A. Winslow, *The Conquest of Epidemic Diseases* (Princeton, N. J.: Princeton University Press, 1943), pp. 207–235.

45. Noah Webster, compiler, *A Collection of Papers on the Subject of Bilious Fevers, Prevalent in the United States for a Few Years Past* . . . (New York: Hopkins, Webb & Co., 1796).

physician he did not hesitate in 1797 to engage in direct controversy over the matter with Currie and other physicians. "I considered and still consider the question," he wrote, "as resting principally on fact, and not on medical skill; therefore proper to be investigated and discussed by any man who has leisure and means, as well as physicians." [46]

The discussion over yellow fever was only a beginning. Since he essentially agreed with Rush in the fundamental identity of fevers, Webster quickly broadened his search for facts to include all epidemic diseases from ancient times down to 1799. In the course of his inquiry, Webster's belief that causes of epidemics lay mainly in local unsanitary conditions was increasingly modified by his new conviction that the effects of such conditions depended upon the epidemic constitution of the atmosphere. The study thus came to include not only all the facts he could find about the diseases themselves and their related mortality, but also facts about the natural phenomena which accompanied the diseases as they occurred through history: weather, climate, volcanic eruptions, famines, meteors, tides, and so on.

Webster began collecting mortality statistics, meteorological observations, and other data for his history by early 1798. He asked medical and other societies to send him details about every epidemic about which they knew — as to time, place, numbers of people affected, state of weather

46. Noah Webster, *A Brief History of Epidemic and Pestilential Diseases*, 2 vols. (Hartford, Ct.: Hudson & Goodwin, 1799), I, viii.

Like many other scientific and medical writers of the age, Webster used the term "History", in the title of his work, in both its broad and its narrow senses. The word thus means here not only a retrospective gathering of information from the past, but, more actively, the explanation of causes.

and climate, evidence of simultaneous natural phenomena, and the appearance of unusual insect invasions or diseases among fish and animals.[47] Several times in 1798 he advertised publicly for such data. In January, in his New York paper, *The Spectator*, he asked sextons of New York City churches for death records of the period 1785 to 1797, and offered to pay for any data furnished. Later that year, after a similar appeal in the *Connecticut Journal*, he thanked the contributors, but, in the next breath, complained that much of "the data were not precise and detailed enough." [48]

Most of the information about ancient epidemics, their mortality and associated environmental phenomena, had to be sifted out of the classics and other standard narratives, and was understandably limited. For more modern times the volume of information increased. When Webster reached his own century and country, his sources of data included the whole range of histories, diaries, medical studies, and journals which colonial Americans had available, as well as recent registers and bills of mortality.

Webster realized that few of his statistical data, whether ancient or modern, were compatible, since the bills of mortality which he obtained rarely covered the same time periods. Still, he had to make do with whatever turned up. In the case of American data, he had to rely principally upon post-Revolutionary bills of mortality, for he discovered early that data of the colonial period were "few and imperfect." [49] Except for Boston and Philadelphia, he was unable to unearth much pre-1770 information beyond that handed down by tradition and hearsay.

Despite the shortcomings of its data, Webster's study was

47. Webster, *Letters on Yellow Fever*, ed. Spector, pp. 105–106.
48. Skeel, *Bibliography*, pp. 346 and 418.
49. Webster, *Brief History*, p. 227.

a bold and original attempt to correlate disease and environment. The physicians who attempted such correlations in emulation of Sydenham's systematic method often bogged down in the minute details of the diseases they were trying to describe. The layman Webster, on the other hand, was struck by the larger quantities involved, the historical trends, the global relationships, and the accumulations of data and experience.[50] Using quantitative methods in connection with his large viewpoint, Webster carried the concept of the epidemic constitution to its logical limits compatible with the knowledge of the times.

With the bills he obtained Webster prepared tables of comparative mortality for various European and American cities during eight particularly serious epidemic periods between 1716 and 1797. He made much of the coexistence of the plague in Europe with various different epidemic diseases in America which assertedly came about because of the same disturbances of the epidemic constitution. Webster also presented tables which compared the annual deaths of five European cities (London, Augsburg, Dresden, Dublin, Paris) and three American cities (Boston, Philadelphia, and Salem). Deaths were set against data on weather, comets or meteors seen, volcanic eruptions, and epidemics of each year.

Faced with the inadequacies of his information sources, Webster came to realize that the data-collecting process he had undertaken could not hope to reveal definitive answers about epidemic diseases, but only the broad outlines. He thus tried to prepare the way for more and yet larger studies by other scholars. He joined Rush and Holyoke in

50. Among Americans, Currie, for instance, though he used historical data in his *History of Climate and Diseases in the United States of America,* showed little sense of the larger continuities.

the hope that bills of mortality could be issued monthly in order to show the progress of epidemics more accurately. At the same time, he knew that "bills of mortality do not exhibit a complete view of epidemics; as some of the more remarkable, especially *influenza*, destroy but few lives, and the bills when that disease alone prevailed, are remarkably low." Meaningful study and effective management of epidemic disease demanded extensive morbidity as well as mortality figures. Webster thus concluded his work by urging that every medical and scientific society promote the systematic collection, registration, and dissemination of disease data. He hoped that they could obtain not only the fact of occurrence of every case of disease, but information as to the time it occurred, location, occupations of patients, weather, unusual celestial phenomena and volcanic eruptions, unusual blights or insect invasions at the time, the position of the moon, and the nature of the tides.[51]

Following the appearance of his book in 1799, Webster's active studies of epidemic diseases quickly ended. He pub-

51. Webster, *Brief History*. The quotation above is from II, 1; his charge to medical societies is from II, 253.

The accumulated interest generated by the eighteenth-century studies of Webster and other Americans of the disease-weather-climate relationship carried over into the nineteenth-century work of Lorin Blodget, Daniel Drake, Samuel Forry, and others. The long-existing American tradition of such studies helped pave the way also for a favorable nineteenth-century reception in the United States for the writings and ideas of Alexander von Humboldt in related areas. The mid-twentieth-century revival of interest in ecology has, therefore, deep historical roots. See J. B. deC. M. Saunders, "Geography and Geopolitics in California Medicine," *Bulletin of the History of Medicine*, 41 (1967), 293–324, for a discussion of the Humboldt influence in the West. Saunders does not attempt to trace the pre-Humboldtian influences in the United States back to Webster or other eighteenth-century writers.

lished résumés of some additional vital statistics, and occasionally repeated his call for the collection and study of such facts. Yet, since the needs of continued data-collecting on the subject were beyond the capacity of a single historian, no matter how industrious, Webster left further work along this line to others. In fact, he saw that an adequate quantitative study of epidemic disease was of such magnitude as to require the ultimate participation of learned societies and governments of every country. He had no illusions as to its feasibility in his own day. Nevertheless, the ultimate benefits were inviting:

> The facts being carefully collected, laid together and compared, would certainly lead to satisfactory conclusions, and furnish the basis of a system for preventing or avoiding the most severe calamities.[52]

52. [N. Webster], unsigned article in *The Spectator* (N. Y.), III, April 30, 1800.

Epilogue

Webster's effort to discover medical order in the phenomena of the physical universe exemplified the ambitious intellectual spirit of the eighteenth century. But the statistical compilations he made represented only one of the types of quantitative activities which men of that age were carrying out. By 1799 the statistical approach to the affairs of governments and societies, to the conduct of science, and to the pursuit of knowledge about human populations and diseases had advanced a considerable way in the Western world. Political arithmetic, in its principles if not its name, had become an accepted tool of statesmen and bureaucrats everywhere for their economic, fiscal, or demographic analyses. Humanitarians and scientists on both sides of the Atlantic by then were using the long cumulations of longevity and mortality records as bases for annuities or life insurance. And the whole complex world of

Western commerce and industry was requiring ever better records and quantitative procedures.

The growth of colonial America coincided with the emergence of the new statistical concepts and practices in Europe. Since the two developments were not unrelated, there was no appreciable time-lag between the introduction of most of these practices in Europe and that in the New World. Nevertheless, some aspects of statistics remained essentially European during this period. For instance, the development of mathematical theories of probability after Pascal and Huygens remained an area in which contributions were made exclusively by Europeans such as the Bernoullis, De Moivre, and Laplace. As for the science of chemistry it was still only in Europe that scientists had the facilities to contribute, toward the close of the century, toward a measure of order and quantitative concepts.[1] Nevertheless, in other developments, notably in their pioneering national census, the Americans were in the mainstream of early statistical developments. European investigators by no means had a monopoly on the use of statistical methods in testing the efficacy of smallpox inoculations. And American historians, economists, and geographers throughout the period were as devoted as European scholars and Encyclopedists to the quantitative cataloging of national resources, institutions, people, and knowledge generally.

Despite such indications of statistical progress, in many areas of life people of every country still used rules of thumb or pure guesswork in place of exact numbers. Statistical method and institutions still had large gaps in 1799, even in Europe. In Great Britain, for example, English

1. See Henry Guerlac, "Quantification in Chemistry," *Isis*, 52 (1961), 196.

reformers did not succeed in obtaining a nationwide census until 1801. And the London Bills of Mortality did not receive their long-needed overhaul until the mid-1830's. Meanwhile, in France, official statistics only began to get the impetus they needed during the administration of Napoleon, while few other European countries obtained adequate data-producing machinery until the Napoleonic influence made itself felt through conquest.

In the United States as well, two centuries of "statistical" activities had not really brought Americans very far beyond a simple quantitative way of looking at things. The process of organizing government, society, and institutions clearly required information-gathering procedures, but the latter were not easy to assure under frontier conditions. The same barriers to good statistical practices deterred the cultivation of mathematics. And advanced mathematics, among other things, was necessary before a people could use statistics in sophisticated ways, not to mention contribute to statistical theory. Seventeenth- and eighteenth-century American uses of demographic, medical, and other statistical data were thus only beginnings. But by 1799 a conscious statistical mind was beginning to emerge from embryo in the United States, just as it was taking shape on the other side of the Atlantic. While the day of the statistical specialist was not yet at hand, the simple beginnings were already starting to give way to a more complex period which would have less room for amateurs and generalists.

Some Americans by 1799 were aware of the shortcomings of their statistical arrangements. Business entrepreneurs knew that they needed broader and more systematic data sources if they were to bring the factory system to America or compete for new markets. Officials, merchants, and scholars alike saw that the federal census was already inadequate in the scope of its inquiries. Investigators were increasingly conscious that orderly procedures and data-gathering were valuable in medical and scientific activities. Medical and scientific societies were giving much attention to parish registers and were generally finding them wanting. Indications were already strong that the substantial traditional role of churches and churchmen in vital statistics registration was inadequate and probably irrelevant in an increasingly secular society, at least in scientific applications. It was equally clear that government, notably at the city level, could and should soon take a larger role in future registration of vital statistics, particularly in the interests of furthering the public health.

As the eighteenth century ended, hints were also detectable, in available vital and population statistics, about the nature of the demographic problems that lay ahead. White Americans who consistently regarded themselves as a chosen people in an ever-bounteous garden had, up to this time, little reason to be other than optimistic demographically. The effervescent beliefs of Price, Priestley, Franklin, and Condorcet in human perfectibility were at a high tide of popularity. The boundless reaches of a yet-unopened continent offered the opportunity of transforming these beliefs into an unparalleled civilization. But substantial clouds threatened to dim the luster of this vision. Many white Americans were already concerned by potentially explosive social, moral, and economic issues which they perceived rising from the growth of Negro slavery around them. Others foresaw and dreaded the inevitable evils which were certain to accompany the coming of the Industrial Revolution to the United States. And, in the passage of the Alien and Sedition Acts of the late 1790's, Americans indicated all too well their awareness of the gnawing dilemma posed by immigration.[2]

At this juncture in history, Thomas Malthus wrote his provocative essay on population. True, the Malthusian doctrines were not aimed at America, but, in the context of the country's emerging demographic problems, they held considerable interest for some Americans. Notably, they constituted a newly pessimistic viewpoint from which nineteenth-century Americans could reconsider the old subject of their rapid population increase.[3]

Americans had a reasonably well-based comprehension of what was happening to them demographically as the eighteenth century ended. They knew that statistical methods helped illuminate the pattern of meaning of their collective vital events and population movements, as well as those of every facet of national life. They went into the nineteenth century with much respect for the developing statistically based demographic sciences as well as with much motivation for using them.

2. The act on aliens, which was in force only two years, included a provision to register immigrants. No data were known to have been collected, however, during that time. See [U. S. Bureau of the Census], *Historical Statistics of the United States, Colonial Times to 1957* (Washington, D. C.: Government Printing Office, 1960), p. 48.

3. Thomas R. Malthus, *An Essay on the Principles of Population,* 1st ed. (London: J. Johnson, 1798). See also J. J. Spengler, "Malthusianism in late Eighteenth-Century America," *American Economic Review,* 25 (1935), 691–707.

Bibliographical Notes

Index

Bibliographical Notes

1. GENERAL

The references given here, even when used in conjunction with the footnotes of the text, are far from exhaustive. They are intended only to suggest types of materials for the historical study of vital, medical, and demographic statistics in early America, with special reference to the men who used them, to ideas about them, and to the growth of statistical institutions. I have selected these materials to illuminate the subject as an element of American civilization rather than merely as a matter for technical analyses.

I have found no special library collections which focus upon the history of American demography and vital statistics in their broad aspects, at least for the period covered by this book. On the contrary, much of the material has had to be sifted from a wide range of subject classifications in large general libraries. I have culled the rest out of the holdings of several specialized libraries, notably the National Library of Medicine, the Library of the Department of Health, Education, and Welfare, that of the Bureau of the Census, the American Philosophical Society Library, and several university and local historical society libraries. Some of the types of sources became apparent only during the course of correspondence with a considerable number of scholars.

2. PRIMARY SOURCES

To a considerable extent, the text of my book is itself a bibliographical essay on sources for the history of American demographic ideas and vital statistics. It points out the variety of early American and British literature (somewhat less in the European) which relates to the subject. It discloses evidence of quantitative concerns not only in scientific and economic literature, but in political, religious, geographical, and historical works; in sermons, pamphlets, broadsides, journals or diaries, letters, almanacs, magazines and newspapers, books, and even in an occasional poem. It demonstrates that a large cross section of the early leaders of the United States, like those of Europe and Britain, utilized the statistical approach in one way or another, although their relevant writings about these uses were often fragmentary or scattered within the substantive works which the statistics served. Relatively few of the primary writings are more than isolated passages. Accordingly, it would serve no important purpose to attempt to list here every passing demographic or statistical reference of the period. The following list includes only some of the most relevant landmark publications, European and American.

Scientific Works: European and British

Achenwall, Gottfried. *Staatsverfassung der heutigen vornehmsten Europäischen Reiche und Folker im Grundrisse.* 5th rev. ed. Göttingen: Vandenhoeck, 1768.

[Arbuthnot, John]. *The Life and Works of John Arbuthnot.* Edited by George A. Aitken. Oxford: Clarendon, 1892.

Bacon, Francis. *Of the Proficience and Advancement of Learning.* London: Parker, 1852.

Black, William. *Observations Medical and Political on the Smallpox . . . and on the Mortality of Mankind at Every Age in City and Country.* London, Johnson, 1781.

Brissot de Warville, J. P. *New Travels in the United States of America, Performed in 1788.* 2nd ed. corr., 2 vols. London: Jordan, 1794.

Buffon, Comte de (Georges Leclerc). *Histoire naturelle, générale et particulière,* 44 vols. vol. II. 2nd ed. Paris: L'Imprimerie royale, 1750.

Condorcet, Marquis de. *Essai sur l'application de l'analyse à la Probabilité des décisions rendues à la pluralité des voix.* Paris: L'Imprimerie royale, 1785.

———— *Outlines of an Historical View of the Progress of the Human Mind.* London: Johnson, 1795.

Cullen, William. *A Synopsis of Methodical Nosology.* Philadelphia: Hall, 1793.

Derham, William. *Physico-Theology.* 3rd Scottish ed. Glasgow: Urie, 1758.

Fothergill, John. *The Works of John Fothergill, M.D.* 3 vols. London: Dilly, 1783–1784.

Graunt, John. *Natural and Political Observations Made upon the Bills of Mortality.* Edited by Walter Willcox.

Baltimore, 1939. Original edition: London: Roycroft, 1662.

[Hakluyt, Richard]. *Hakluyt's Collection of the Early Voyages, Travels and Discoveries of the English Nation.* 5 vols. III. London: Evans, Mackinlay, and Priestley, 1810.

[Halley, Edmund]. *Degrees of Mortality of Mankind.* Edited by Lowell Reed. Baltimore, Md.: Johns Hopkins Press, 1942. (This is the editor's composite title for Halley's two communications to the Royal Society.)

Heysham, John. *Observations on the Bills of Mortality in Carlisle* (Carlisle, 1780–1787).

Jurin, James. *An Account of the Success of Inoculating the Smallpox in Great Britain.* London: Peele, 1724.

[Kalm, Peter]. *The America of 1750: Peter Kalm's Travels in North America.* 2 vols. New York: Wilson-Erickson, 1937.

[King, Gregory]. *Two Tracts by Gregory King.* Edited by George E. Barnett. Baltimore: The Johns Hopkins Press, 1936.

Linnaeus, Carl von. *Genera, morborum in auditorium usum publicata.* Uppsala, Steinert, 1763.

Montesquieu, Baron de. *The Spirit of Laws.* 2 vols. New York: Colonial Press, 1899.

Percival, Thomas. *Essays Medical and Experimental.* 2nd rev. ed. London: Johnson, 1773.

[Petty, William]. *The Economic Writings of Sir William Petty.* Edited by Charles H. Hull. 2 vols. Cambridge University Press [Eng.], 1899.

———— *The Petty Papers.* Edited by Marquis of Lansdowne. 2 vols. London: Constable, 1927.

[Price, Richard]. *Letters to and from Richard Price, D.D.,*

F.R.S. Cambridge, Mass.: John Wilson & Son, Harvard University, 1903.

—— *Observations on Reversionary Payments; On Schemes for Providing Annuities for Widows, and for Persons in Old Age; On the Method of Calculating the Values of Assurances on Lives; and On The National Debt; to which are added Four Essays on Different Subjects in the Doctrine of Life Annuities and Political Arithmetic.* London. Cadell, 1771.

Pringle, John, *Observations on the Diseases of the Army in Camp and Garrison.* London: Millar, Wilson, and Payne, 1752.

[Randolph, Edward]. *Edward Randolph.* Edited by Alfred T. S. Goodrick. 6 vols. Boston: The Prince Society, 1909.

Sauvages de la Croix, Francois Boissier de. *Nosologica medica, sistens morborum classes, genera et species.* 3 vols in 5. Amsterdam: Fratres de Tournes, 1763.

Short, Thomas. *A Comparative History of the Increase and Decrease of Mankind in England, and Several Countries Abroad.* London: Nicoll and Etherington, 1767.

—— *New Observations, Natural, Moral, Civil, Political, and Medical on City, Town, and Country Bills of Mortality.* London, Longman and Miller, 1750.

Süssmilch, Johann Peter. *Die Göttliche Ordnung in den Veränderungen des Menschlichen Geschlechts, aus der Geburt, dem Tode, und der Fortpflanzung desselben erwiesen.* 4th ed. 3 vols. Berlin: Buchhandlung der Realschule, 1775.

[Sydenham, Thomas]. *The Works of Thomas Sydenham, M.D.* Edited by R. G. Latham. 2 vols. London: The Sydenham Society, 1848 and 1850.

Vincent, Thomas. *God's Terrible Voice in the City.* New London: Green, 1770.

Scientific Works: The United States

[Adams, John]. *The Works of John Adams.* Edited by Charles Francis Adams. 10 vols. Boston: Little, Brown, 1850–1856.

Barton, William. *Observations on the Progress of Population and the Probabilities of the Duration of Human Life, in the United States of America.* Philadelphia: Aitken, 1791.

Belknap, Jeremy. *History of New Hampshire.* 2nd ed. 3 vols. Boston: Bradford and Read, 1813.

Beverley, Robert. *The History and Present State of Virginia.* Edited by Louis B. Wright. Chapel Hill, University of North Carolina Press, 1947.

Boylston, Zabdiel. *An Historical Account of the Smallpox Inoculated in New England upon all Sorts of Persons, Whites, Blacks, and of all Ages and Constitutions.* 2nd ed., corr. London: Chandler, 1726, and repr. Boston, 1730.

[Byrd, William]. *The Writings of Colonel William Byrd of Westover in Virginia, Esqr.* Edited by John Spencer Bassett. New York: Doubleday, Page, 1901.

Carey, Mathew. *A Short Account of the Malignant Fever Lately Prevalent in Philadelphia with a Statement of the Proceedings that Took Place on the Subject in Different Parts of the United States.* 3rd impr. ed. Philadelphia: Carey, 1793.

Chalmers, Lionel. *An Account of the Weather and Diseases of South Carolina.* 2 vols. London: Dilly, 1776.

Coxe, Tench. *A View of the United States of America.* London: Johnson, 1795

Currie, William. *An Historical Account of the Climates and Diseases of the United States of America.* Philadelphia: Dobson, 1792.

Douglass, William. *The Abuses and Scandals of some late Pamphlets in favour of Inoculation of the Smallpox Modestly Obviated.* Boston: Franklin, 1722.

———— *Dissertation Concerning Inoculation of the Smallpox.* Boston: Henchman, 1730.

———— *The Practical History of a New Epidemical Eruptive Miliary Fever, with an Angina Ulcusculosa which Prevailed in Boston New-England in the Years 1735 and 1736.* Boston: Fleet, 1736.

———— *A Summary, Historical and Political, of the first Planting, progressive Improvements, and present State of the British Settlements in North America.* 2 vols. Boston: Rogers and Fowle, 1749–1751.

Fitch, Jabez. *An Account of the Numbers that have died of the Distemper in the Throat, Within the Province of New Hampshire, with some Reflections Thereon.* Boston: Russel, 1736.

[Foulke, John]. "Oration Pronounced by Doctor Foulke Before the American Philosophical Society, February 7 [1789]." Unpaged Manuscript at N. Y. Historical Society.

Franklin, Benjamin. *Observations Concerning the Increase of Mankind, Peopling of Countries, &c.* Boston: Kneeland, 1755.

———— *The Papers of Benjamin Franklin.* Edited by Leonard W. Labaree *et al.* New Haven, Ct.: Yale University Press, 1959– .

———— *Poor Richard Improved, for 1750.* Philadelphia: Franklin, 1749.

Gordon, William. *The Plan of a Society for Making Pro-*

vision for Widows, by Annuities for the Remainder of Life, and for Granting Annuities to Persons after Certain Ages, with the Proper Tables *for calculating what must be paid by the Several Members, in order to secure the said Advantages.* Boston, Edwards and Fleeming, 1772.

[Hamilton, Alexander]. *The Papers of Alexander Hamilton.* Edited by Harold C. Syrett. New York: Columbia University Press, 1961– .

Holyoke, Edward A. "A Bill of Mortality for the Town of Salem, for the Year 1782," American Academy of Arts and Sciences, *Memoirs,* I (1785), 546–550.

——— "An Account of the Weather and of the Epidemics, at Salem, in the County of Essex, for the Year 1786. To which is added, a Bill of Mortality, for the same Year," Massachusetts Medical Society, *Medical Communications,* I, 1787, 17–40.

——— "On Meteorological Observations and Bills of Mortality," (letter from Holyoke to Edward Wigglesworth dated Feb. 22, 1790), American Academy of Arts and Sciences, *Memoirs,* II (1804), 58–61.

Jefferson, Thomas. *Notes on the State of Virginia.* Edited by William Peden. Chapel Hill: University of North Carolina Press, 1955.

[———] *The Papers of Thomas Jefferson.* Edited by Julian P. Boyd. Princeton, N. J.: Princeton University Press, 1950– .

[———] *Writings of Jefferson.* Edited by A. E. Bergh, 20 vols. Washington, D. C.: Jefferson Memorial Association, 1903.

Johnson, Edward. *Johnson's Wonder-Working Providence, 1628–1651.* Edited by J. Franklin Jameson. New York: Scribners, 1910.

[Lining, John]. "A Letter from Dr. John Lining at Charlestown South Carolina to James Jurin, M.D. Statical Experiments Made on Himself for One Whole Year Accompanied with Meteorological Observations, and Six General Tables," Royal Society, *Philosophical Transactions*, 42 (1743), 491–498. Also see supplementary letter in *ibid.*, 43 (1743), 318.

[Madison, James]. *Letters and Other Writings of James Madison.* 4 vols. Philadelphia: Lippincott, 1865.

———— *The Papers of James Madison.* Washington: Langtree and O'Sullivan, 1840.

Mather, Cotton. *The Christian Philosopher.* London: Matthews, 1721.

———— *Diary of Cotton Mather,* in *Collections of the Massachusetts Historical Society,* 7th ser., VII (1911) and VIII (1912).

———— "The Way of Proceeding in the Smallpox Inoculated in New England," Royal Society, *Philosophical Transactions* 31 (January–March 1722), 370.

Morse, Jedidiah. *The American Geography.* 2nd ed. London: Stockwell, 1792.

Porcupine, Peter (pseud. of William Cobbett). *The Rush Light.* New York: Cobbett, 1800.

Prince, Thomas, "Observations on the State of the Smallpox at Boston, in 1752," *Gentleman's Magazine,* 23 (September 1753), 414–415.

Ramsay, David. *The Charleston Medical Register for the Year MDCCCII.* Charleston, S. C.: Young, 1803.

———— *A Sketch of the Soil, Climate, Weather, and Diseases of South Carolina.* Charleston: Young, 1796.

[Rush, Benjamin]. *The Autobiography of Benjamin Rush.* Edited by George W. Corner. Princeton, N. J.: Princeton University Press, 1948.

—— *Essays, Literary, Moral and Philosophical.* 2nd ed. Philadelphia: Bradford, 1806.

[——] *Letters of Benjamin Rush.* Edited by L. H. Butterfield. 2 vols. Princeton, N. J.: Princeton University Press, 1951.

—— *Medical Inquiries and Observations.* 4th ed. 4 vols. in 2. Philadelphia: Carey, 1815.

[Smith, John]. *Travels and Works of Captain John Smith.* Edited by Arber and Bradley. 2 vols. Edinburgh: Grant, 1910.

Stiles, Ezra. *A Discourse on the Christian Union.* Boston: Edes and Gill, 1761.

[——] *Extracts from the Itineraries and other Miscellanies of Ezra Stiles.* Edited by Franklin B. Dexter. New Haven, Ct.: Yale University Press, 1916ff.

—— *A Funeral Sermon, Delivered Thursday, July 26, 1787.* New Haven: Green, 1787.

[——] *Letters and Papers of Ezra Stiles.* Edited by Isabel M. Calder. New Haven: Yale University Library, 1930.

[——] *The Literary Diary of Ezra Stiles.* Edited by Franklin B. Dexter. 3 vols. New York: Scribners, 1901.

—— *The United States Elevated to Glory and Honor.* New Haven: Green, 1783.

Webster, Noah. *A Brief History of Epidemic and Pestilential Diseases.* 2 vols. Hartford: Hudson and Goodwin, 1799.

Wigglesworth, Edward. *Calculations on American Population.* Boston: Boyle, 1775.

—— "Observations on the Longevity of the Inhabitants of Ipswich and Hingham and Proposals for Ascertaining the Value of Estates held for Life, and the Reversion of Them." American Academy of Arts & Sciences, *Memoirs,* I (1785), 565–568.

———— "A Table shewing the Probability of the Duration, the Decrement, and the Expectation of Life, in the States of Massachusetts and New Hampshire formed from sixty-two Bills of Mortality on the files of the American Academy of Arts and Sciences, in the Year 1789." *American Academy of Arts & Sciences, Memoirs,* II (1793), 131–135.

Periodicals

Virtually all colonial and Federal newspapers issued in the area of the present United States are valuable sources and need further investigation of their demographic content. Those for the urban centers of Boston, New York, and Philadelphia far outweigh the others. Chief among publications of the scientific organizations of the day are the *Philosophical Transactions* of the Royal Society, the *Transactions* of the American Philosophical Society, and the *Memoirs* of the American Academy of Arts and Sciences. *The Gentleman's Magazine* of London, together with a few other popular journals, was a more general eighteenth-century outlet for statistical and demographic literature, as well as for the London Bills of Mortality. A serial source of much importance has been the *New England Historical and Genealogical Register,* which, from its establishment in 1847, has gathered and published much seventeenth- and eighteenth-century statistical material in its original form. Other journals of local history and genealogy include much similar material. Only small numbers of early board of health reports or broadsides of American bills of mortality exist, but they are essential. Equally valuable are the many volumes of the *Calendar of State Papers, Colonial Series, America and West Indies,* which summarize and index large amounts of official material for the colonial period. These must be supplemented by the original documents in the Public Record Office of Great Britain, together with such publications as the *Journal of the Commissioners for Trade and Plantations.*

3. SECONDARY SOURCES

Like the primary sources, some of the secondary materials for this study are easily identified; others are fragmentary and scattered. There have, however, been no previous over-all historical accounts, either 1) of American demographic thought throughout the seventeenth and eighteenth centuries; 2) of the roots, establishment, uses, and early growth of vital and medical statistics in what is now the United States; or 3) of the development of the statistical mind in America as a part of the total American intellect. Equally there is no thorough technical history of American statistics as a branch of science, though there are several European statistical histories. And there is nothing focusing on scientific quantification in the United States like the splendid collection of papers mostly concerning Europe which emerged from the 1959 Conference on the History of Quantification in the Sciences (See *Isis,* vol. 52, June 1961). The very existence of the statistical component of the American mind has never really been adequately acknowledged, let alone grappled with by historians. An exception is Stella H. Sutherland's "Colonial Statistics" (*Explorations in Entrepreneurial History,* Fall 1967), seen only after this volume had gone to press.

A few historians, however, have examined some elements of the development of American human statistics and demography. Their publications have included a few analyses of old registers by newly active historical demographers, together with some socio-historical works on matters related to the American family, as well as limited numbers of specialized studies of colonial censuses, population concepts, vital registers, and public health practices or data. Besides these, my study owes much to both general and special bibliographies. It relies upon collections of the laws and court records of the respective colonies or states, though these records need much further study. Many of the publications of the WPA Historical Records Survey made nearly thirty years ago provide useful guides or indices to vital statistics, church records, and public archival materials in the respective states, as well as brief historical notes. Equally useful are the compilations of local records prepared by many New England towns as well as by communities in other regions. Not least in value, finally, are the standard texts and special studies of the colonial and early Federal period: the political, economic, social, and intellectual histories, supplemented by the smaller number of histories of science, medicine, and public health.

Taken together, the various sources have provided many indications as to the nature and extent of the statistical mind of early America as it was manifested in censuses, life insurance projects, population theories, immigration data, and church registers, as well as in medical and official vital statistics. The attempted synthesis of the text thus relies considerably upon the perceptiveness of large numbers of scholars. It would be impracticable to cite here all such secondary sources. The following lists include only some of the most directly relevant works.

Europe and General: Some Histories
of Demography, Economics, Medicine,
Science, and Statistics

Annales de démographie historique (Yearly publication of Société française de la démographie historique). Paris, 1966– .

Bancroft, T. A. "Statistics," *The Encyclopedia Americana*, 25 (1964), 530–536a.

Beattie, Lester M. *John Arbuthnot, Mathematician and Satirist*. Cambridge, Mass.: Harvard University Press, 1935.

Becker, Carl. *The Heavenly City of the Eighteenth Century Philosophers*. New Haven, Ct.: Yale University Press, 1962.

Bonar, James. *Theories of Population from Raleigh to Arthur Young*. London: Allen & Unwin, 1931.

Buer, M. C. *Health, Wealth and Population in the Early Days of the Industrial Revolution*. London: Routledge, 1926.

Burn, John Southerden. *The History of Parish Registers in England*. London: Suter, 1829.

Clark, G. N. *Science and Social Welfare in the Age of Newton*. Oxford: Clarendon, 1937.

Cone, Carl B. *Torchbearer of Freedom, The Influence of Richard Price on Eighteenth Century Thought*. Lexington: University of Kentucky Press, 1952.

Cox, J. Charles. *The Parish Registers of England*. London: Methuen, 1910.

Creighton, Charles. *A History of Epidemics in Britain*. 2 vols. Cambridge University Press [Eng.], 1891–1894.

Crum, Frederick S. "The Statistical Work of Süssmilch," *American Statistical Association, Publications*, n.s., VII, no. 55 (September 1901), 1–46.

David, Florence N. *Games, Gods and Gambling*. New York: Hafner, 1962.

Davis, Kingsley. "Vital Statistics," *Encyclopedia Americana*, 28 (1964), 177–179.

Dewhurst, Kenneth. *John Locke, 1632–1704, Physician and*

Philosopher. London: Wellcome Historical Medical Library, 1964.

Edge, P. Granville. "Vital Registration in Europe," *Journal of the Royal Statistical Society* (London), n.s., 91, no. 3 (1928), 346–393.

Egerton, Frank N. III, "The Longevity of the Patriarchs," *Journal of the History of Ideas,* 27 (1966), 575–584.

Faber, Knud. *Nosography in Modern Internal Medicine.* New York; Hoeber, 1923.

Fox, R. Hingston. *Dr. John Fothergill and his Friends.* London: Macmillan, 1919.

Garrison, Fielding H. *An Introduction to the History of Medicine.* 4th ed., repr. Philadelphia: Saunders, 1961.

Glass, D. V. "Gregory King and the Population of England and Wales at the End of the Seventeenth Century," *The Eugenics Review,* 37 (January 1946), 170–183.

———— "John Graunt and his *Natural and Political Observations,*" Royal Society of Biology, *Proceedings,* 159 (1963–1964), 1–37.

———— and D. E. C. Eversley, eds. *Population in History.* Chicago: Aldine, 1965.

Goubert, Pierre. "Régistres paroissiaux et démographie dans la France du XVIe siècle," *Annales de démographie historique, 1965.* Paris: Société de démographie historique, 1966.

Greenwood, Major. *Medical Statistics from Graunt to Farr.* Cambridge University Press [Eng.], 1948.

Hogben, Lancelot, ed. *Political Arithmetic: A Symposium of Population Studies.* London: Allen & Unwin, 1938.

Kargon, M. Noel. "An Inquiry into Various Death-Rates and the Comparative Influence of Certain Diseases on the Duration of Life," *Annals of Eugenics,* 4 (1931), 279–302.

King, Lester S. *The Medical World of the Eighteenth Century.* Chicago, Ill.: University of Chicago Press, 1958.

Koren, John, ed. *The History of Statistics.* New York: Macmillan, 1918.

Lewis, John E. "A Short History of Taxonomy from Aristotle to Linnaeus," *Medical Arts and Sciences,* 17 (1963), 106–123.

Letwin, William. *The Origins of Scientific Economics.* Garden City, N. Y.: Doubleday, 1965.

Meitzen, August. *History, Theory, and Technique of Statistics.* Translated by Roland P. Falkner. Philadelphia: American Academy of Political and Social Science, 1891.

Miller, Genevieve. *The Adoption of Inoculation for Smallpox in England and France.* Philadelphia: University of Pennsylvania Press, 1957.

Mullett, Charles F. *The Bubonic Plague and England.* Lexington: University of Kentucky Press, 1956.

Ornstein, Martha. *The Role of Scientific Societies in the Seventeenth Century.* Hampden, Ct.: Archon, 1963.

Peel, Roy V. "Census," *Encyclopedia Americana,* 6 (1964), 194–198.

Rosen, George. "Economic and Social Policy in the Development of Public Health," *Journal of the History of Medicine,* 8 (1953), 406–430.

——— *A History of Public Health.* New York: MD, 1958.

——— "Problems in the Application of Statistical Analysis to Questions of Health, 1700–1880," *Bulletin of the History of Medicine,* 29 (1955), 27–45.

Rosengarten, G. G., ed. and trans. *Achenwall's Observations on North America, 1767.* Philadelphia, 1903. (Reprint from *Pennsylvania Magazine of History and Biography,* January 1903.)

Seguin, J. A. R. *The London Annual Bill of Christenings and Burials (1732–1799 in Ten Tables)*. Jersey City, N. J.: Paxton, 1964.

Shryock, Richard H. *The Development of Modern Medicine*, 2nd ed. New York: Knopf, 1947.

Singer, Charles, and E. A. Underwood. *A Short History of Medicine*. New York: Oxford University Press, 1962.

Spengler, Joseph J., and Otis D. Duncan. *Population Theory and Policy*. Glencoe, Ill.: Free Press, 1956.

Strauss, Eric. *Sir William Petty: Portrait of a Genius*. Glencoe, Ill.: Free Press, 1954.

Thomas, Roland. *Richard Price, Philosopher and Apostle of Liberty*. London: Oxford University Press, 1924.

Todhunter, I. *A History of the Mathematical Theory of Probability from the Time of Pascal to that of Laplace*. New York: Stechert, 1931.

Underwood, E. Ashworth. "The History of the Quantitative Approach in Medicine," *British Medical Bulletin*, 7 (1951), 265–274.

[United Nations]. *Handbook of Vital Statistics Methods*. New York: Statistical Office of the United Nations, 1955.

Vincent, Paul E. "French Demography in the Eighteenth Century," *Population Studies*, 1 (1947–1948), 44–71.

Westergaard, Harald L. *Contributions to the History of Statistics*. London: King, 1932.

Whipple, George C. *Vital Statistics*. New York: Wiley, 1919.

Winslow, C.-E. A. *The Conquest of Epidemic Diseases*. Princeton, N. J.: Princeton University Press, 1943.

Wolf, Abraham. *A History of Science, Technology and Philosophy in the Eighteenth Century*. 2nd ed. rev. London, Allen & Unwin, 1952.

Woolf, Harry, ed. *History of Quantification in the Sciences.* In *Isis,* 52 (1961), 133–354. Of especial relevance are the articles by Paul Lazarsfeld, Richard H. Shryock, and Joseph J. Spengler.

The United States — General Works

Bailyn, Bernard. *The New England Merchants in the Seventeenth Century.* New York: Harper & Row, 1964.

Billington, Ray A. *Westward Expansion.* New York: Macmillan, 1949.

Blake, Nelson M. *The Road to Reno: A History of Divorce in the United States.* New York: Macmillan, 1962.

Boorstin, Daniel. *The Americans: The Colonial Experience.* New York: Random House, 1958.

Bridenbaugh, Carl. *Cities in Revolt.* New York: Knopf, 1955.

——— *Cities in the Wilderness.* New York: Ronald, 1938.

Brown, William G. *The Life of Oliver Ellsworth.* New York: Macmillan, 1905.

Bruce, Philip A. *Economic History of Virginia in the Seventeenth Century.* 2 vols. New York: Macmillan, 1895.

——— *Institutional History of Virginia in the Seventeenth Century.* 2 vols. New York: Putnam's, 1910.

——— *Social Life of Virginia in the Seventeenth Century.* 2nd ed. New York: Ungar, 1964.

Calhoun, Arthur. *A Social History of the American Family.* 2nd ed., 3 vols. New York: Barnes & Noble, 1960.

Cooke, Jacob E., ed. *The Federalist.* Middletown, Ct.: Wesleyan University Press, 1961.

Curti, Merle. *The Growth of American Thought,* 3rd ed. New York: Harper & Row, 1964.

Dorfman, Joseph. *The Economic Mind in American Civilization, 1606–1865.* 2 vols. New York: Viking, 1946.

Faulkner, Harold U. *American Economic History*, 6th ed. New York: Harper, 1949.

Hall, Michael G. *Edward Randolph and the American Colonies, 1676–1703*. Chapel Hill: University of North Carolina Press, 1960.

Hansen, Marcus L. *The Atlantic Migration, 1617–1860*. Cambridge, Mass.: Harvard University Press, 1940.

Howard, George E. *A History of Matrimonial Institutions*, 3 vols. Chicago, Ill.: University of Chicago Press, 1904.

Jacobson, Paul H. and Pauline F. *American Marriage and Divorce*. New York: Rinehart, 1959.

Johnson, Amandus. *The Journal and Biography of Nicholas Collin, 1746–1831*. Philadelphia: New Jersey Society of Pennsylvania, 1936.

Jones, Howard Mumford. *O Strange New World*. New York: Viking, 1964.

Jones, Maldwyn A. *American Immigration*. Chicago, Ill.: University of Chicago Press, 1961.

Jordan, Winthrop D. *White Over Black: American Attitudes toward the Negro, 1550–1812*. Chapel Hill: University of North Carolina Press, 1968.

Kraus, Michael. *The Atlantic Civilization: Eighteenth Century Origins*. New York: Russell and Russell, 1961.

Martin, Edwin T. *Thomas Jefferson: Scientist*. New York: Schuman, 1952.

Marx, Leo. *The Machine in the Garden*. New York: Oxford University Press, 1967.

Miller, John C. *Origins of the American Revolution*. Boston: Little Brown, 1943.

Miller, Perry. *The New England Mind — The Seventeenth Century*. New York: Macmillan, 1939.

——— *The New England Mind — From Colony to Province.* Cambridge, Mass.: Harvard University Press, 1953.

Morgan, Edmund S. *The Gentle Puritan, A Life of Ezra Stiles, 1727–1795.* New Haven, Ct.: Yale University Press, 1962.

——— *The Puritan Family.* Boston: Boston Public Library, 1944.

Morison, Samuel E. *The Intellectual Life of Colonial New England.* 2nd ed. New York: New York University Press, 1956.

——— and Henry S. Commager. *The Growth of the American Republic.* 4th ed., rev. & enl. 2 vols. New York: Oxford University Press, 1955.

Savelle, Max. *The Foundations of American Civilization.* New York: Holt, 1942.

Skeel, Emily E. F., compiler. *A Bibliography of the Writings of Noah Webster.* New York: New York Public Library, 1958.

Smith, Abbot E. *Colonists in Bondage.* Chapel Hill: University of North Carolina Press, 1947.

Smith, Henry Nash. *Virgin Land.* Cambridge, Mass.: Harvard University Press, 1950.

Spalleta, Matteo. "Divorce in Colonial New York," *New York Historical Society Quarterly Bulletin* 39 (October 1955), 422–440.

Van Doren, Carl. *Benjamin Franklin.* New York: Viking, 1938.

Warfel, Harry R. *Noah Webster, Schoolmaster to America.* New York: Macmillan, 1936.

Wetzel, W. A. *Benjamin Franklin as an Economist.* Baltimore, Md.: Johns Hopkins Press, 1895.

Winslow, Ola E. *Meetinghouse Hill*. New York: Macmillan, 1952.

The United States — Histories of Census and Population

Aldridge, Alfred O. "Franklin as Demographer," *Journal of Economic History*, 9 (1949–1950), 29–44.

Benton, Josiah H., Jr. *Early Census Making in Massachusetts, 1643–1765*. Boston: Goodspeed, 1905.

Carey, Lewis J. *Franklin's Economic Views*. New York: Doubleday, Doran, 1928.

Dexter, Franklin B. "Estimates of Population in the American Colonies," American Antiquarian Society, *Proceedings*, n.s., 5 (1888), 22–50.

Greene, Evarts B., and Virginia Harrington. *American Population before the Census of 1790*. New York: Columbia University Press, 1932.

Greven, Philip J., Jr. "Family Structure in Seventeenth Century Andover, Massachusetts," *William and Mary Quarterly*, 3rd ser., 23 (1966), 234–256.

Karinen, Arthur. "Numerical and Distributional Aspects of Maryland Population," *Maryland Historical Magazine*, 54 (1959), 365–407; 60 (1965), 139–159.

Lockridge, Kenneth A. "The Population of Dedham, Massachusetts, 1636–1736," *Economic Historical Review*, 2nd ser., 19 (1966), 318–344.

Merriam, William R. "The Evolution of American Census-Taking," *The Century Magazine*, April 1903, pp. 832–833.

Moller, Herbert. "Sex Composition and Correlated Culture Patterns of Colonial America," *William and Mary Quarterly*, 3rd ser., 2 (1945), 113–153.

Rossiter, W. S. *A Century of Population Growth*. Washington, D. C.: Government Printing Office, 1909.

Spengler, Joseph J. "Malthusianism in Late Eighteenth Century America," *American Economic Review*, 25 (December 1935), 691–707.

———— "The Political Economy of Jefferson, Madison and Adams," in David K. Jackson, ed., *American Studies in Honor of William K. Boyd*. Durham, N. C.: Duke University Press, 1940.

Sutherland, Stella H. *Population Distribution in Colonial America*. New York: Columbia University Press, 1936.

Taeuber, Irene B. *General Censuses and Vital Statistics in the Americas*. Washington, D. C.: Government Printing Office, 1943.

[United States Bureau of the Census]. *Historical Statistics of the United States, Colonial Times to 1957*. Washington, D. C.: Government Printing Office, 1960.

Wright, Carroll D., and William C. Hunt. *The History and Growth of the United States Census*. Washington, D. C.: Government Printing Office, 1900 (Senate Document no. 194, 56th Cong., 1st sess.).

Zirkle, Conway. "Benjamin Franklin, Thomas Malthus, and the United States Census," *Isis*, 48 (1957), 58–62.

The United States — Histories of Life Insurance

Fowler, J. A. *History of Insurance in Philadelphia for Two Centuries (1683–1882)*. Philadelphia: Review, 1888.

Gudmundsen, John. *The Great Provider, The Dramatic Story of Life Insurance in America*. South Norwalk, Ct.: 1959.

Knight, Charles K. *The History of Life Insurance in the*

United States to 1870. Philadelphia: University of Pennsylvania Press, 1920.

Mackie, Alexander. *Facile Princeps: The Story of the Beginning of Life Insurance in America.* Lancaster, Pa.: Presbyterian Ministers' Fund, 1956.

Stalson, J. Owen. *Marketing Life Insurance, Its History in America.* Cambridge, Mass.: Harvard University Press, 1942.

The United States — Histories of Church and Vital Registration

Blake, John B. "The Early History of Vital Statistics in Massachusetts," *Bulletin of the History of Medicine,* 29 (1955), 46–68.

Coats, R. H. "Beginnings in Canadian Statistics," *Canadian Historical Review,* 27 (1946), 109–130.

Gutman, Robert. *Birth and Death Registration in Massachusetts, 1639–1900.* New York: Milbank Memorial Fund, 1959.

Kirkham, E. Kay. *A Survey of American Church Records.* 2 vols. Salt Lake City, Utah: Deseret Book Company, 1959–1960.

Kuczynski, Robert R. "The Registration Laws in the Colonies of Massachusetts Bay and New Plymouth," *Journal of American Statistical Association,* n.s., 7 (1900), 1–9.

Locke, L. Leland. *The Ancient Quipus, or The Peruvian Knot Record.* New York: American Museum of Natural History, 1923.

Oberholzer, Emil, Jr. *Delinquent Saints.* New York: Columbia University Press, 1956.

Parrot, Paul. "History of Civil Registration in Quebec," *Canadian Public Health Journal,* 21 (1930), 529–540.

Pine, Leslie G. *American Origins*. Garden City, N. Y.: Doubleday, 1960.

Worthley, Harold F. "Pilgrim-Puritan Church Records," *Bulletin of the Congregational Library*, 13 (October 1961), 4–7.

The United States — Histories of Medicine and Public Health

Ashburn, Percy M. *A History of the Medical Department of the United States Army*. Boston: Houghton Mifflin, 1929.

Beall, Otho T., Jr., and Richard H. Shryock. *Cotton Mather: First Significant Figure in American Medicine*. Baltimore, Md.: Johns Hopkins Press, 1954.

Blake, John B. *Public Health in the Town of Boston, 1630–1822*. Cambridge, Mass.: Harvard University Press, 1959.

Brunhouse, Robert L., ed. *David Ramsay, 1749–1815: Selections from his Writings*. American Philosophical Society, *Transactions*, n.s. 55, pt. 4, 1965.

Caulfield, Ernest. *A True History of the Terrible Epidemic Vulgarly Called the Throat Distemper which Occurred in his Majesty's New England Colonies Between the Years 1735 and 1740*. New Haven, Ct.: *Yale Journal of Biology and Medicine*, 1934.

Duffy, John. *Epidemics in Colonial America*. Baton Rouge: Louisiana State University Press, 1953.

Guerra, Francisco. *American Medical Bibliography 1639–1783*. New York: Harper, 1962.

Howard, William T., Jr. *Public Health Administration and the Natural History of Disease in Baltimore, Maryland, 1797–1920*. Washington, D. C.: Carnegie Institution of Washington, 1924.

Marti-Ibañez, Felix, ed. *History of American Medicine.* New York: MD, 1959.

Packard, Francis R. *History of Medicine in the United States.* 2 vols. New York: Hafner, 1963.

Powell, John R. *Bring Out Your Dead.* Philadelphia: University of Pennsylvania Press, 1949.

Rosen, George. "Noah Webster — Historical Epidemiologist," *Journal of the History of Medicine,* 20 (1965), 97–114.

Shryock, Richard H. *Medicine and Society in America: 1660–1860.* New York: New York University Press, 1960.

——— *Medicine in America — Historical Essays.* Baltimore, Md.: Johns Hopkins Press, 1966.

Smillie, Wilson G. *Public Health, Its Promise for the Future.* New York: Macmillan, 1955.

Stearn, E. Wagner and Allen E. *The Effect of Smallpox on the Destiny of the Amerindian.* Boston: Humphries, 1945.

Top, Franklin H., ed. *The History of American Epidemiology.* St. Louis, Mo.: Mosby, 1952.

Waring, Joseph I. *A History of Medicine in South Carolina, 1670–1825.* Charleston, S. C.: South Carolina Medical Association, 1964.

Weaver, George H. "Life and Writings of William Douglass, M.D.," *Bulletin of the Society of Medical History of Chicago,* 11 (1921), 229–259.

The United States — Histories of Science

Boorstin, Daniel. *The Lost World of Thomas Jefferson.* New York: Holt, 1958.

Cajori, Florian. *The Early Mathematical Sciences in North and South America.* Boston: Badger, 1928.

Chinard, Gilbert. "Eighteenth Century Theories of America as a Human Habitat," American Philosophical Society, *Proceedings*, 91 (1947), 27–57.

Gruman, Gerald J. *A History of Ideas about the Prolongation of Life.* Philadelphia: American Philosophical Society, 1966. (American Philosophical Society, *Transactions*, n.s. 56, pt. 9 [1966].)

Hindle, Brooke. *The Pursuit of Science in Revolutionary America.* Chapel Hill: University of North Carolina Press, 1956.

Hornberger, Theodore. *Scientific Thought in the American Colleges, 1638–1800.* Austin: University of Texas Press, 1945.

Kilgour, Frederick G. "The Rise of Scientific Activity in Colonial New England," *Yale Journal of Biology and Medicine,* 22 (1949), 123–138.

Kraus, Michael. "Scientific Relations between Europe and America in the Eighteenth Century," *Scientific Monthly,* 55 (1942), 259–272.

Smith, David E., and Jekuthiel Ginsburg. *A History of Mathematics in America before 1900.* Chicago: Mathematical Association of America, 1934.

Index